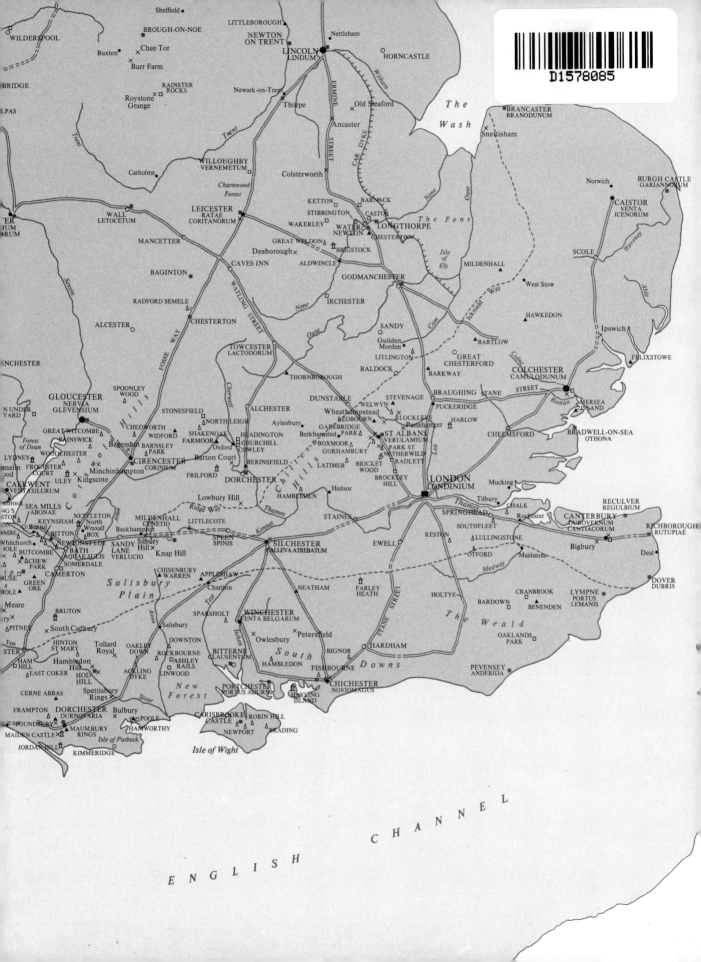

ROMAN BRITAIN

ROMAN BRITAIN
was edited and designed by
The Reader's Digest Association Limited,
London

First edition
Copyright © 1980
The Reader's Digest Association Limited,
25 Berkeley Square,
London W1X 6AB
Reprinted with amendments 1982

Copyright © 1980
Reader's Digest Association
Far East Limited
Philippines Copyright 1980
Reader's Digest Association
Far East Ltd

® READER'S DIGEST
is a registered trademark of
The Reader's Digest Association, Inc.
of Pleasantville, New York, U.S.A.

Printed in Hong Kong by South China Printing Co.

Reader's Digest

LIFE IN BRITAIN

ROMAN BRITAIN

LIFE IN AN IMPERIAL PROVINCE

Keith Branigan

PROFESSOR OF PREHISTORY AND ARCHAEOLOGY, UNIVERSITY OF SHEFFIELD

PUBLISHED BY THE READER'S DIGEST ASSOCIATION LIMITED

London New York Montreal Sydney Cape Town

CONTENTS

FOREWORD

By Barry Cunliffe
Professor of European Archaeology, University of Oxford

For nearly 400 years Britain was occupied and governed by an alien power – Rome. Yet, remarkably, the impact of that long period of rigid control on the island's subsequent development was comparatively slight. Why this should be is one of the more fascinating questions in British history.

The reasons are complex and interwoven. To begin with, pre-Roman Britain, or more precisely the south-east corner of the country, was by no means uncivilised. This much Julius Caesar realised when he raided the island in 55 and 54 BC. In his war commentaries he says that by far the most civilised inhabitants lived in the area that is now Kent, but that the further inland one went the more primitive was the tribes' way of life.

Caesar's over-simplification had grains of truth in it. By the time he arrived, trading links had been established between the communities of the Thames estuary and their Gaulish neighbours, and between those of the Hampshire-Dorset coast and their compatriots in Brittany and further afield. Metals, slaves and other commodities were exported to the civilised world; luxuries like Mediterranean wine flowed into the households of British chieftains.

Caesar's conquest of Gaul brought Roman civilisation to the doorstep of Britain, and for the next 90 years the British communities in the south-east of the country developed dramatically. The use of coins became widespread, market centres sprang up and the political organisation seems to have changed from one of petty warring chieftains to more unified state systems. In fact, by the time the armies of Emperor Claudius arrived in AD 43 to conquer the country, much of the south-east had already reached a high level of political and economic organisation. Roman administrative genius simply observed the state of the country and moulded the new administrative system around what already existed. Flourishing communities were taken over, Romanised and joined by roads, tribal groupings became units of local government and the native aristocracy moved into the governing class.

Outside the south-east – roughly defined by the line taken by the Roman Fosse Way from Exeter to Lincoln – in regions where native social and economic organisation was comparatively undeveloped, the Romanised urban system, and the villa estates which supported it, failed to take root.

But this is not to deny the Roman achievement. The Roman administrative system admittedly had faults – heavy taxation to pay for a vast standing army and a huge bureaucracy, corruption among the provincial officials, and the harsh repression of dissident elements. For those willing to accept the new rules, however, there were untold benefits, not least of which were peace and material prosperity on an unprecedented level. Moreover, the new social system allowed able men to rise to positions of prestige and power unfettered by the constraints of the rigid Celtic class system, while the capitalist workings of the Roman economy encouraged the creation of a new class of *nouveaux riches*. In this atmosphere of exuberance, towns grew and were aggrandised by their citizens, while the wealthy landowners built sumptuous villas for themselves adorned with mosaics and paintings often of exceptional quality.

The Roman system was, however, doomed to failure: its hollow centre consumed the wealth created in the provincial fringes. All the while the empire was expanding, bringing new areas of productivity into the Roman orbit, a degree of stability could be maintained; but from the moment when the constraining frontiers were drawn by Hadrian in the early decades of the 2nd century AD the beginning of the inevitable disintegration can begin to be seen. Increasing inflation, population decline and barbarian pressures from beyond the frontiers hastened the collapse.

In Britain the end was spectacular. In the 380s Britain seems to have been a comparatively prosperous part of the Roman world; yet within 30 years the province was in ruins, centralised government had collapsed, the monetary system had virtually ceased to operate and industrial production had ground to a halt. Barbarians began to pour in as Britain dissolved into anarchy.

The new immigrants naturally chose the fertile developed land of the south-east in which to settle, leaving the north and west untouched. Thus, largely by geographical accident, the thoroughly Romanised area of Britain was swamped by peoples of Germanic descent, while the more distant fringes of the island remained with their essentially native social and economic structure intact, virtually untouched by both Roman and Germanic invasions alike. What emerged was a Britain divided between a Celtic north and west and a Germanic south and east – Roman culture had all but disappeared.

However, many relics of the occupation – road patterns, the remains of baths, temples, a palace, villas, walls and forts – remain permanent features of the British landscape. Over the years, too, archaeologists have recovered from the ground objects ranging from rich mosaics and bronzes to safety pins, dockers' tools, cooking pots and children's toys, all of which help to build up a picture of what life was like in Britain during Roman times.

The dramatic history of Roman Britain – its forceful creation, its long period of peaceful life and its spectacular end – has fascinated generations of readers. Keith Branigan's elegant approach in the pages that follow presents the story to us with a new vividness.

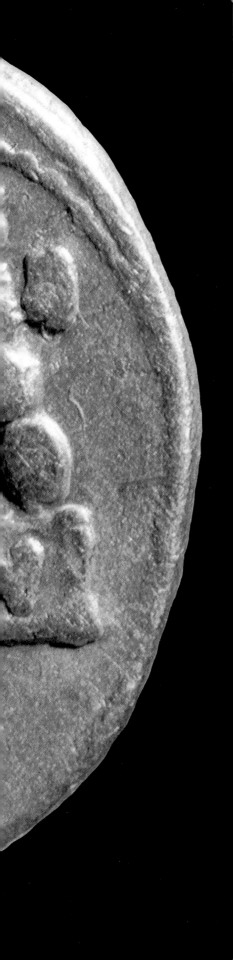

CHAPTER ONE

The Conquest and the conquered

The world of warrior-kings and peasants, barbaric splendour and primitive squalor, that confronted the invading legions of Rome

Victor and vanquished
To Emperor Claudius, the conquest of Britain meant plaudits and triumphal arches (left). But to tribesmen who defied him, as to these Gallic prisoners (below), the legions brought chains and death.

The war trumpets sound
The harsh, brassy notes of the great Celtic war trumpets were meant not only to urge warriors into battle, but also to intimidate the enemy. The trumpets were about 4 ft long, and were held upright as they were sounded. Their range of notes was limited, but they were probably used also to sound signals. These are on a silver bowl of around 100 BC.

P EERING THROUGH FLYING SPRAY AT THE TOWERING CLIFFS AHEAD, GAIUS JULIUS CAESAR WAS FORCED TO THE conclusion that this might not be the right place – or the right time – to test the fighting qualities of the British.

Facing him and his 12,000 legionaries, as their ships bucketed beachwards through the steep Channel waves, waited a fearsome deterrent: massed war parties of chariots and cavalry, long lines of fierce-eyed, wild-haired spearmen. Helmets and armour flashed in the morning sun, swords and javelins were brandished aggressively. Brazen war trumpets brayed the alarm, and hoarse challenges rent the air.

The beach was narrow, and from those tall cliffs, javelins and missiles could rain down on the legionaries as they struggled ashore through the surf. Furthermore, as luck would have it, the ships bearing the Roman cavalry were late, delayed by adverse winds; and several transports were also lagging behind.

Caesar's order was brief, and passed swiftly through the fleet: 'Drop anchor!'

The order was given at about 9 a.m. By 3 p.m. all the stragglers except the cavalry – who never turned up – had joined the rest of the fleet off the coast near Dover, and fresh plans had been laid. Anchors were raised, all bows swung sharp right, and the whole assault force headed north-east, slanting shorewards 7 miles further up the coast, towards the flatter beaches between Walmer and Deal.

But the Britons had seen Caesar's move. Their chariots and cavalry thundered along the coast after him, with the foot soldiers making the best time they could behind. Charioteers and horsemen reached the beach ahead of the Roman ships, racing into the surf to confront the enemy anew.

Even the iron legions of Rome were taken aback by the swift reaction of the natives and their ferocious eagerness for battle. There was a moment when nobody wanted to be first over the side to engage them – and history hung in the balance.

Caesar himself later described that moment, and the soldier who rose to it:

'The man who carried the eagle of the Tenth Legion prayed to the gods and cried out, "Come on lads! Jump, if you don't want to lose your eagle to the enemy!" . . . He then leapt into the water and began wading towards the shore. The others followed, shouting that they must not shame themselves by losing their eagle.'

The tough, disciplined and determined assault troops of Rome, once committed, hacked and smashed and stabbed their way

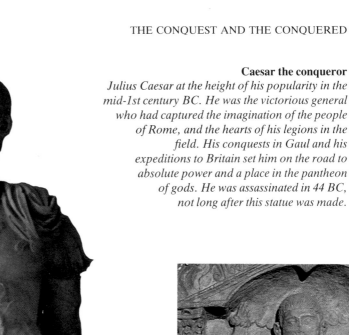

Caesar the conqueror

Julius Caesar at the height of his popularity in the mid-1st century BC. He was the victorious general who had captured the imagination of the people of Rome, and the hearts of his legions in the field. His conquests in Gaul and his expeditions to Britain set him on the road to absolute power and a place in the pantheon of gods. He was assassinated in 44 BC, not long after this statue was made.

Where eagles dared

It was the eagle-bearer who led Caesar's reluctant Tenth Legion ashore against the British in 55 BC. The man above carries the eagle of the Fourteenth Legion, an important unit in Claudius's conquest nearly a century later.

ashore, to secure a foothold in Britain that would later lead to the four centuries of Roman rule, and change the face of the country.

Their presence is all around us still, not only in the buildings and countless artefacts they left, but also in the political and legal traditions they brought, the outgoing and cosmopolitan attitudes they encouraged, and in the English language itself.

Roman tastes and Roman ways were often remarkably close to those of modern society, and though the Roman Empire itself drowned eventually in a sea of decadence, it built on the Greek experience and laid the foundations of Western civilisation.

Punishment – or glory?

By Caesar's own account, his attack on Britain in 55 BC was a punitive expedition against the tribal chieftains for sending warriors across the Channel to aid his enemies in northern Gaul – recently occupied but seething with revolt. His private reasons were probably concerned more with winning personal glory.

Whatever his motive, he grossly underestimated the British. His legions, even after fighting their way ashore in a vicious, confused battle, made little impression on the natives, and no progress into the interior of Kent. Within a few weeks, Caesar was back in Gaul.

A year later, with his reputation and perhaps his command at stake, Caesar assembled a massive force bent on winning a resounding victory. Thirty thousand crack legionaries, 2,000 cavalry and an unknown number of auxiliary troops crossed the Channel in a fleet of more than 800 ships. They landed unopposed, stormed through Kent, crossed the Thames – perhaps near Tilbury – and invaded the tribal territory of the Catuvellauni. Their king, Cassivellaunus, ruled an area that probably covered present-day Buckinghamshire, Hertfordshire and Bedfordshire.

Caesar wrote later that Cassivellaunus was able to muster about 4,000 chariots, as well as foot soldiers, against the Romans. But the British king had made enemies among the surrounding tribes – particularly the Trinovantes of present-day Essex, whose king he had already killed. The Trinovantes and other minor tribes became Caesar's allies and betrayed the king's stronghold to him.

Caesar describes this British capital as 'protected by forests and marshes, and filled with a large number of men and cattle . . . It was of great natural strength, and extremely well fortified.' Traces of that great defensive ditch and bank are still visible at Wheathampstead, on the west bank of the River Lea, near Welwyn.

Caesar's armada
For his second assault on Britain in 54 BC, Caesar flung across the Channel a massive army of 32,000 men in an armada of more than 800 ships. There were no fewer than five legions, each of 6,000 crack troops, plus another 2,000 cavalry. The fleet included powerful galleys driven by banks of oarsmen, like the ship in this relief from the Vatican Museum. Many more, however, were probably merchant ships used as transports, and smaller vessels.

Cavalry trumpeter
The first serious opposition Caesar encountered during his second invasion came from the army of Cassivellaunus, king of the Catuvellauni tribe, whose capital was in Hertfordshire. Caesar wrote that they mustered about 4,000 charioteers, as well as cavalry and infantry. This coin issued by the Catuvellauni, now in the British Museum, shows one of their mounted warriors, possibly brandishing a war trumpet. The inscription on the bottom of the coin, 'SEGO', is so far unexplained. The Romans easily overran the capital of the Catuvellauni.

However, the highly trained legionaries overran it without difficulty, though Cassivellaunus and most of his army escaped.

Soon afterwards, Cassivellaunus came to terms with the Romans and Caesar withdrew, never to return, having taken hostages and fixed an annual tribute to be paid by the Britons.

There was another important condition attached to the withdrawal: that the Catuvellauni should respect Trinovantian territory. Evidence that the Romans took their guarantees to the Trinovantes seriously long after Caesar had left came to light in 1924, during excavations at one of the richest prehistoric burials found in Britain. This was the grave of a Trinovantian king who died at about the time of the birth of Christ, and which had laid hidden beneath a great burial mound at Lexden near Colchester for nearly 2,000 years.

The king's personal riches – the possessions he most valued – had been buried with him to accompany him into the after-life. There were pieces of his chain-mail armour, some bronze ornaments, and wine jars from the Continent. But the most exciting of all was a Roman medallion, struck in 17 BC and bearing the portrait of Emperor Augustus, Julius Caesar's heir and successor.

It seems likely that the medallion was sent to the British king – believed to have been named Addedomarus – as a token of support while Augustus was on a personal visit to Gaul in 16 BC. The gesture would be a sign that the Romans still regarded as binding the agreement Caesar had made with the Catuvellauni 40 years earlier. It may also have been inspired by a further attack by the Catuvellauni on their neighbours in 17 BC. They must have briefly occupied the Trinovantian capital – present-day Colchester – for in that year, and that year only, Catuvellaunian coins carried the mark of the Colchester mint.

Support for an ally
This small silver medallion was among the personal possessions of a British king that were found when his grave was excavated at Lexden, near Colchester. It bears the head of Emperor Augustus, heir and successor to Caesar, and was struck in 17 BC. The buried king is believed to have been Addedomarus, of the Trinovantes tribe, and the medallion was possibly sent to him as a token of support by Augustus while the emperor was visiting Gaul in 16 BC: evidently the king was a trusted ally of Rome.

Britons as allies of Rome

By that time conditions in Britain had changed a great deal. Caesar had referred to 11 different tribes or kingdoms in the south-east corner of the island, but by the end of the century there were probably only three survivors – Catuvellauni, Trinovantes, and the Cantiaci of Kent. Immediately beyond them were perhaps two more kingdoms: to the west the Atrebates, and to the north-east the Iceni. The smaller tribes and kingdoms had been absorbed by the larger, and the Catuvellauni in particular were now poised to begin the domination of their principal rivals.

At the same time many, perhaps all, of these kingdoms had

Eve of battle
The map shows the approximate distribution of British tribes at the time of the invasion. Tribal names are probably Latinised versions of what the various peoples called themselves.

14

Roman 'help' becomes an invasion

Several British kings seem to have made treaties with Rome, particularly the kings of the Atrebates, who were descended from Caesar's old Gallic ally, Commius. Last of these Atrebatan kings was Verica, whose coin, seen above, not only shows one of his mounted warriors, but also boasts in large letters the title 'REX'. Use of this Latin term for king may imply that Verica claimed more than mere friendship with Rome, and in effect claimed Roman recognition of his title. When the Catuvellauni attacked him in about AD 41–42, he asked Emperor Claudius for help. Claudius replied by invading Britain and making it a Roman province.

established treaty relationships with Rome. Strengthened political contacts had encouraged a growth of trade between Britain and Roman Gaul, and with Rome and the Mediterranean. The most important centre for this trade was Colchester, and the Trinovantian capital was clearly a major prize for the aggressive Catuvellauni.

By AD 7 the greatest of all Catuvellaunian kings, Cunobelinus, had captured Colchester and made it his capital. He made such a strong impression on history that he was still remembered by Shakespeare, who called him Cymbeline.

In succeeding years the kingdom of Cunobelinus expanded its grip in all directions, particularly to the west and south-west. Within a year or two of his death, about AD 40, the last enclave of the Atrebates, in southern Hampshire, succumbed. This stronghold had been ruled by a king named Verica, whose use of the Latin title *rex* suggests that he was probably a treaty ally of Rome. He appealed to the emperor for help against the Catuvellauni. He got far more 'help' than he had bargained for.

The emperor to whom Verica appealed was Claudius, the shy, stammering cripple, newly and surprisingly elevated to the throne by the army after the assassination of his nephew, Caligula. To secure his shaky throne, Claudius needed a spectacular military victory. The historian Suetonius, writing about 80 years later, dryly summed up the situation: 'The Senate had already voted (Claudius) triumphal regalia, but he thought it beneath his dignity to accept these, and decided that Britain was the country where a real triumph could be most readily earned.'

So, in AD 43, Claudius seized the opportunity presented by Verica's appeal to undertake a conquest that promised to be both easy and prestigious – prestigious because it might achieve what the great Julius Caesar had failed to do a century before.

But despite the emperor's confidence, Roman authors of the time reveal that very little was known of the land Claudius proposed to conquer. Indeed, the Greek historian Dio Cassius writes that Claudius's troops refused at first to embark for Britain, believing it to be beyond the limits of the known world.

Privilege and poverty

The situation in Britain by AD 43 was that the whole south-east had been overrun by the Catuvellauni. But the conquered Trinovantes, Cantiaci and Atrebates all shared with the Catuvellauni a common ancestry – they were founded and peopled by the Belgae, immigrants from what is now northern France, the first of whom reached

Under the thatch
The Celtic farmers' building technique becomes more obvious inside the hut (right). A large number of thin poles are lashed together at the top, which is braced with a frame of shorter poles. This light but strong roof construction was able to support a thick layer of thatch.

Home for a Celtic Briton
The timbers, wattle walls and thatched roofs of Celtic houses have long since rotted away, but sufficient evidence remained to make possible this modern reconstruction of a Celtic round house at Petersfield in Hampshire.

Britain around 100 BC. They formed a number of independent tribes, speaking various dialects of a common Celtic tongue; the names by which the tribes are known today are those they used themselves, or Latinised forms of them.

The political unity created by Cunobelinus and his sons was therefore imposed on people with a common cultural background, which can be traced over the whole area east of the River Test in Hampshire and the River Cherwell in Oxfordshire, and south of the River Nene in Northamptonshire.

Principal settlements in this Belgic heartland were *oppida*, the most important of which were on the sites of present-day Colchester, St Albans, Canterbury, Silchester and Chichester-Selsey. The Latin word *oppidum*, which strictly means 'town', was the best word Caesar could find to describe these places, the Celtic name for which is lost. They were indeed not much like Roman towns, being sprawling settlements spread over very large areas.

The greatest of all the *oppida* was at Colchester. The Romans called it Camulodunum, the Latin form of a Belgic place-name

meaning the fortress of Camulos, a Celtic war god. Camulodunum at its greatest extent covered an area of more than 12 sq. miles. But not all, or even most, of this area was built over. Caesar's description of the *oppidum* at Wheathampstead makes no mention of buildings, and the Greek geographer Strabo, apparently referring to the tribal *oppida*, writes:

> 'Forest thickets are their "cities". They fence round a wide clearing with felled trees and here they make themselves huts and keep their cattle.'

Archaeological excavations in modern times have revealed many more details of Cunobelinus's capital, and of other *oppida*. Camulodunum was defended by the natural barriers of the River Colne and its marshes to the north and east, and by the River Roman – a name derived from the conquerors – to the south. On the western side, four or five massive dykes were dug to present a complex and formidable obstacle to attackers.

Within these defences, almost every kind of human activity was carried on. Houses, workshops, rubbish pits, cemeteries and at least one major place of worship have all been discovered. The testimony of Caesar and Strabo that cattle were kept – and presumably grazed – inside has been confirmed by the size of the clear, uncultivated and uninhabited areas found within the defences.

Most of the buildings discovered so far at Colchester seem to have been roughly circular huts, rarely more than 20 ft across, with plain clay floors. The walls were of wattle-and-daub construction: panels of interwoven twigs, daubed with clay and supported by solid timber posts. None is of any special size or style that might identify it as the 'palace' of a great king such as Cunobelinus. But in the rubbish pits beside one were found quantities of imported glassware and superb Italian pottery, showing that the people who lived there were wealthy, with Romanised tastes. This hut had apparently been singled out for thorough destruction soon after AD 43, and has been claimed as that of Cunobelinus himself, or of one of his retainers.

Noisy, dirty and chaotic

Some *oppida* had their own workshops, many of them for metal-working, and the one at Colchester – among others – minted coins of gold, silver and bronze. Debris found at St Albans includes almost complete moulds for casting coin blanks, as well as crucibles.

To a visitor from abroad – say, a Roman merchant – places like Colchester and St Albans must have seemed confusing and

Celtic craftsman's art
Workmanship of extraordinary delicacy and inventiveness by a Celtic artist-craftsman appears on the reverse of a bronze mirror found at Desborough, Northamptonshire. The flowing scroll decoration dates from the 1st century AD.

The warrior's emblem
Celtic huntsmen knew from experience the fierce, fighting qualities of the boar, and warriors used it as a symbol on chariots, and as a crest on their helmets. This bronze boar was found in the Lexden burial.

A Celt's last sleep
It was the custom for both men and women of the Celtic nobility to be buried with some of their finest and most treasured possessions around them. This woman has been laid out as if asleep, with her round bronze mirror close to hand.

chaotic, far removed from the ordered town life of his homeland.

Religious ceremonial at Colchester probably took place in a square enclosure at nearby Gosbecks. Set apart by a massive ditch more than 13 ft deep and 35 ft wide, this enclosure later became part of a large Roman sanctuary dedicated to Mercury. Traces of a similar enclosure lie beneath the forum, or market place, of the Roman town at St Albans, which later incorporated two Roman temples. There were special funeral rituals, and cemeteries have been found in the *oppida* at Colchester and St Albans. Colchester's Lexden cemetery contained not only the burial mound of Addedomarus, but also at least 20 other graves that were clearly those of wealthy nobles and their families. Imported wine jars and other belongings there included a bronze mirror, a coral-inlaid cup and a bronze bucket or large drinking vessel. Equally rich burials were found in the St Albans cemetery. They are clear evidence of a brisk trade with Europe and the Mediterranean, and of the Romanised tastes of the Belgic nobility. They also confirm Caesar's observation that Celtic society consisted of two classes: the privileged, and the rest – peasants, craftsmen and slaves.

Tankards and a bear skin

Some of the nobility seem to have lived outside the 'towns', on isolated farmsteads in the countryside, and they were buried near them. A number of these rural graves have disclosed evidence of considerable wealth. One at Panshanger, Hertfordshire, for example, contained five Italian wine jars, 36 other pottery vessels, an imported silver cup, a bronze serving dish and strainer bowl, and a set of 24 glass gaming pieces – six of each in white, blue, yellow and green. There were also traces of wooden vessels decorated with bronze – tankards, perhaps – and of a bear skin. In contrast, six other burials around this grave contained nothing but cremated human remains – possibly those of the nobleman's slaves.

Only 220 yds away are traces of a hut farmstead, doubtless the nobleman's home. Huts in farmsteads at Gorhambury, Lockleys and Park Street, near St Albans, were rectangular, up to 30 ft long, and often had a compacted chalk floor. Walls were probably of timber and wattle-and-daub, and there was usually a hearth inside. At Park Street a second, oval hut stood close by, which may have been slaves' quarters, for a pit near by contained an iron slave chain.

Slaves, like cattle, were an important form of wealth in Belgic Britain, and were among the exports listed by Strabo: 'Corn, cattle, gold, silver, iron ... together with hides, slaves and dogs useful for hunting.' Strabo also provides evidence that Belgic wealth and power were largely built on successful farming. Even Caesar remarked that farmsteads, like those around St Albans, were to be seen in great numbers across the landscape. Others have, indeed, been found at places such as Barton Court, in Oxfordshire, and Owlesbury, Hampshire.

It is certain that the Belgic tribes made better use of the land than earlier British farmers. Traces that remain give a fair idea of what these farmlands looked like when the Romans arrived. Small, squarish fields enclosed by banks and hedges were devoted to growing spelt – a hardy form of wheat – and barley. Beyond the fields were areas of open pasture where herds of Celtic short-horn cattle were grazed. By their skilled management of the land and ability to organise their labour force, the Belgic nobility built a firm economic basis for themselves and their overseas trade.

Home cooking
This reconstructed Celtic clay oven at Petersfield proved to be remarkably efficient. Food could be roasted, boiled or baked by standing it on an inside ledge above the fire.

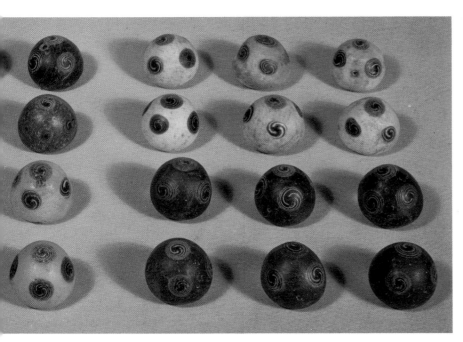

Skill and chance
The rules governing the movements of these fine glass gaming counters have long been forgotten, but they were doubtless familiar to the Romano-British chieftain in whose grave in the Panshanger estate of Welwyn Garden City the pieces were found. He must have been a convivial soul for, in addition to his favourite game, he was also supplied in his grave with five wine amphorae, a wine strainer, a silver drinking cup and numerous flagons and bowls.

Home consumption
The amount of corn grown on most Celtic farms would feed only the family; there was little to spare for sale or barter. It was ground in querns like this one in Petersfield, the grain being poured through the hole in the upper stone, which was then rotated against the lower one.

Home comforts
Hides were used for bedding and clothing. The skins of animals were cured by the women of the house, then hung around the main living-hut, as shown in this detail from the reconstructed Iron Age settlement at Butser Hill, south of Petersfield. The smoke from the central fire would help in tanning.

Hill-forts of the west

Further west and north lived other peoples, either partly Belgic in origin or people who had adopted some of the trappings of the Belgic tribes, and had even submitted to Belgic rulers. The principal tribes concerned were the Durotriges of present-day Dorset and south Somerset, the Dobunni of Avon, Gloucestershire, Warwickshire, Hereford and Worcester, and the Coritani of the north and east Midlands.

But in all this great arc of territory, only one or two *oppidum* sites have been found. One of about 200 acres, enclosed by a dyke at Bagendon, just north of Cirencester, was probably the Dobunnic capital, though there is an even larger dyked enclosure at Minchinhampton. In Coritanian territory there were major settlements at Old Sleaford and Leicester.

The coins of these two tribes have inscriptions suggesting that they were ruled by kings. But the Durotriges' coins were seldom inscribed – the tribe was probably a confederacy formed from local chiefdoms without a single centre.

Among the Durotriges the hill-fort, a form of settlement whose origins lay in the Bronze Age, 1,000 years before Caesar, seems to have been the focal point of each chiefdom. Hill-forts are common, too, on the Mendips and Cotswolds, in Dobunnic territory. Excavations have shown that many were thickly crowded with huts.

Forts such as Hod Hill, Maiden Castle and South Cadbury in Wessex probably embraced circular huts together housing several hundred people. These huts were of timber and thatch, the larger ones up to 35 ft across. With skins or straw on the floor and a good fire going they could have been warm, if not comfortable. Some of the smaller huts were stores or workshops.

Crafts like spinning and weaving were practised, and near two huts at Pilsdon Pen, in Dorset, two outdoor hearths and a crucible containing traces of gold have been found. At the South Cadbury fort, the discovery of a small gold bar reveals that a goldsmith once worked there, while on the crest of the hill was a bronzesmith's workshop, revealed by its furnaces and ovens. Tools such as iron punches, chisels and scribers were also found, along with bronze punches and several whetstones. Products of this workshop, discovered near by, include shield-bosses and rims, daggers, spearheads and scabbard ornaments, as well as cauldron or bucket handles. The best find of all is a superbly decorated bronze shield-boss, with typical Celtic decoration based on a scroll design.

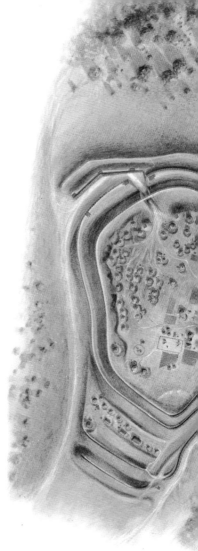

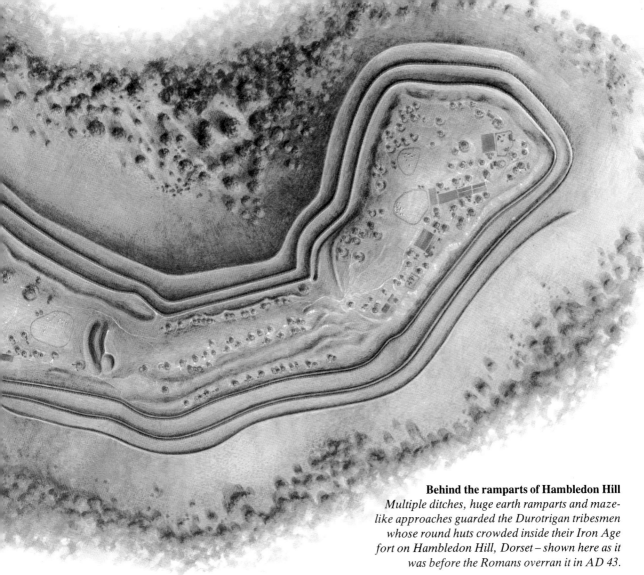

Behind the ramparts of Hambledon Hill
Multiple ditches, huge earth ramparts and maze-like approaches guarded the Durotrigan tribesmen whose round huts crowded inside their Iron Age fort on Hambledon Hill, Dorset – shown here as it was before the Romans overran it in AD 43.

Warp and woof
Wool from Celtic sheep was spun on spindles, then woven on simple looms like this reconstruction at Petersfield. The warps – vertical threads – were kept straight on the wooden frame by means of clay weights on the lower ends. The wool would have been dyed with vegetable dyes, perhaps woven in a tartan-like pattern.

Celtic pastoral
The reconstructed Iron Age settlement at Butser Hill, near Petersfield, Hampshire, shows how Celtic farming families lived and worked about the time of the Roman invasion. Haycocks, animal pens and living quarters were surrounded by wattle fencing, and frequently the entire settlement would be enclosed within a stockade to protect it from wild beasts and cattle raiders.

Close by the bronzesmith's workshop stood a hut quite different from any other found there – an 8 ft square room fronted by a porch. Lining the approach to it were pits in which sheep, cows and pigs had been buried. These were surely sacrifices, and the building itself, a shrine.

Other hill-fort shrines have been found at Pilsdon Pen and Maiden Castle. The Pilsdon sanctuary was quite elaborate: two circular huts stood within a timber palisade enclosing an otherwise empty area nearly 200 ft square. At Maiden Castle, the shrine was a large circular hut reached by a street from the east gate. A young child was buried in front of the hut entrance, and later, during the Roman occupation, the local people built a temple there to some part-Roman, part-Celtic god. At both Maiden Castle and Hod Hill, huts and workshops were crowded together in narrow lanes, and from the evidence found, life in these crowded hill-forts must have been lived in a cacophony of noise and continuing bustle more like that of a busy town of the Middle Ages.

Village and farm

Something approaching town life was obviously evolving in the south and south-west before the Romans arrived. Similar signs appear further north: the Coritani, though seldom occupying hill-forts, still lived in large settlements such as those at Dragonby and Ancaster, in Lincolnshire. These, moreover, were not fortified.

The most complete picture of village life at this time has emerged from the famous, but misleadingly named, 'lake-villages' of Glastonbury and Meare in Somerset. These were unusual in that they were built on the edge of marshland, on artificial platforms made of earth and brushwood. But otherwise, in their history and range of remains found, they seem to have been like the more conventional settlements. However, they are particularly interesting because the damp conditions have helped to preserve traces of wood and cloth articles that would have been destroyed elsewhere.

Glastonbury had dozens of round huts with wattle-and-daub walls and clay floors. Some floors were covered with wooden boards, and each house had a clay hearth. A variety of bronze and shale rings, bracelets, mirrors, needles, bone dice and a bone dice-box have been found there. Iron, Cornish tin and Mendip lead were used and worked. Dozens of bone carding combs – used in the initial stages of weaving – suggest a woollen industry.

However, despite the evidence of such relatively large centres of population, many more people of the Coritani, Dobunni and

Ceremonial finery
Most of what is known of the armour and equipment of the Celtic warrior is gleaned from occasional finds such as this bronze helmet and shield discovered in the River Thames. Neither, however, would have been very efficient in combat, and they were probably intended for ceremonial use only.

Durotriges lived outside, in isolated farmsteads of single-family huts, or hamlets of perhaps three or four related families. Such a hamlet was the settlement of ten round huts, that were both houses and stores, discovered at Colsterworth, Lincolnshire. A typical family farmstead with a single round living hut and rectangular granaries has been totally excavated at Tollard Royal, Wiltshire.

Life on such farmsteads must have been a year-in, year-out round of labour, but other items unearthed in the territory of these tribes indicate that there, too, a wealthy nobility existed. Their wealth was sometimes hoarded in the form of flat iron bars used as currency, but it was also expressed in collections of bronzework like that buried in the Polden Hills, Somerset, including horse ornaments and shield-bosses suggesting a warrior élite.

Further north, in the territory of the Coritani, fewer treasures from the pre-Roman period have been found. Some discoveries, such as gold neck-rings from the area immediately south of the Humber, indicate that certain Coritanian chieftains became quite wealthy. Coritani lands were rich in iron, and in an age when inter-tribal warfare was frequent, those who produced iron for swords and spears must have flourished.

British weaponry and defences were designed, of course, for Celtic warfare. Individual prowess was highly regarded, but ideas of siege warfare were fairly rudimentary. In both respects the British differed totally – and as it was to prove, fatally – from the Romans. The Roman army of Claudius, which landed in Britain nearly a century after Caesar, was a disciplined machine to which a few earthen ramparts presented little obstacle.

The coming of the conquerors

Claudius's army, assembled under the command of Aulus Plautius in AD 43, was made up of four regular legions – about 24,000 men – and an unknown but probably equal number of auxiliary troops. The auxiliaries included cavalry and infantry units, and also some specialist regiments such as the Batavians, recruited in the Low Countries, who were skilled in attacking across rivers. The army landed at Richborough, established a supply base there, and then moved westwards to the Medway. There a decisive battle was fought, probably somewhere near Rochester. The British put up a

The Romans in battle
For a number of reasons that included the need for a victory to bolster his shaky throne, Emperor Claudius (above) unleashed the disciplined fury of the legions upon the British tribes in AD 43. No pictorial record of the invasion exists, but the battles that followed the landings must have resembled this mêlée of Romans and Germanic warriors depicted on a sarcophagus in Rome of about the same period.

stiff resistance, but were eventually forced to fall back upon the Thames. Here, as on the Medway, it was the auxiliaries – probably the Batavians – who forced a river-crossing, enabling Plautius to establish a bridgehead and supply base on the north shore. There the Romans paused to lick their wounds – casualties had been heavy – and to await the arrival of the Emperor Claudius, who wished to partake in the final victory. Claudius arrived early in August with a large retinue of nobles, relatives, detachments of the Praetorian Guard, his personal physician, and a troop of elephants. The latter at least must have deeply impressed the British.

The army, now under Claudius's command, advanced upon Colchester against what seems to have been fairly light opposition; Roman sources differ on the subject. In any event, the Emperor, probably attended by his elephants, rode in triumph into the *oppidum*, and there he received the submission of a number of tribes. After little more than a fortnight, he returned to Rome before autumn gales made the Channel crossing too hazardous.

According to Suetonius, Claudius celebrated a second triumph on his return to Rome, and news of his conquest spread throughout the Empire. Arches commemorating the victory were erected in Rome and at Cyzicus in Asia Minor, while a group of touring athletes from the eastern Mediterranean sent Claudius a gold crown to salute his achievements: his letter of thanks survives today, in the British Museum.

These formalities accomplished, the army was now free to hammer out the new Roman province. The first objective was the subjugation of the land east of a rough line from Lyme Bay to the Humber, and to achieve this, Aulus Plautius divided his army into three divisions, each with a legion at its head; the remaining legion, the Twentieth Valeria, he left in reserve at Colchester. The Ninth Hispana was dispatched towards Lincoln, the land of the Coritani, while the Fourteenth Gemina marched west through what is now Leicestershire and into the West Midlands. Responsibility for the conquest of the lands of the Atrebates, Dobunni and the Durotriges – roughly Wessex – was given to the crack Second Augusta under the command of the future Emperor Vespasian.

Between AD 43 and 47 these three armies successfully completed their tasks, and established a frontier which ran somewhere to the north-west of the Fosse Way – a road probably built to supply a line of frontier forts that ran from the mouth of the Severn to that of the Humber. What kind of resistance was encountered by the Ninth and the Fourteenth is unknown, but a combination of archaeological evidence and a single, but informative, sentence in Suetonius's biography of Vespasian, give a glimpse of the conquest

Victory remembered
A fragment from a triumphal arch in Rome recalls Emperor Claudius's personal participation in the conquest of Britain. It tells how Reges Brit . . . *'Kings of Britain', submitted 'without loss' – that is, to Roman arms.*

Imperial guards
The relief from the Louvre (right) is said to portray members of the Praetorian Guard. A unit of this élite corps accompanied Claudius to Britain, but also returned to Rome with him two weeks later.

Gratitude of an emperor
This letter (below) written in Greek by the erudite Claudius, records the emperor's thanks to the Guild of Touring Athletes who, from Antioch in Syria, had sent him a golden crown to commemorate his conquest of Britain. The letter is now in the British Museum.

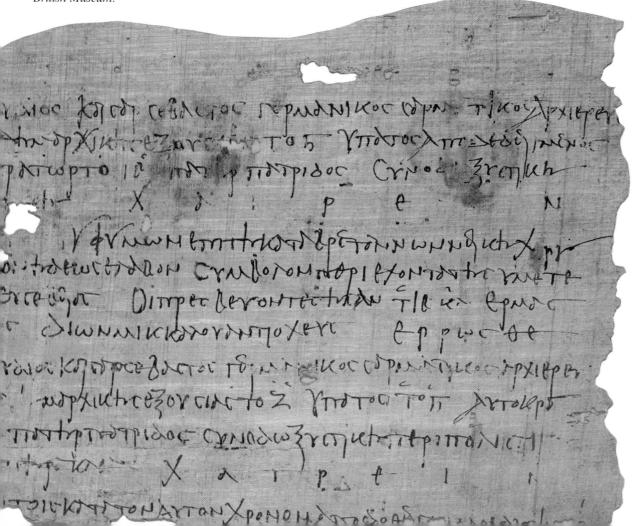

Campaigns of the Legions in Britain

→ IInd Augusta AD 43-84
→ IXth Hispana AD 43-84
→ XIVth Gemina AD 43-66
→ XXth Valeria AD 43-87

IInd Aduitrix was brought into Britain in AD71 and held in reserve at Lincoln until AD78, when it was transferred to Chester; it remained there until AD 87, when it was withdrawn from Britain.

○ YORK [AD 71] Legionary fortress, and the year in which the legion was first stationed there.

of the south-west. Recounting Vespasian's days in Britain, he says that between AD 43 and 47, Vespasian 'fought 30 battles, subjugated two warlike tribes, and captured more than 20 towns, besides the entire Isle of Wight'.

There is little doubt that the two warlike tribes were the Durotriges and the Dobunni. From a base at Fishbourne, on Chichester harbour, in the friendly territory of Verica's Atrebates, Vespasian launched a co-ordinated land and sea attack along the southern flank of the north Dorset hills, and up the valleys of the rivers Stour and Avon. Resistance was at first fierce, if unavailing. At Spettisbury Rings the remains of more than 100 slaughtered Britons were found, together with fragments of weapons and shields. A little further south-west it was the turn of the seemingly impregnable fort of Maiden Castle. There the legionaries faced up to four rings of deep ditches and high banks, pierced by intricately

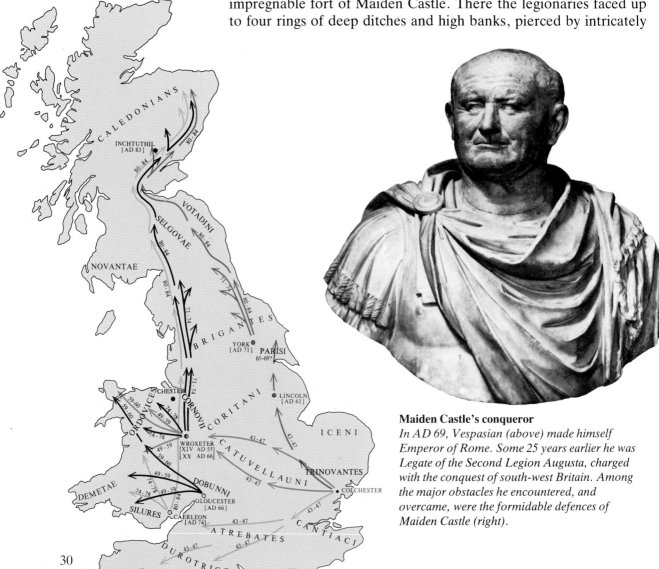

Maiden Castle's conqueror

In AD 69, Vespasian (above) made himself Emperor of Rome. Some 25 years earlier he was Legate of the Second Legion Augusta, charged with the conquest of south-west Britain. Among the major obstacles he encountered, and overcame, were the formidable defences of Maiden Castle (right).

30

winding entranceways designed to confuse and delay attackers. These entrances were defended by slingers, whose piles of ammunition have been found on the ramparts.

The Roman solution to the problem was simple, brutal and totally effective. The legionary artillery laid down a barrage of ballista bolts, with devastating results. A Briton whose spine was pierced by one of the heavy, pointed missiles – it was still lodged there when found almost 1,900 years after the battle – must have been one of many similar casualties. The barrage was followed by an attack on the east gateway, possibly under cover of smoke from burning huts outside the fort, and probably in the protection of the testudo, or 'tortoise', a shelter of overlapping shields. The wooden gates were fired, the legionaries swept in, and there followed an indiscriminate massacre of the defenders, whose bodies were later thrown into shallow graves near the ruined gates.

The events of Spettisbury and Maiden Castle clearly demonstrated the futility of attempting to defend hill-forts against the legions, and further west and north in Durotrigian territory there was now a marked change both in Roman tactics and in the British response. At Hod Hill, in the valley of the Stour, the Romans set up a single ballista. This soon found the range and bearing of a large hut within the fort – possibly the chieftain's house – and poured a concentrated fire into it.

This show of strength seems to have been sufficient to persuade the defenders of Hod Hill to surrender, for the gates were not destroyed and there was no massacre. To the north-west of Maiden Castle, single ballista bolts found near the shrine at Pilsdon Pen and in the farmstead at Tollard Royal to the north-east, suggest similar token displays for the benefit of wavering tribesmen. In the territory of the Dobunni, however, the Romans seem to have had to repeat the lesson handed out at Maiden Castle, for at Worlebury hill-fort, above Weston-super-Mare, there are again indications of a battle and a massacre of the defenders.

By about AD 47, the Romans were firmly established over the whole of southern and central England, and had built garrison forts at strategic points throughout the country. The western and north-western frontiers still posed a problem. In the north, the Trent seems to have been used as a tenable if not entirely satisfactory frontier, which the Romans attempted to make more secure by making a treaty with the Brigantes, the tribe occupying most of the highland zone to the north of the river.

Between Newark-on-Trent and Gloucester, at the mouth of the Severn, there was a very unsatisfactory frontier which was neither marked nor defended by any significant natural features.

Ammunition dump
The Durotrigian defenders of Maiden Castle poured spears and slingstones upon the heads of the Second Legion as they fought their way up the hill, rampart by rampart. A dump of slingstones still lies among the defences.

Silent witness
*It was not the Roman practice
to grant quarter to vanquished
enemies, as can be seen from
the butchered remains of men,
women and children in south-
western forts. This defender of
Worlebury, Avon, was severely
wounded by a sword cut on the
back of the head.*

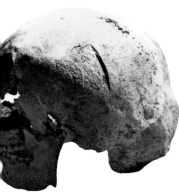

Death from afar
*Roman discipline and Roman
artillery were the deciding
factors in the conquest of the
hill-forts. These eloquent
remains from Maiden Castle
show the power of a ballista
whose bolt, fired from beyond
the ramparts, tore through a
Briton's spine.*

The Welsh tribes, particularly the Silures of south-east Wales and
the Ordovices of central Wales, were fiercely resisting any Roman
threat to their independence. Their leader was Caratacus, one of
Cunobelinus's surviving sons.

Between AD 47 and 60 the Romans were impelled, perhaps
unwillingly, to a frontier on the Severn and thence into Wales,
moving first to the River Wye and then to the River Usk at the foot
of the Black Mountains. In AD 59 and 60, in preparation for the
total conquest of Wales, two legions under the command of
Suetonius Paulinus, Governor of Britain, were launched against
north-west Wales and Anglesey.

The island of Anglesey, or Mona as it was known to the
Romans, seems to have been the last surviving centre of the Druidic
cult in Britain. Classical writers, in describing the Druids, generally
laid stress upon their human sacrifices, and the particularly un-
pleasant manner in which these were carried out.

Julius Caesar paints a vivid and terrifying picture of their
rituals: 'Some of them make use of gigantic wickerwork images, the
limbs of which are packed with living men; they are set alight and
the men perish in the inferno.'

Tacitus adds: 'It was their religion to drench their altars in the
blood of prisoners and consult their gods by means of human
entrails.'

When Paulinus attacked Anglesey in AD 60, the defenders
were urged on by the Druids, who stood close by, 'raising their
hands to heaven and screaming dreadful curses'. Swimming his
cavalry across the Menai Strait, Paulinus embarked his infantry in
flat-bottomed boats and launched a ferocious assault on the island.
Having taken it, he slaughtered the Druids and demolished their
sacred groves.

With the capture of Anglesey the Romans were poised for a
major series of campaigns that would bring Wales into the province.
But all plans were thrown into disorder by disastrous news from
eastern England.

The Iceni rise

The Iceni were a fierce warrior tribe occupying present-day Norfolk
and parts of Suffolk and Cambridgeshire. Little is known of them in
the pre-Roman era, except that their rulers appear to have been
exceptionally wealthy, and were able to employ goldsmiths to
produce exquisite gold neck-rings. Several hoards of these have
been unearthed, including more than 40 at Snettisham and five at

Ipswich. To judge, too, from the fine trappings for horses and chariots that have been discovered in Iceni territory, the Icenian aristocracy had a passion for martial display.

At the time of the Roman invasion, the tribe was ruled by a king named Antedios. He became an ally of the Romans by treaty, thereby preserving the independence of his kingdom and the wealth of his dynasty. In AD 49 the Iceni, or more probably a part of them, revolted when the Romans disarmed them, as a means of protecting their rear when the reserve legion at Colchester was sent to fight the Welsh. About this time Antedios died, and was succeeded by Prasutagus, who managed to perpetuate the alliance with Rome. But in AD 60 Prasutagus also died, and although he had been wily enough to make the Emperor Nero his co-heir, the Romans decided to incorporate his entire kingdom into the province. The men sent to accomplish this were both brutes and fools; what happened is described by the historian Tacitus, whose father-in-law, Julius Agricola, was serving in the army in Britain at that time:

'Kingdom and household alike were plundered like prizes of war, the one by Roman officers, the other by Roman slaves. As a beginning, his (Prasutagus's) widow Boudicca was flogged and their daughters raped. The Icenian chiefs were deprived of their hereditary estates . . . So they rebelled. With them rose the Trinovantes and others . . . They particularly hated the Roman ex-soldiers who had recently established a settlement at Camulodunum. The settlers drove the Trinovantes from their homes and land . . .'

The fury of the rebels was beyond anything the Romans could have dreamed of. Led by Boudicca, they moved against the hated colony at Colchester and burnt it to the ground, massacring its inhabitants when they sought refuge in the still-unfinished temple of Claudius. The nearest legion, the Ninth, who were in winter quarters at Longthorpe and Newton-on-Trent, attempted to intervene, but were defeated and forced to retire in disorder. Now the rebels moved on London, a rich prize, and also the obvious point for the arrival of Roman reinforcements. Like Colchester, it had as yet no walls to defend it and was an easy prey for the rebels. Paulinus, the governor, made a desperate dash with cavalry from north Wales to London, but although he arrived before Boudicca he could do little to defend the town, and instead retreated to the Midlands to await his two legions marching south-east along Watling Street.

London suffered the same fate as Colchester; thick layers of burnt debris still lie beneath both cities, marking the passage of Boudicca's tribesmen. In pursuit of the retreating Paulinus, they swung north along Watling Street, and engulfed St Albans in a wave

Claudius the god
This life-size head may well be a portrait of Emperor Claudius, snatched from the blazing ruins of his temple at Colchester by the Iceni, and later thrown away as they fled from the legions of Paulinus.

of fire. The Trinovantes especially had old scores to settle, and swept over the earthwork defences as though they hardly existed. The town and its surrounding farmsteads were razed to the ground.

According to Suetonius, Nero at some point in his reign considered withdrawing from Britain. If so, this must surely have been the time. Had he done so, the history of Roman Britain would have covered no more than 17 years, and the history of Britain and the British people would have been very different. As it was – perhaps while Nero still wavered – Paulinus gathered two legions and their accompanying auxiliaries somewhere in the Midlands and prepared to meet Boudicca in the battle that would decide the fate of Britain. Although Paulinus was heavily outnumbered, Roman discipline and superior weaponry prevailed. It was, in Tacitus' words, 'a glorious victory, comparable with bygone triumphs. According to one report almost 80,000 Britons fell. Our own casualties were about 400 dead.'

Roman vengeance was terrible. Fugitives from the battle were hunted down relentlessly, and as they ran, they cast aside the spoils gathered in the sacking of Colchester and London. From time to time, some of this loot still turns up in East Anglia – like the life-size head of Claudius found in the River Alde and a bronze helmet at Hawkedon, Suffolk. Boudicca herself is said to have taken poison.

About AD 65, the Romans began to reorganise in a way that suggests that they were once more considering the conquest of Wales, and possibly an extension of the northern frontier. But before either could be undertaken, there remained the irksome question of the far south-west – a block of unconquered territory that presented a potential threat to the Roman flank.

Icenian craftsmanship
The Icenian aristocracy grew rich on the fine farmlands of East Anglia, and spent their wealth on adorning themselves and their horses and chariots. These harness pieces in bronze and enamel typify the skills of their craftsmen.

Expansion to the west

Vespasian's Second Legion, in the initial south-western campaign, does not seem to have penetrated further west than Exeter, which became a fort and supply base at one end of the Fosse Way. Beyond Exeter lay the tapering peninsula occupied by the Dumnonii, a poor people by comparison with their neighbours to the east. They issued no coins, built no large settlements, but lived instead in groupings of defended enclosures, the homes of local chieftains, and the small farmsteads of their dependants.

On the coasts, the defended enclosures were 'cliff castles' – promontories protected by the sea on three sides and by ramparts on the fourth. The best known of these is The Rumps, near Padstow. Further inland, settlements consisted of hundreds of farmsteads and a number of fortified enclosures, defended by two or three rings of banks and ditches protecting ten or a dozen huts. Such wealth as the Dumnonian chieftains possessed is likely to have come as much from trading in tin rather than rearing sheep or cattle. The discovery of Durotrigian and Dobunnic coins in Dumnonia shows that the Dumnonii traded with these tribes, as does the appearance of Cornish tin at Glastonbury. Coins from Brittany testify to cross-Channel trade contacts, and it was through this link that Cornish tin reached the Mediterranean.

Tin may well have been a factor in the Romans' decision to conquer the region. The fort at Nanstallon, built about AD 65, yielded evidence of the exploitation of local tin. Other forts in Dumnonia are as yet scarcely known, although there were watching posts on the cliff-tops along the Bristol Channel to guard against raiders from south Wales and to keep an eye on Roman supply ships proceeding to the base at Sea Mills near the mouth of the Avon.

Sea fort
The Dumnonii of the south-west peninsula were politically fragmented and ruled by local petty chieftains who lived in fortlets or on coastal promontories like this one (above) at The Rumps, near Padstow. Secured by cliffs and the sea on three sides, landward access was protected by ramparts and ditches whose remains are still clearly visible.

Problems in the north

If the invasion of the Cornish peninsula in the mid-60s was intended to provide a jumping-off ground for the final conquest of Wales, then, like Paulinus's Anglesey expedition in AD 60, it ended in frustration. In AD 69, Rome exploded into civil wars that one way and another embroiled army units throughout the Empire, including those in Britain.

At the same time, the whole Roman strategy on the province's northern frontier collapsed in ruins. Since AD 43 the security of this frontier had depended as much on the treaty alliance with the

Masterpiece in miniature
This small bronze mount, found among the debris of Venutius's conquered stronghold at Stanwick, reflects the simple elegance of Celtic craftsmanship. Two opposed 'trumpet scrolls', and a pair of almond-shaped eyes, create a superb caricature of a doleful horse.

Bastion of the Brigantes
The Brigantian forces that blocked the Roman advance to the north were centred upon a fortified settlement at Stanwick, North Yorkshire. The defences, which have been reconstructed (left), consisted of ditches and stone walls. But they were overwhelmed by the Ninth Legion, and the Brigantian king, Venutius, was slain in the battle.

End of the race
Two great iron tyres and the traces of wooden spokes mark the grave of a Parisi charioteer whose vehicle had been buried with him. Ten similar burials have been found in eastern Yorkshire, usually in cemeteries, and surrounded by much simpler interments.

The horse soldiers
Julius Caesar himself tells how the Celts used their chariots in battle. The driver would control the horses, while the warrior behind him would hurl javelins at the foe before leaping off to fight on foot. This lively representation on a Gallic coin bears out Caesar's account.

Brigantes as on the Roman forts along the Trent and in the west Midlands. But Cartimandua, the pro-Roman queen of the Brigantes, had been under increasing pressure from rebels within her own kingdom, and particularly from Venutius, her ex-husband. Venutius finally succeeded in toppling Cartimandua, and the Romans could do little more than rescue the queen and hold the existing frontier. Overnight the northern frontier had become the immediate and major problem, whose only solution was the conquest of the Brigantes.

This was not a task to be undertaken lightly. The tribe was probably the most numerous in Britain, and its bleak Pennine heartland was a difficult territory to conquer. On the other hand,

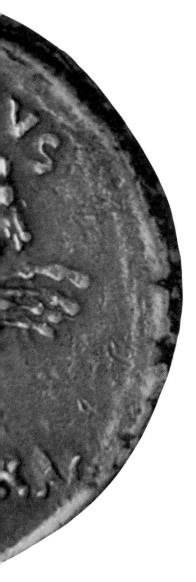

Celtic gold
So far as is known, the Parisi of Yorkshire minted no money, yet their cousins in northern Gaul – who gave their name to Paris – created a coinage that included this handsome gold stater.

the Brigantes had relatively few hill-forts. Although some of these forts, such as Almondbury near Huddersfield, were defended against the Roman advance, it appears that most of them had ceased to be occupied by the mid-1st century AD. The Brigantes seem to have been socially more fragmented than the tribes of southern Britain, perhaps because many of them led a nomadic existence as shepherds, moving their flocks from pasture to pasture. Perhaps Julius Caesar was thinking of the Brigantes when he wrote: 'Most of the tribes in the interior do not grow corn, but live on milk and meat, and wear skins.' Strabo, too, spoke of some of the British who 'have plenty of milk, but do not know how to make cheese; and they know nothing of planting or of any sort of husbandry'.

The outlines of Iron Age fields have been found in Brigantia, but there is little or no sign of storage pits and querns, to suggest that the Brigantes practised extensive agriculture. Poor soils, the steepness of the land, and the wet climate all suggest that their fields were used mainly for grazing, rather than for cultivation.

However, the existence of a well-to-do warrior élite is revealed by occasional finds of iron swords and decorated scabbards, by warrior graves such as those at Thorpe and Clotherholm, and by a similar find at the great fortress at Stanwick in North Yorkshire. Within no more than 20 years, this settlement had developed from a 17 acre fort to a massive fortified enclosure covering more than 700 acres, and defended by deep, rock-cut ditches dug in front of high, stone-faced ramparts.

Although circular living huts stood inside the defences, most of the enclosed area was intended as safe grazing for cattle. The size of these herds and of the labour force needed to build the defences, together with the quantity of military equipment found there, all suggest that Stanwick was the stronghold of Venutius.

The task facing the Romans in AD 69 was not an enviable one, but the Brigantians possessed two weaknesses that the Romans were able to exploit. The first was the very size and nature of the Brigantian homeland; it made campaigning difficult, but it also made it difficult for Venutius to unite his forces or even co-ordinate their activities. The second was an exposed eastern flank, due to the presence of the Parisi, an independent people of Gallic descent who lived in what is now eastern Yorkshire and Humberside.

To judge from aerial photographs, these industrious farmers built dyke systems dividing much of their territory into estates containing pasture and arable land, with separate areas for burial and settlement.

Their orderly cemeteries – small burial mounds within square, ditched enclosures – give evidence of the affluence of the Parisi and of their skilled craftsmanship. Of the hundreds of graves in some of the larger cemeteries, most contained a joint of meat, some pots, or a personal item such as a brooch or a spear. But the most impressive are the chariot burials. These show that the Parisi were the kind of warriors that Caesar described, charioteers who raced into battle:

'... hurling javelins, and generally the terror inspired by the horses and the noise of the wheels is sufficient to throw their opponents' ranks into disorder. Then, after making their way between the squadrons of their own cavalry, they jump down from the chariots and engage on foot ... they attain such proficiency that even on a steep incline they are able to control the horses at full gallop, and to check and turn them in a moment. They can run along the chariot pole, stand on the yoke, and get back into the chariot as quick as lightning.'

The most obvious route by which the Romans might attack the Brigantian stronghold at Stanwick was through the territory of the Parisi, where dry, firm ground could be guaranteed, and where there was no immediate danger of a flank attack coming down from the Pennines. A line of four forts from Brough-on-Humber to Malton marks the line of this initial Roman advance, which may have taken place between 69 and 71, and paved the way for three years' hard campaigning under the general Petilius Cerialis.

Despite their chariots and magnificent warrior skills, the Parisi seem to have offered little opposition to the Roman advance. This was due to a mixture of sound sense and economic wisdom. The Parisi apparently had flourishing trade contacts with the Roman province; and in any case, for nearly 30 years the Romans had been poised at the Humber, on their southern borders. When the larger and more powerful tribes of the south-east had failed to stop the Romans, there was little hope of the Parisi doing so.

Details of Cerialis's campaigns against the Brigantes are obscure, largely because Tacitus, the historian of the conquest, was much more concerned with glorifying the achievements of his father-in-law Agricola, and so understates the role that Cerialis played. Tacitus grudgingly admits that 'after a series of battles, some not uncostly, Petilius had operated, if not actually triumphed, over the major part of their (the Brigantes) territory'.

The general impression created by Tacitus' brief summary is confirmed by the limited archaeological evidence. Cerialis used two legions to attack Brigantia. The Twentieth, commanded by Agricola, was ordered to march up the west side of the Pennines; the Ninth, under Cerialis himself, moved against the eastern flank from its springboard in the Parisi territory.

The remains of fired huts and demolished defences show that

War chariot
Though much of Wales was unsuited to the use of the chariot, the remains of ten of these vehicles have been discovered in Anglesey. From them it was possible to reconstruct a Welsh war chariot of the 1st century AD. With its two-man crew, it would have been hauled by ponies.

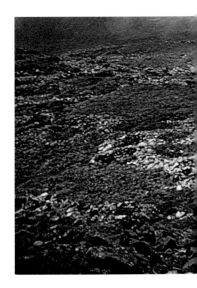

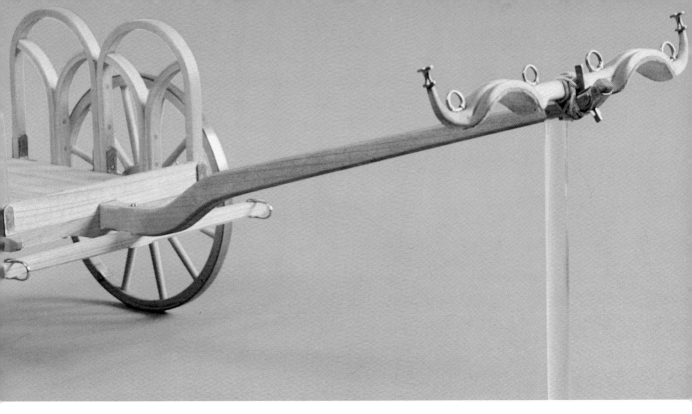

Security in the clouds

On the summit of Tre'r Ceiri, the tribesmen of north-west Wales built a settlement of about 80 huts, including outbuildings, surrounded by stone ramparts; doubtless the inhabitants grazed their sheep on the nearby bleak hillsides. Considerable remains of the settlement (below) survive.

Stanwick and Almondbury were attacked and captured, and in one of the battles Venutius was killed, leaving the Brigantes intimidated and leaderless. Cerialis's line of advance is indicated by the three marching camps his legion built in the Stainmore pass, on its way to join up with Agricola's Twentieth at Carlisle. Having done so, Roman intentions towards the Brigantes were made abundantly clear by the establishment of a legionary fortress at York, from which the whole eastern flank of the tribal territory could be dominated. Now, at last, the Romans felt able to turn their attention to the long-overdue solution of the Welsh problem.

The march on Wales

Despite the campaigns of the 50s and the preparations of the mid-60s, the tribes of Wales were still free and still posed a constant threat to the western parts of the province. The Roman frontier stood along the foot of the mountainous heartland of Wales and, in the south, on the lower reaches of the River Usk. Beyond stood tribes whose hatred of Rome was implacable – the powerful Silures and Ordovices, together with a number of lesser peoples.

The swarthy, curly haired Silures, who faced the Roman garrisons along the Usk and the edge of the Black Mountains, may originally have established their capital in the 5 acre hill-fort at Llanmelin Wood. They appear also to have occupied other hill-forts in the eastern part of their territory until the time of the Roman invasion. Otherwise, they lived much as their Cornish cousins, in defended cliff-top sites and small walled farmsteads scattered among the hills. There is little to suggest from any of the sites so far discovered that the Silures possessed much in the way of riches; yet their fighting qualities and knowledge of their wild terrain placed them among the most obdurate enemies of Rome.

The Ordovices, tribesmen of Snowdonia and central and north-western Wales, put up an equally ferocious fight based largely upon their hill-forts. On the flat tops of steep, rock-girt hills and mountains, the Ordovices built strong stone ramparts enclosing large villages of up to 100 huts. Traces of them, on cloud-girt Garn Boduan and Tre'r Ceiri, can be seen to this day. The huts cluster in groups, each group seemingly representing the house, workshops and stores of a single family, with its cultivation plots. Again, there is little sign of prosperity, yet if the great hoard of objects found in a peat bog at Llyn Cerrig Bach, on Anglesey, is any guide, the Ordovices managed to accumulate large quantities of expensive metalwork. The find consisted of more than 130 objects, some of which came from south-west England, Ireland and Brigantia. The remainder were presumably Ordovician in origin, and included swords, spears, harness, shield embellishments, and the wheels of at least ten chariots, the tribute and ritual gifts sent from a wide area to this Druidic cult centre.

So when the new Roman governor, Julius Frontinus, began his Welsh campaigns in AD 74, he was faced both by difficult terrain and by fierce and resolute enemies. Tacitus makes little mention of Frontinus's campaigns, but in the space of three years the Roman governor is said to have subdued the Silures and begun the task of conquering the Ordovices. Victory was nailed down by the establishment of legionary fortresses at Caerleon and Chester, the two key strongholds on which control of Wales was to be based. In addition, a series of infantry and cavalry forts was built to stand at strategic points through the Welsh valleys, so controlling the movements of the tribes.

Julius Agricola returned to Britain in AD 78, this time as provincial governor. He swiftly put the finishing touches to Frontinus's campaigns by finally crushing the Ordovices and completing the garrisoning of Wales. Next year he rounded off his conquests with a rapid and apparently indiscriminate campaign of terror in Brigantia, making assurance doubly sure with a complex of garrison forts controlling the eastern and western flanks of the Pennines and the Pennine passes. By AD 79, what is now England and Wales was firmly under Roman occupation.

Lonely capital
Wild, legend-haunted Eildon Hill, Borders, was the tribal capital of the Selgovae. The ramparts enclosed some 500 huts and outbuildings – room for about 1,000 people.

Man-made isle
A favourite form of defence in the north-western fringes of Britain was the crannog, an artificial island in a lake. This reconstructed example (below) is in Co. Clare, Ireland.

The island conquered

Family dwelling
So enduring are the massive double walls of Dun Telve broch (left) near Glenelg, that they still stand to a height of 30 ft and more, even after the passage of 2,000 years. Brochs, which had rooms built into the thickness of the walls, are fairly common in northern Scotland and the Isles, and seem to have been built to defend family groups against the depredations of their neighbours. The inhabitants probably made their living from fishing, primitive farming and a little piracy and slave-trading.

Already the frontiers of the province of Britannia had been pushed far beyond those envisaged at the time of the invasion, and it might be supposed that the Romans would now rest content. It seems clear, however, both from the speed and determination of Agricola's actions in 78 and 79, and from the single-mindedness of his subsequent campaigns, that Vespasian – now Emperor of Rome – had made up his mind to attempt the conquest of the whole island. The army must now prepare to march north of Brigantia, into territories completely unknown and against tribes that can have been little more than names to the Roman commanders.

From east to west across the southern uplands of Scotland were the lands of the Votadini, the Selgovae and the Novantae. Small hill-forts or defended settlements are numerous in the territory of the Votadini and Selgovae, although in the 1st century unwalled settlements of stone-built huts, or small enclosed farmyards with just two or three buildings in them, were becoming common. The impressive hill-fort at Traprain Law was the capital of the Votadini, and the one at Eildon Hill probably played a similar role for the Selgovae.

South-west Scotland – the country of the Novantae – presents a different, and less-peaceful picture of scattered, isolated farmsteads, almost invariably fortified. Some are crannogs – artificial platforms built on the edge of lochs and approachable only by boat or a narrow causeway. Others are duns – roughly oval or circular enclosures defended by a strong stone wall. Other farms still were centred on brochs – massive stone towers up to 40 ft high.

Brochs have been found as far north as Orkney, while between the firths of Forth and Moray lie a number of defended settlements. The inhabitants of the whole of this northern part of Scotland were collectively labelled 'Caledonians', whom Tacitus describes as being red-haired and large of limb.

Agricola set out to conquer this vast and largely inhospitable area with the same mixture of ruthlessness and drive that had marked his campaigns against the Welsh and the Brigantes. Between AD 80 and 81 he brought the whole of southern Scotland under Roman domination, and began the construction of two roads to the forts that would guarantee his supply routes and secure the southern uplands. The Novantae were brought to submission in 82, leaving Agricola free to prepare for the final northern push.

With a fleet in support, securing his supplies and launching surprise attacks on coastal settlements, Agricola marched north of the Tay with three legions and supporting auxiliaries. His line of advance can still be traced by the camps of his legions.

In AD 84, Agricola managed to provoke the Caledonian leader, Calgacus, into fighting a pitched battle. Somewhere just north-west of Inverurie, perhaps near the marching camp at Durno, the two armies clashed in the battle of Mons Graupius. While the three legions were held in reserve, a force of 8,000 auxiliary infantry and 3,000 cavalry fought and destroyed a Caledonian force estimated at more than 30,000 men. When the Caledonians broke and fled the field, the cavalry pursued them relentlessly and cut them down. Ten thousand are said to have fallen. Tacitus describes the great emptiness that greeted the Romans next morning:

'A grim silence reigned on every hand, the hills were deserted, only here and there was smoke seen rising from chimneys in the distance, and our scouts found no one to encounter them.'

Behind the victorious Romans stretched thousands of square miles over which they were the undisputed masters, but had hardly yet explored. Now their task was to shape it to the Roman image. In

Imperial optimism
Successive emperors claimed to have completed the conquest of Britain and to have at last established its frontiers. This coin was issued by Antoninus Pius in the 2nd century to celebrate his northern victories; it shows Britannia, looking remarkably like her representation on old pennies, symbolising the final pacification of Britain.

Hill-fort hoard
Looming forbiddingly above its surrounding fields, Traprain Law was the capital of the Votadini tribe, in Lothian. Earthen ramparts enclosed 40 acres in this 500 ft high hill-fort. Its inhabitants traded with the Roman province, and much Roman ware was found there. A fine hoard of silver now in the Edinburgh Museum of Antiquities may be trade goods or raiders' loot.

the north and west this would never be easy, for there lived people of fiercely independent spirit, with little to lose, and a way of life that had nothing in common with that of the conqueror, whose incursions they continued bitterly to resist.

In the south and east, however, a century of contact with the Roman Empire engendered a native population whose social and economic background was not totally different from that of Rome. Indeed, while Caledonian warriors were dying on Roman swords at Mons Graupius, people in southern Britain were building new towns and learning to run local affairs. The *pax Romana* had arrived.

45

THE PUZZLE

Clues from cemeteries, dumps and lonely hillsides rebuild the portrait of a long-vanished society

If written records were all that remained, then present-day knowledge of Roman and pre-Roman Britain would be slight indeed; a few accounts of battle and conquest, a number of names on tombstones, a few miraculously preserved letters. But of day-to-day life, practically nothing would be known at all.

That a considerable amount is known, is due very largely to archaeology – a science that involves not only excavation, but the endless and exhaustive collation, comparison and interpretation of finds that over years builds up a picture of a vanished age. Careful sifting of the rubble of a building long razed to the ground and buried beneath the turf reveals tiles and window-glass, door-fixings, drains and wall-plaster, as well as the fragments of a hundred discarded everyday objects, from which the life style and occupations of successive owners of the building can be deduced.

Burials, especially where they occur in large cemeteries, reveal a good deal about life expectancy, disease and diet in a particular period, while the articles buried with the deceased tell much about religious beliefs and craftsmanship. Rubbish pits, too, rich with ancient debris, add their quota to the portrait, while insect and plant remains hint at the vegetation of 20 centuries ago.

Despite the intensive cultivation of the last couple of hundred years or so, the outlines of thousands of acres of Romano-British landscape still survive. On moor and mountainside, archaeologists have managed to identify the remains of ancient droveways, animal pens and cultivated plots, and can recognise, in the shadows that appear at sunset on the Downs of southern England, the long, narrow outlines of Roman field patterns.

All this constitutes the solid background of Romano-British archaeology, but very occasionally a treasure-hoard is unearthed that highlights some moment of drama or crisis that took place during the 350 year occupation. Such discoveries may have great monetary value, but vastly more important to the scholar are the circumstances in which they were found, and the questions of when they were buried or jettisoned, by whom, and why? The study of a hoard of coins, for example, may provide a useful guide to the economy of a particular period, while famous finds like the Appleshaw pewter, the Mildenhall treasure and the priest's regalia unearthed at Barkway, Hertfordshire, probably reflect times of invasion, brigandage or religious persecution.

Money talks

Ancient coins reflect the political history of the times. The two smaller coins were struck in Rome, about 40 BC. One showing Gallia, the personification of Gaul, recalls the creation of the province in 51 BC, while the other may portray Vercingetorix, the leader of the Gallic resistance defeated by Julius Caesar. The distribution of Belgic coins, like the one found in Buckinghamshire (below), helps to trace the spread of Belgic domination in southern England.

Urn burial

Much – perhaps even a major part – of the field archaeologist's life is taken up with emergency digs in advance of the invading bulldozers. While Britain's motorway scheme has been responsible for the discovery of hundreds of archaeological sites, it has also destroyed a vast number, and often no more than a few days can be allowed for study before the tractors move in. The grave shown here is one of many in a large 2nd-century Romano-British cemetery discovered during the construction of the Puckeridge by-pass in Hertfordshire. Excavated by the East Herts Archaeological Group, the grave is chiefly remarkable for containing the cremated remains of two people. The ashes have been placed in two large urns, surrounded by platters, flagons and flasks – all that the dead might require for their sojourn in the next world. Even a brief study of such sites can reveal much about the religious beliefs, prosperity and degree of craftsmanship of the period and community.

47

CHAPTER TWO

Masters of Britain

Disciplined killer and versatile craftsman: the Roman soldier at war, work and play

Trooper of Rome
The footslogging legionaries were the backbone of the Roman army, but the cavalry were its wings. The tombstone (left) celebrates the fighting spirit of the horse-soldiers, while the horse mask (below) suggests the brilliance of their turn-out.

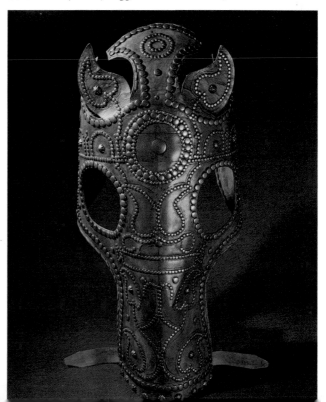

LUCIUS VITELLIUS TANCINUS WAS PROBABLY A MAN OF HUMBLE ANCESTRY, BORN INTO MODEST CIRCUMSTANCES. It is unlikely that he ever saw himself as a member of a ruling élite, or as a part of the most ruthless and efficient fighting machine the world had ever seen; yet that is just what he became. Tancinus was born in the Roman province of Spain, perhaps around the time of Augustus's death in AD 14. He was a tribesman of the Vettones, and lived in their city of Caurium, about 150 miles west of Madrid. At the age of 20 he enlisted in the cavalry regiment raised in his region – the *Ala* of Vettones. These were auxiliary troops, the second line of the Roman army; for Tancinus, not being a Roman citizen, was not eligible to join the legions. Ten years after Tancinus joined the army, his regiment was put under the command of Aulus Plautius as one of the many auxiliary regiments selected to support the legions in the invasion of Britain.

Very shortly after the initial landings, Tancinus and his comrades were fighting in the West Country, under the direct command of Vespasian, and they may well have taken part in the storming of Maiden Castle, Hod Hill and Spettisbury Rings. Once the territory was conquered, they would certainly have ridden many patrols in Dorset and Somerset. In AD 47, when Silures from Wales launched one of their attacks across the Severn, Tancinus's regiment may have distinguished itself and won a great victory. Certainly, around this time, the regiment was given a block grant of Roman citizenship for valour, and Tancinus, on becoming a citizen, followed the usual custom of adopting the forenames of some distinguished Roman contemporary. The names he chose – Lucius Vitellius – are those of one of the consuls elected in Rome in AD 47. The new-fledged citizen of Rome completed his 25 years' service at just about the time of Boudicca's revolt, but perhaps due to the emergency, did not receive his discharge. He was probably still in the army when he died at Bath, aged 46, about AD 60.

This brief biography of a Roman soldier reflects the lives of so many of his kind who, for the best part of two millennia, have lain in graves so far from home. Among the 40,000 to 60,000 Roman troops stationed in Britain at any one time, were men from almost every part of the Empire. They came from North Africa, Syria, Turkey, Greece, Eastern Europe, Germany, France, Spain and, of course, Italy itself. They left families, friends, a familiar way of life, and often a warm, dry land to come to a strange, still largely untamed country with a climate that was already notorious, and where they faced at best suspicious provincials, and at worst hostile savages. Why did they do it?

Some of these soldiers had been conscripted, but most had

Joining up
Whatever the advantages of 'following the Eagles', it was still a big step for the 18-year-old recruit to sign away a quarter-century of his life, knowing that in all probability he would finish his service, and spend his last days, in some far-off corner of the Empire and never see his family again. The gravity of joining the legions is depicted in this relief from Rome in which a recruit signs on, takes the oath of allegiance, and dons uniform and shield before going off to make sacrifice to Mars, god of war.

volunteered, well aware of the conditions of service and its likely dangers. To some, danger and excitement would have been sufficient lure to join the army, just as it is today; but most recruits were attracted by other considerations. Again, like modern regular armies, that of Rome offered a secure, reasonably well-paid profession with the opportunity to learn a craft and earn promotion, under conditions which were no worse, and often better, than those of the civilian population. But the main attraction was the ultimate prize, gained on retirement – for the Roman legionary, an award of land or cash, and for the auxiliary from the provinces, the gift of citizenship, with all its attendant privileges.

To earn these rewards, both legionary and auxiliary signed on for 25 years. The only short-term engagements were for the senior officers. These men, the legion's commander and the military tribunes who assisted him, held their posts for only a few years at a time, in between a variety of civilian administrative postings. The enduring strength of the army and the real element of continuity lay with the long-service men – the rank and file and the non-commissioned officers, which included the centurions.

Bronze bonnet
*What appears to be a peak on
this eminently practical
legionary helmet – now in the
Verulamium Museum – is
actually a neck-guard.
Additional protection was
provided by cheek-pieces.*

The new recruit

Such were the attractions of army life that the Romans could afford to be particular about whom they recruited. High standards of physical fitness were demanded: a broad chest, strong arms, an upright carriage and bright eyes. Some of these requirements, however, might be waived if the recruit possessed a letter of introduction from a father or a friend who had been a soldier, and who knew someone of importance in the unit.

There were other qualifications, too. A man had to prove that he was a freeman and was of good character. Above all, the recruit to the regular legions had to be a Roman citizen. Possession of the rights and privileges of citizenship, including full protection under the law and eligibility for government office, meant that the soldier had a vested interest in the state, and would be loyal to it. In addition, a cavalryman had to meet a height qualification of 5 ft 8 in.

Having measured up thus far, the successful applicant would be sent to his unit, bearing a document declaring his name, age and description. For the most part, the new recruits would be young men of 18 to 22 years of age; but the legionary Marcus Valerius Latinus, who died at the age of 35 and was also buried at Bath, apparently joined up at 15.

The new recruit took an oath of loyalty to the emperor, which also embraced loyalty to his unit, to its sacred eagle standards, and to his comrades. If he did not already know Latin, he would have to

Cavalry splendour
*These attractively decorated clips
and studs of silvered bronze
once embellished the uniform of
a Roman cavalryman. They
were found in Yorkshire.*

The legion's honour

Standard-bearers, like this one in a Roman relief, were senior NCOs who fought always at the forefront of the battle. The standards they carried were both a rallying-point and a sacred symbol of the legion's honour; to lose them was a disgrace that reflected upon every man in the unit, and the troops would willingly die in their defence.

Parade dress

Unlike the auxiliaries, whose uniforms varied enormously, the regular legions dressed to a fairly standard pattern throughout the Empire. This fine bronze portrays a legionary of the 2nd century AD wearing a crested parade helmet and the overlapping bronze armour of the period. Despite the corselet's heavy appearance, a cunning arrangement of straps, buckles and thongs permitted remarkable ease of movement. Soldiers serving in the chillier provinces were issued with leather breeches and heavy red cloaks, and often stuffed their open-toed boots with fur.

learn at least enough to understand words of command. He was then issued with his uniform. For the legionary at the time of the invasion of Britain this consisted of a short-skirted leather tunic and, if serving in the cold climate of northern Europe, a pair of leggings. Strong leather boots protected his feet. Over the tunic he wore a cuirass of iron hoops protecting shoulders and trunk, and a breastplate and backplate. His head was protected by a metal helmet with a neck guard and cheek-pieces. Centurions wore a slightly different uniform, with shoes, a leather corselet shaped to fit the body, and bronze greaves to protect the shins. The uniforms of auxiliaries varied from one unit to another, but a leather tunic with chain or scale armour over it was common in most. All troops serving in northern Europe were issued with warm woollen cloaks.

The uniform was expensive, and its cost was deducted from the soldier's pay, as was that of subsequent replacements. This was not his only expense. Accounts from Egypt reveal that debits were made for weapons, bedding, a share in the tent used on campaign, the annual camp dinner, the unit's burial fund, and even for rations. Food, the most expensive item, would cost a legionary about one-third of his year's wages. If weapons or uniform had to be replaced, then with other stoppages the soldier might end up with no more than one-fifth of his pay to spend. Even so, he was better off than an unskilled labourer in civilian life.

The rates of pay varied from one type of unit to another. Crack legionary troops at the time of Emperor Hadrian (AD 117–38) are thought to have earned about 300 silver denarii a year, a trooper in the cavalry 200, a cavalryman in a part-mounted regiment 150, and a private in an auxiliary infantry unit 100 denarii. Non-commissioned officers were paid on higher but related scales, junior NCOs receiving one-and-a-half times the basic rate, and the more senior NCOs double.

Discipline was strict to the point of harshness. Centurions carried canes which they appear to have used freely, and loss of rank, seniority or privileges were frequent punishments. Dishonourable discharge meant losing both the shelter of the unit and more important, the grant of land or citizenship on retirement. Men found guilty of barrack-room theft or of desertion could be, in military law, beaten to death by their comrades. Cowardice in battle sometimes led to decimation – literally, the execution of every tenth man in the unit concerned; the survivors were put on a ration of barley. But the greatest disgrace that could befall a legion, after an ignominious defeat perhaps, was disbandment and dispersion. This may have happened to a legion stationed in Britain, the Ninth Hispana, though the circumstances are uncertain.

The professional
Caecilius Avitus, who died at Chester aged 34, was an optio, *a senior NCO of long service. His modern equivalent, depending on his seniority, might be sergeant or company sergeant-major.*

The centurion
Marcus Facilis carries the vinewood staff that was both his badge of office and a means of instant punishment. He may have risen through the ranks, been appointed from the Praetorian Guard or even, if of good family, have entered the army as a centurion.

The hammers of Rome

Probably never before, and not for centuries after, was there a military formation that could equal the power and efficiency of a Roman legion. Ultimately, the strength of Rome rested upon the iron shoulders of its legions, of which there were generally about 30 stationed at various places throughout the Empire. Each one consisted of between 5,500 and 6,000 men. Of these, apart from 120 cavalry scouts and messengers, the vast majority were heavy infantry. The remainder included doctors, veterinary surgeons, secretaries, blacksmiths, engineers and carpenters. The foot soldiers were divided into ten cohorts, nine of which were subdivided into six centuries, each of 80 men, while the First Cohort consisted of five centuries of 160 picked troops apiece. The cohorts were led by

The legate
Caelius, commander of the Eighteenth Legion, was a man of considerable administrative experience, both civilian and military. His decorations were awards for bravery in the field.

their senior centurions, the First Cohort being under the command of the *primus pilus*, 'first javelin', or most senior centurion in the entire legion. Over all were the senior officers, consisting of a legate and six military tribunes.

Below the centurions were the sergeants and corporals – the *optios, signifers* and *immunes* – who between them controlled the day-to-day destinies of the rank and file, the tough, magnificently trained legionaries known throughout the Empire as the *caligatae*: the 'booted ones', or 'footsloggers'.

Promotion was slow. A legionary who was conscientious and had acquired a skill might hope to become a junior NCO after perhaps six or seven years, but only the best, and that after about 15 years' service, could expect to become a centurion. The centurion, in turn, would look for promotion within his own cohort, and hope eventually to become a centurion in the First Cohort. Considering the degree of competition, the *primus pilus* must have been a remarkable man indeed.

Auxiliary troops were organised in smaller units than the legions. Infantry units and mixed – that is, part-mounted – formations were usually organised as cohorts of 480 infantry and, in the case of the part-mounted units, 128 cavalry, each commanded by a Roman prefect. Cavalry regiments or *alae* were of approximately the same size as an infantry cohort.

Apart from regular infantry and cavalry, the auxiliaries also included a number of specialist units, such as the famous Syrian archers. A cohort of these bowmen served at Carvoran on Hadrian's Wall and Bar Hill on the Antonine Wall. Similarly, the Batavians from the Low Countries, who were specialists in river crossings, probably played an important role in the conquest of Britain and appear again as a garrison on Hadrian's Wall at the fort of Carrawburgh.

Rome marches

The Roman army on campaign was an awesome sight, and moved in much the same way whether in Judaea or Caledonia, covering up to 30 miles a day on forced marches. Flung out ahead of the main body were the auxiliary infantry, acting as scouts and advance guard. Behind them marched the leading legion, supported by cavalry. Then came the men who would build the marching camp for the force, consisting of ten men drafted from each century, and the pioneers who prepared the route for the main column.

At the head of the main body was the baggage of the

Foraging party
At the close of each day's march, each soldier set about his appointed task – some to build fortifications, some to pitch tents, some to forage for food and fodder.

Digging in
With entrenching tools such as this, legions on campaign built nightly marching camps. The traces of many of these camps are stamped on the British landscape to this day.

Marius's mules
A nickname for a legionary was mulus Marianus – *General Marius's mule – recalling the time when the general cut down the number of the legions' baggage animals and made the troops carry most of their equipment themselves. This relief of a legion crossing a bridge comes from Trajan's Column in Rome, a monument whose continuous frieze depicts army life during Emperor Trajan's campaigns in eastern Europe, about AD 100.*

headquarters staff, protected by cavalry, followed by the commanding officer and his escort. Behind him came the combined cavalry of the legions, followed by the remaining staff officers – legates, tribunes and prefects, with their escorts. At last, came the main legionary force. Each legion, six abreast, was preceded by its eagle bearer, surrounded by the standard bearers of the centuries. They marched at attention, accoutrements jingling, javelin heads glinting in the sun, to the endless, ominous rhythm beaten out by thousands of iron-shod boots.

When a halt was called for the night, sentries were posted and foragers for food and fuel were sent out. Meanwhile, other men would erect a camp in which the army could sleep in safety. The ability to construct one of these 'marching camps' in no more than two or three hours was one of the many remarkable features of the Roman army.

Normally, its defences consisted of a shallow ditch and low bank, surmounted by a palisade. On each of the four sides of the camp was a gateway, protected either by a detached length of bank and ditch running parallel to the main defences, or else by a curving and overlapping spur of the main bank and ditch. Marching camps with the second type of gateway all belong to the years AD 70–100, which includes the period of Agricola's Scottish campaign. Traces of his camps, still visible, enable the course of the invasion to be followed to this day. Marching camps vary greatly in size, but those used by Agricola in Scotland were either 30 acres or about 110 acres in extent. The first may have accommodated a single legion and up to six auxiliary cohorts, but the larger camps are big enough to have sheltered Agricola's entire force of nearly 30,000 men.

In the morning, breaking camp was carried out with the same disciplined efficiency. Tents were struck at a single trumpet call and loaded on to baggage animals at the sound of a second. Then the army formed up and continued its advance, until the enemy was discovered and brought to battle.

The killing-machine

Provided that the enemy was an undisciplined horde, as was usually the case, the superior weaponry and training of the legions made their mark quickly. The legionary was equipped with four weapons. His throwing weapon was a 7 ft javelin, which had a long, slender iron head on a wooden shaft, and was particularly effective at a range of about 30 yds. High on his right side, the legionary wore a *gladius*, a short sword, whose 20 in. blade had straight edges and a sharp point. He also carried an iron dagger which, like his sword, was worn in a richly decorated scabbard. In most armies, the shield was regarded as a means of defence, but the Roman legionary used his as a weapon, to push and batter an opponent off his feet. The legionary shield was semi-cylindrical in shape, and made of leather-covered laminated wood bound with bronze strips. It had an iron or bronze boss in the centre of its outer face and metal emblems that may have been unit markings.

The auxiliary units were less lavishly armed than the legionaries and usually carried oval shields. Auxiliary weapons, like auxiliary uniforms, varied considerably from one unit to another. Specialist units had their own weapons, such as the powerful composite bows of the Syrians – deadly up to 400 yds – and the lead bullets and slings of the Celts. Auxiliary cavalrymen carried two weapons – a lance and the *spatha*, a 29 in. slashing sword.

In battle, the cavalry were generally drawn up on the flanks, while the legions occupied the centre. The auxiliary infantry fought as skirmishers on the wings, though a number were also held in reserve. At Mons Graupius in Scotland, however, Agricola reversed the usual order and kept his legions in reserve while flinging the auxiliaries into the main attack.

But in the main, legionary battles were fought to a rigid pattern of tight formations held together by iron discipline. The

Victory in Caledonia
The crushing of the Caledonian tribes by the army of Antonius Pius in the years after AD 140 is celebrated here in a relief found on the Antonine Wall – the turf fortification that Antonius built between the Forth and Clyde. The Roman forces were over-extended, however, and within 20 years they had withdrawn southwards to the line of Hadrian's Wall. This was to remain the northern frontier of the province of Britain – and, indeed, of the whole Roman Empire – until the end of the occupation.

Fighting tortoise
This detail from Trajan's Column shows legionaries storming a Dacian stronghold in 'tortoise' formation, protected above and around by locked shields. The tactic was also employed in Britain, and was generally highly successful – provided the defenders had no boiling oil.

Missile launcher
Ballistas, represented here by a model in Newcastle Museum, were fearsome weapons against massed infantry, cavalry and even the defenders of the hill-forts that the legions encountered in southern Britain. The heavy bolts discharged by the machines could far outrange any missiles put up by a tribal enemy. Each legion was equipped with about 50 ballistas which were used to lay down a barrage of bolts in the 'softening-up' process preceding a general advance.

attack began with an intimidating discharge of javelins, that was intended not so much to kill as to force their opponents to discard their shields. Seven feet of javelin stuck into a man's shield made it unwieldy, if not a positive menace to his comrades. Before the enemy warriors could recover from the confusion, the legionaries were upon them, smashing iron shield bosses into faces and shoving their adversaries back in disorder. All the while, the short swords flickered and stabbed with deadly effect.

Few enemies could stand against the legions in pitched battle, and those who had tried it, including the British, generally tried to find other means of continuing the fight. The most successful seems to have been hit-and-run guerrilla tactics, such as those employed by the Silures of South Wales between the years AD 47–52. Perhaps the only other course open to an enemy of Rome was to shut himself up in a stronghold. But Britain had no strongholds capable of successful defence against the legions, who had developed siege warfare to a high degree. However, the mobile siege towers and battering rams that were used to overcome the defences of the

Jewish stronghold of Masada were not needed when storming native hill-forts like Maiden Castle. Neither probably were the large catapults known as onagers ('wild asses'), which could throw 150 lb stone balls 200 yds and more, though they were used in Britain as part of the defences of outlying forts on the northern frontier.

The siege weapon used against the British hill-forts was the smaller ballista, which rather resembled a monster cross-bow. These, too, could discharge stone balls, but iron bolts such as those discovered at Maiden Castle, Hod Hill and Pilsdon Pen were the more usual ammunition. Ballistas could kill at up to 400 yds and were remarkably accurate. With a barrage from these machines keeping the enemies' heads down, the legions could rush the slopes of a hill-fort and set fire to its gates.

This initial assault might be led by a testudo, or 'tortoise', comprised of a group of 27 men, who, formed up in four ranks, gained all-round protection by locking their shields overhead and on all sides. According to Tacitus, the testudo was used at least once in Britain, in a battle between Ostorius Scapula and Caractacus's Welshmen in AD 51. Apparently, the troops 'crossed the river without difficulty, and reached the ramparts ... Under a roof of locked shields, the Romans demolished the crude and clumsy stone embankment'.

For valour

As a reward for defeating Caractacus, Scapula received the highest honour the Empire could bestow upon a successful general – a triumph, or ceremonial procession held in his honour through the streets of Rome, and paid for by the State. No doubt there would have been lesser awards distributed to troops who had played a particularly valiant role in the battle. Tacitus mentions that only a couple of years previously, Scapula's own son had been awarded the *corona civica* (Citizens' Crown) for saving the life of a fellow-Roman during the Iceni revolt of AD 49. Other awards are known to have been won by soldiers on active service in Britain. Among them were two soldiers of the Eighth Legion, elements of which formed part of the invading force in AD 43. An inscription found in

Rome's last argument
Though adept with the throwing-spear, the legionary's principal weapon was the gladius, *or short sword. Despite the sword's two sharp edges, it was rare for the legionary to use more than its point in battle, when the blades flicked out in short, vicious thrusts from behind the wall of shields. The grip was of bone or wood, and the leather scabbard was embellished with medallions.*

Turin records that Gaius Silvanus, who had been *primus pilus* in the Eighth Legion, had been awarded neck-chains, armlets, medals and a gold crown for his part in the invasion, and a tribune of the Eighth, Lucius Candidus, was also awarded a gold crown for being the first man over an enemy rampart. The site of his heroic deed is not known, but it could have been the battlements of Maiden Castle.

Not only soldiers, but units too were awarded honours for outstanding conduct. The Sixth Legion, for example, was given the title *Victrix Pia Fidelis* – 'Victorious, Faithful and True'.

The occupying power

Apart from the Twentieth, firmly settled in Colchester, the other legions based in Britain during the first 15 years of the occupation were split up into detachments that, amalgamated with units of auxiliaries and cavalry, garrisoned forts up and down the country. Some of these early forts covered 30 acres, but whether large or small they were all built of timber and turf. The one at Longthorpe, near Peterborough, is typical. Sheltering a detachment of the Ninth Hispana and two troops of cavalry, it was defended by double ditches and turf ramparts topped by a timber palisade standing overall some 15 ft high. Within the defences were a headquarters building, a granary, stables and barrack accommodation for 2,500 men – the whole thing looking not unlike the forts built on the American frontier some 1,700 years later.

As the wars of conquest came to an end, and the garrison role of the army was established, the legions were brought together in fortresses of 40 to 50 acres, while the auxiliary units were re-assigned to smaller forts of 3 to 5 acres. At the same time, timber and turf were gradually replaced by stone. From the end of the 1st century onwards there were three permanent legionary fortresses in Britain; at Caerleon, Chester and York. Little is known and less can be seen today of the fortresses at Chester and York, but at Caerleon barracks, defences and an amphitheatre are still visible.

The clearest picture of what a full-sized legionary stronghold was like is provided by the most northerly fortress of the Roman Empire. In AD 83, at Inchtuthil, about 17 miles west of the present-day Dundee, Agricola planted the Twentieth Legion as the linchpin to his hold on Scotland. As it turned out, the Twentieth were to remain at Inchtuthil for only four years, and their great fortress was still unfinished when the order came to demolish it and march south to reinforce the army on the German frontier. Although Inchtuthil was a timber fortress, it was clearly built to the same general design

Consolidation
Victory accomplished, the army consolidated its conquests with turf and timber forts set up at strategic points throughout the new territory. Like everything the legions did, the building was swift, efficient and to a set pattern – even the turves were cut to a uniform size of 18 in. × 12 in. The turf walls, which could be

as the three permanent legionary fortresses, and because the site has never been built over, virtually its entire plan has been identified.

In its hey-day, it was impressive indeed – far more so than Longthorpe would ever have been. Its 53 acres were surrounded by earthen ramparts fronted by a stone wall, and a ditch 20 ft wide and more than 7 ft deep. This in turn was protected by a low bank with dry thorn clumps set into it.

Within its four gateways, the camp was a model of legionary organisation and discipline. The 20 ft wide street leading to head-quarters was flanked by storehouses fronted by verandas. Beyond the storehouses were barrack rooms arranged in blocks of six, one block for each cohort.

The southern half of the fortress contained a number of houses for senior officers, though apparently the legate's house was still not built when the legion marched out for the last time. In the northern half were wagon sheds, accommodation for a cavalry unit, a workshop and a very large hospital, as well as barracks.

remarkably long-lasting, were protected by ditches, palisades and heavy timber gateways. This detail from Trajan's Column shows troops building such a fort somewhere in eastern Europe, but exactly similar procedures were followed in many parts of Britain during the early years of the Roman occupation.

Senior officers' quarters were fairly luxurious. A covered walkway round an open courtyard or garden led to living rooms, bedrooms, kitchen and domestic quarters. The centurions of the First Cohort also appear to have lived in courtyard houses, though smaller than those of the senior officers. The centurions of the other cohorts, as was customary in the Roman army, lived in the barrack blocks. Even so, their living conditions were far superior to those of the men they commanded. A centurion was given four or five rooms, while the legionaries lived and slept eight men to a room measuring 17 by 14 ft, though the squad also had a smaller room in which to store their equipment. The crowded conditions may have had their advantages; at least they helped to dispel some of the chill of the Caledonian winters.

The fort contained granaries with raised floors to keep out vermin, and a legionary workshop where wagons were repaired. Apart from being a repair and maintenance depot, this was also probably the blacksmith's shop; when the building was abandoned a pit was dug and filled with iron tyres and nearly a million nails.

Opposite the workshop stood the legionary hospital, built around a courtyard or garden with 60 wards opening off a single, continuous corridor. The operating theatre also overlooked the central courtyard; the surgical implements departed with the legion, but in a fortress at Neuss in West Germany were found scalpels and *spatulae* – instruments that are still used for medical examination. At Neuss, too, were found the remains of five medicinal herbs, together with lentils, figs and garden peas, all of which are recommended in Roman medical texts for the treatment of invalids. No doubt similar implements and special foods were kept at Inchtuthil, to be dispensed by medical orderlies or doctors. At least one legionary doctor has been identified – a Greek called Hermogenes, who was doctor to the Twentieth Legion when it was stationed at Chester.

Finally, there was the headquarters building, located at the junction of the streets running from the gates of the fortress to its centre. This was built around an arcaded courtyard, at the rear of which was the entrance to a transverse wing. Beyond this, at the centre of a range of seven rooms, stood the legion's shrine. Here the Eagle and the other standards were kept, and the pay-chest too, where it could be protected by the standards and the gods as well as by more earthly sentinels. The three rooms on one side of the shrine were occupied by the adjutant and clerks, and those on the other side by the standard-bearers, whose duties included dealing with pay and savings, as do those of colour-sergeants in British regiments.

The legionary fortress contained every facility for the smooth

Stone springboard
The stone-built cavalry fort at Chesters on Hadrian's Wall was a base for Roman horsemen. They formed a mobile striking force that could be swiftly summoned to deal with emergencies along the Wall, or deep into the wild lands, north and south.

Imprint of Rome
The neat rectangle of a Roman fort superimposed upon British defences at Hod Hill, Dorset, eloquently declares a legion's victory.

Trouble spot
Reconstructed in modern times by men of the Royal Engineers, the fort at Baginton, Warwickshire, was originally built about AD 60. Its purpose was probably to keep an eye on the tribes after Boudicca's revolt. Later, it was used as a cavalry training depot.

65

running of the legion as a military machine. But for entertainment, the legionary had to go outside the ramparts. Close by the fortress there were generally baths and an amphitheatre, though there is no trace of either at Inchtuthil. Usually, too, a civilian settlement grew up outside the walls to meet those demands for which the military authorities made no provision – shops, women and drink.

Life in the legion

Recruits trained from dawn to dusk, but the qualified soldier drilled in the mornings only. Basic training lasted about four months, during which the recruits learned to keep military pace, step and dressing, generally with 50 lb packs on their backs. They were given dummy weapons to attack wooden stakes driven into the ground, and taught how to use shields and real swords. Those who could not swim were taught to do so.

From dummies, recruits moved on to real arms and human opponents – their comrades – but fought with the tips of their swords covered. Trained soldiers kept up their weapon training, and made five-hour, 20 mile route marches three times a month. Sloppy drill or poor weapon handling were rewarded by a crack from the centurion's cane, or by a few days on barley and water.

As well as drills and training in barracks, there were manoeuvres and fort-building exercises. Dummy forts and camps are known in several parts of Britain, but the most impressive are on Llandrindod Common in central Wales, where as many as 18 can still be seen – permanent testimony to the labours of Roman troops stationed in the fort at Castell Collen.

In Scotland, at Woden Law and Burnswark, there is evidence of Roman troops practising siege warfare on abandoned hill-forts. At Burnswark, siege camps were constructed around the fort, the plan of a gateway was laid out in paving slabs over a blocked entrance, and clay missiles were shot at the mock gateway from prepared catapult platforms.

Much of this sort of activity probably struck the average Roman soldier as a waste of time and effort. In the 2nd, 3rd and 4th centuries, wars or even large-scale rebellions by subject peoples were few and far between, and most troops stationed in Britain would have lived through their military careers having seen no more than one or two skirmishes. Very likely, patrols, scouting expeditions and punitive raids may have actually been welcomed by the troops as a break from barracks routine.

This, at any rate, is the impression gained from inscriptions on

Daily bread
Ensuring that there was sufficient food in store to see the troops through the winter was a constant preoccupation of every garrison commander. Large stone granaries, like the one at Corbridge (right), were features of every permanent fort. The walls were buttressed, and the floors raised to keep the contents dry.

Army issue
Like everything else in the Roman army, food supplies were carefully regulated. This stamp was used to mark issue bread.

Granary reborn
1st-century granaries, like most fortress buildings of the period, were built of timber. This reconstruction at Baginton, Warwickshire, shows the pattern of a typical Roman military granary.

slabs recording successful cavalry skirmishes. One was set up by Calpurnius Concessinus, a regimental commander, after the slaughter of a band of tribesmen called the Corionotatae. Another, found at Carlisle and dating from around AD 180–90, was also erected by the commanding officer of an ala 'after the slaughter of a band of barbarians', an action that took place somewhere north of Hadrian's Wall. Apart from patrols and raids beyond the frontiers, there would also have been frequent patrols of the areas garrisoned by the army, especially through the Pennines and central Wales.

Patrols and raids could never have occupied more than a small part of a legion or regiment at any one time, and the remainder would be engaged in far more routine activities. Gates, towers and the headquarters building had to be guarded, and the commander's house as well. Weapons and armour had to be cleaned and there were always barracks, bath-house and latrine fatigues for defaulters. Pack animals and officers' horses had to be supplied with fodder, and fuel had to be found for cooking, for the baths and the commander's house, and perhaps for braziers to warm barrack rooms in winter.

Sign of the legion
Legionary works depots supplied everything the legion needed – weapons, armour, uniforms, pottery and building materials, including tiles like this one. The Twentieth Legion established a depot at Holt, not far from their fort at Chester. Some of the tiles made there bear the legion's boar crest.

All these duties were allocated by an NCO and written on a roster on the barrack-room wall. These rosters have long since vanished except, amazingly, for one found in Egypt and dating from the 1st century AD. It is probably little different from the duty rosters posted up in dozens of forts throughout Britain.

The ten soldiers whose names appear on the sheet would seem to have been inmates of a single barrack room, and their duties for the first ten days of October are listed. On October 7 Julius Valens was on bath-house fatigues, Julius Octavianus guarded the headquarters and Clodius Secundus drew gate duty.

One soldier had the centurion's boots to clean, while policing patrols are suggested by the allocation of 'camp-market duties' to Secundus and Longus Sipo on October 1–3. Similarly, on Hadrian's Wall, regular duty would have included checking civilians passing through the Wall and overseeing the collection of customs dues.

As for Marcus Arrius Niger, whose name is sixth on the roster, he was clearly unlucky. Whereas his comrades have been given a variety of duties, Niger has been put on barrack fatigues for a week – no doubt for one of those minor crimes that have been leapt upon by NCOs since armies first began.

The Roman legionary was not only a soldier, but also a skilled carpenter and builder too. In 1st-century Britain, this involved

Britannia's thanks
This magnificent slab was found at Hutcheson Hill, just 4 miles from the west end of the Antonine Wall. It records a victory over the Caledonians, two of whom flank the central panel in which a standard-bearer acknowledges the gratitude of a well-dressed lady – probably Britannia. However, the monument's main purpose was to celebrate the Twentieth Legion's achievement in building 3,000 ft of the Wall.

cutting turf for the ramparts and timber for parapet, gates and buildings. The quantity of timber used even in a small fort was immense, and the Romans often used seasoned timber sent up from base workshops. When fortresses like Inchtuthil were abandoned, they were carefully dismantled and the timbers taken away for use elsewhere. Indeed, the regularity of design and size of many 1st-century gate structures suggests that gateways may have been prefabricated in supply bases and then transported to the sites of new forts under construction.

Every soldier was trained to build sloping ramparts of turf. These could be just as formidable as stone ones – the Antonine Wall in Scotland, and almost half of Hadrian's Wall in its original form,

Paving the way
Legionaries could turn their hands to anything, and probably spent far more of their service in construction work than in fighting. This relief from Trajan's Column shows troops cutting timber and clearing the way for the engineers following, who will build the roads that were the lifelines of the garrison fort system.

MASTERS OF BRITAIN

were built of turf – but maintenance was always a problem and the timberwork and defensive ditches also required constant attention. Once Roman rule was established, building and maintenance might well have been the principal occupation of the army.

From the 2nd century onwards, almost all fortifications were built in stone and maintenance work on defences and buildings became less frequent. But building was still the work of the legions, who added stonemasonry to their long list of skills.

Records of quarrying and building round Hadrian's Wall show that the work was carried out by legionaries working under centurions or their deputies. Units commemorated particular achievements with inscriptions that very often included the names of commanding officers and of the reigning emperor. A typical example is one found at Lanchester fort:

'The Emperor Caesar Marcus Antonius Gordianus Pius Felix Augustus restored the headquarters building and armouries, which had fallen in, through the agency of Maecilius Fuscus, emperor's propraetorian legate, the work being under the charge of Marcus Aurelius Quirinus, prefect of the First Cohort of Lingonians, styled Gordiana.'

Originally the Lingonians came from Dijon, but by this time – around AD 240 – they would have had many native-born Britons in their ranks.

Such inscriptions tell of the restoration and repair of just about every kind of military building – gateways and aqueducts, bath-houses and granaries. At Netherby in Cumbria in AD 222 the First (Part-Mounted) Cohort of Spaniards completed the construction of a cavalry drill-hall 'whose foundations were laid long ago', and it is also on record that the Seventh Cohort of the Second Augusta rebuilt their barracks at Caerleon about 20 years later.

It was legionaries, too, who undertook the lion's share of building the northern frontier defences – Hadrian's Wall and the Antonine Wall. Sections were built by legionary working parties who proudly recorded the length of wall they had completed. Perhaps a certain amount of inter-unit rivalry was involved: slabs found on either side of the fort of Duntocher on the Antonine Wall read:

'For the Emperor Caesar Titus Aelius Hadriano Antoninus Augusta, father of his country, a detachment of the Sixth Legion Victrix Pia Fidelis, built the rampart for 3240 feet.'
and:
'For the Emperor Antoninus Augustus Pius, father of his country, the Second Legion Augusta built this for 3271 feet.'

The legionaries also bore the brunt of road-building, canal digging

Wintering on the Wall
Winters were hard for the troops manning the forts strung along Hadrian's Wall. The reconstruction on pages 72–73 shows Housesteads, gripped by ice and blanketed by snow – but still seething with activity. The great wall itself runs along the edge of a steep escarpment (1) and forms the northern rampart of the fort, which has four gateways. Each gate has a double carriageway, and a platoon of troops is marching in through the nearest (2), and along the via praetoria towards the headquarters building (3) at the centre of the fort. Alongside it to the left is the commandant's house (4) built around an open courtyard; on its right is a pair of granaries (5), heavily buttressed to help take the weight of the garrison's winter store of wheat.

Most of the other buildings within the walls are long barrack blocks (6), each housing 80 men, but there is also a workshop and a messroom. Behind the headquarters building is a hospital (7), and tucked into the left nearside corner, behind the tower, is the latrine (8).

Outside the fort, a civilian

70

and bridge construction throughout the province. There must have been times when the legionary wished he was not so highly trained, and entertained moments of envy for the life of the auxiliary who, though not so well paid, at least spent most of his time soldiering.

Lentils and vinegar

One of the legionary's compensations was that his rations were almost certainly better than the auxiliary's, and his better pay enabled him to supplement his rations. The basis of the army diet was wheat, which the soldier ground into flour, together with soup, vegetables and lard, all washed down with vinegar or sour wine. But there was considerable variety within this basic diet. The choice of vegetables, for instance, might have included lentils, beans, cabbage and celery, and the soldier was also issued with a wide variety of meats. Animal bones recovered from fortress rubbish dumps show that mutton, lamb, beef, veal, pork and goat were all eaten in large quantities. Legionaries at Longthorpe also acquired a variety of waterfowl, hare, deer and fresh mullet, while those at Hod Hill ate cod, and at Chester, perch.

settlement clusters near to the walls. There are houses with their own small gardens and cultivation areas (9), but the buildings near the main gate-house are taverns and shops (10), catering for the troops' needs and offering a little relaxation from their arduous service life.

Accounts found at Chesterholm, dating from around AD 105, tell of incoming supplies of barley, garlic, wine, Celtic beer, hay, vinegar, brine, salt, fish sauce and pork fat. The garlic, wine and fish sauce were probably imported from the Mediterranean, and may reflect the tastes of the garrison's commander rather than those of his troops. But wine was a popular drink among the men, and in the case of Chesterholm it is unlikely that the consignment of 146 gallons recorded on June 22 was all meant for the commander – particularly since another large quantity was delivered to the fort two days later.

Inscriptions on amphorae found at Brough-on-Noe in Derbyshire and in a watch-tower on the Cumbrian coast indicate that they once contained plums and olives. These prove that imported luxuries could find their way beyond the legionary fortresses to small forts and even to tiny detachments occupying watch-towers. A consignment of olives or Spanish wine must have eased the lot of the eight men crouched around a fire in their dank tower by the Solway Firth, while the sentry on duty peered over the black waters outside.

For these men, and for the troops of other small garrisons, there was little enough to occupy their off-duty hours. Gambling was probably the most common pastime, and at the little Cumbrian fort at Biglands, part of a stone gaming board was found. The garrisons of the larger forts were more fortunate; they had their own bath-houses and the civilian settlements near by provided further entertainment.

Military bath-houses were almost invariably outside the fort, since their furnaces made them a serious fire hazard. The facilities varied in size and quality, often according to the strength and status of the garrison. The larger forts provided not only hot and cold rooms, but also a separate changing room, and often an exercise area as well, giving the bath-house the atmosphere of a social club. Here, the off-duty soldier could exchange gossip, gamble or write letters home, usually with a plea for money, food or clothes. Sometimes he was lucky; a letter found at Chesterholm seems to contain a reply to a request of this sort:

'I have sent you . . . pairs of socks, and from Sattia two pairs of sandals; and two pairs of underpants. . . .'

Romans did not normally wear socks or underpants, but no doubt old habits changed on the Wall in winter.

A soldier who had no one to ask for such things could buy them from British shopkeepers. Outside the gates of Chesterholm, for example, there was a substantial civilian settlement, or *vicus*, which included a public inn for travellers, and a whole range of shops and taverns. The shops provided food as well as clothes and

Rest and recreation
The regimental bath-house was much more than a place to wash and brush up; it was a club, in which all ranks could relax, chat, gamble or exercise at the end of the working day. To the troops garrisoning lonely forts, especially, it must have been a boon and a blessing. One of the best-preserved of such baths in Britain is that at Chesters, beautifully sited overlooking the North Tyne. The section shown here is the changing room, with alcoves where the bathers could leave their uniforms and gear, before joining their comrades in a game of dice.

leatherwork. There were even souvenir shops, it seems, to judge by two small bronze cups decorated with a picture of Hadrian's Wall found as far away as Wiltshire, and at Amiens, France.

Sweethearts and wives

Inevitably, garrison troops formed relationships with local women. Until the 3rd century, soldiers were not allowed to marry, but many had common-law wives. On retirement, the men often legally married their girl-friends and set up house in the village with their families. There are many records of these mixed marriages, though few tell so poignant a story as two tombstones found at South Shields and Corbridge. The one at South Shields reads:

> 'To the spirits of the departed and to Regina, his freedwoman and wife, a Catuvellaunian by tribe, aged thirty; Barates of Palmyra set this up.'

Regina, who came from the country just north of London, is shown in a long-sleeved robe, with her work-basket of wool and her distaff and spindle. Her Syrian husband had added to the Latin text a few sad words in his own Palmyrene script: 'Regina, the freedwoman of Barates, alas.' How much older than his wife Barates was can never be known, nor by how long he survived her, but the old soldier eventually died and was buried at Corbridge, about 25 miles from the last resting place of his beloved wife:

'To the spirits of the departed ... Barates of Palmyra, a standard-bearer, lived sixty-eight years.'

On the emperor's service
Not the least remarkable of Imperial institutions was the cursus publicus, a network of courier services which covered the entire Empire from the Balkans and Africa to Hadrian's Wall. Its efficient running demanded changes of horses and post houses every few miles; it was not, however,

popular, since these amenities had to be paid for by local councils. Many of its messengers galloped prodigious distances on horseback, but the service also provided fast carts, like this one on a tombstone in Belgrade, to convey high-ranking officials and their servants between towns and provinces.

Barates, and thousands like him, would have been able to see his wife and children only when he was off-duty and could slip away from the fort. Commanding officers were more fortunate. In their spacious and well-appointed houses fort commanders could live in domestic comfort with their wives and families. Excavations in the rubbish dump of the commander's house at Chesterholm produced vivid confirmation of this, for along with military accounts and a medal, were found the shoes of women and children, and a gold pendant earring. The wife of the commander would have been the only woman in the fort's population of about 500.

On detached service

One way for a soldier to escape the tedium of garrison life was to be seconded for a time to the civil administration. A post of this kind often occupied by soldiers was that of *beneficiarius*, a police officer with special responsibility for the supervision of traffic along main roads, through major junctions and across frontiers. *Beneficiarii* may have been in command of police posts erected for this purpose, and certainly the distribution of altars erected by various holders of the office suggests that they travelled widely to both civilian and military destinations. One altar at Catterick is appropriately dedicated to 'the god who devised roads and paths', though in fact it was erected by two men, a *beneficiarius* and a *singularis*. They might quite easily have travelled together, since both were employed by the governor's office, and the *singularis* was both an official messenger and an overseer of supply routes and communications.

The governor also employed a number of *speculatores*, military police, who were drawn from the legions as ceremonial guards, messengers and official executioners. A 1st-century London tombstone names four *speculatores* who had been seconded from the Second Legion Augusta.

The Imperial Procurator, who controlled the financial affairs of the province, also employed soldiers to oversee the workers and production on imperial estates. Some of these estates were large farms whose produce was imperial property, while others were concerned with the extraction and working of minerals. Lead and silver were both obtained from the same mines, all of which were at first under military control. Near a small fort at Charterhouse in the Mendips were found pigs of lead stamped with the insignia of the Second Legion Augusta. The troops were employed not as miners, but as overseers to the convict gangs who were the normal work force in the mines. There may have been an iron-producing establishment, run along similar lines, in the Weald of Kent, but here it appears to have been the navy rather than the army that was in control.

At Catterick there was a depot for working hides, presumably collected from the farmers of Brigantia, for the manufacture of footwear, uniforms, tents and shields. The Twentieth Legion, based at Chester, had a works depot at Holt and a barracks there big enough to accommodate two centuries. The principal purpose of this depot was to supply pottery and tiles to the legion, so apart from workshops the base at Holt contained drying sheds and huge kilns. Other legions had their own potteries, too, and so did some of the auxiliary forts, though local British potters increasingly took over manufacture of the wares supplied to the army. All in all, it seems there was little that the legionary could not turn his hand to.

However, the legionary's adaptability, like everything else about him, was all employed to one end – the maintenance of the army in Britain as an instrument of conquest and repression. It was to ensure efficiency in this role that the training, the weapons, the fortresses, the roads, the supply depots and the workshops were all designed. They were the essential parts of the machine that, rolling relentlessly through England, Wales and much of Scotland in turn, inflicted humiliating defeats on all who opposed it. Once the conquest was complete, the army's task was to ensure that it was never challenged, so that the government of the province could proceed without interruption or opposition.

Old soldiers undying

In a sense, the Roman soldier's work was never done, for when he retired it was intended that he should settle amongst the civilian population and, by example, teach them the Roman way of life. Legionary veterans were often settled as a group in *coloniae* such as Colchester, Gloucester and Lincoln, and Tacitus, describing the foundation of the colony at Colchester in AD 49, puts the case plainly: 'Its mission was to protect the country against revolt and familiarise the provincials with law-abiding government.' By giving a legionary land, the emperor was ensuring that the veteran stayed in the province where he was demobilised. And though the auxiliary received no land, the chances were that he would not go home either – to Spain, Syria, Romania, or wherever it might be. The journey would be long and expensive, and in any event, after 25 years, his real home was among his regimental comrades, and perhaps with a local girl whom he was now free to marry.

Discharged with honour
Having served with Tampius's First Pannonians for 25 years, auxiliary cavalryman Reburrus was demobilised on January 19, AD 103, and was presented with a bronze diploma to prove it. It records the emperor's edict granting permission to a number of units to discharge their veterans on that day; Roman demobilisations were generally carried out in batches, often on public holidays. It also records the

It is estimated that about half of those who joined up at 18 survived to retirement in their 40s. Although nowadays this seems a poor prospect for a recruit, his chances of surviving to 40 were probably as good in the army as in civilian life, and perhaps better.

Some retired soldiers lived to a good age. Flavius Natalis, for example, died at the age of 65 in the township outside the fortress at Caerleon, and one of his former comrades in the Second Legion Augusta, Julius Valens, survived to become a centenarian. Some veterans moved away from the fort when they retired and went to live in larger towns where their knowledge of Latin and the Roman system of government was invaluable. Many ended up as local councillors and magistrates.

One such was the ex-auxiliary Marcus Ulpius Januarius. He became an *aedile*, an official in charge of local roads and public buildings, on the council of the town of Brough-on-Humber. Around AD 140, he presented the community with a new stage for the theatre, and his generosity is recorded on a stone dedication slab now in Hull Museum. It was in situations like this, mirrored throughout the Empire, that soldier and civilian were finally brought together in peace and prosperity.

name of the Pannonians' commanding officer, C. Valerius Celsus, and that of the current governor of Britain, Lucius Neratius Marcellus. Of greatest interest to Reburrus, however, was the fact that it announces his admission to Roman citizenship and his right to make a legal marriage. Since the diploma was found at Malpas, it looks as though the old soldier settled down as a farmer in Cheshire.

UNEASY BORDERS

Britain's security depended upon mighty fortifications and the constant vigilance of their garrisons.

Though the province of Britannia – more or less present-day England and Wales – was conquered and settled fairly swiftly, its frontiers were always uneasy. From the 1st century onwards, the Romans found it necessary to maintain a fleet in British waters to guard against pirates and raiders, while the only land boundary, to the north, was defended against the Caledonians by Hadrian's formidable coast-to-coast barrier and, for a brief period, by the Antonine Wall further north. The enormous commitment of men and materials steadily increased through the time of occupation. By the 4th century, a system of coastal forts and watch-towers ringed the province from Lancashire, round Wales and the western and southern shores, to East Anglia and Yorkshire. But in AD 367, all of these forts, as well as those on Hadrian's Wall, appear to have been overwhelmed by a concerted attack by tribes from Ireland, the Western Isles and Scotland, acting in unison with Franks and Saxons from the Low Countries. Order was restored within 18 months by Theodosius, a general sent from Rome, who also strengthened the south-coast defences and built a series of watch-towers along the Yorkshire coast from Huntcliff to Filey.

When the British frontiers were overrun for the last time in the 5th century, these front-line posts were the first to succumb. Skeletons of men, women and children found among the fire-blackened ruins of Goldsborough tower tell of the defenders' last stand. Among them was the skeleton of a tall man, sprawled over that of a large dog. The animal's head was at the man's throat; it had fought to the end and had taken one of the enemy with it.

Northern frontier
The great wall, erected on the orders of Emperor Hadrian in the years following his visit to Britain in AD 122, delineates the northernmost boundary of Rome's mighty empire. First built partly of turf, then entirely of stone, it runs for 73 miles from sea to sea.

Southern bastion
Portchester, and other forts, were erected around Britain's southern shores as a defence against cross-Channel raiders.

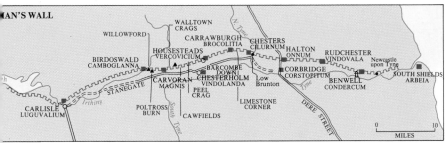

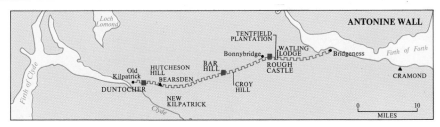

MAN'S WALL

WILLOWFORD
WALLTOWN
CRAGS
CARRAWBURGH
BROCOLITIA
CHESTERS
CILURNUM
HOUSESTEADS
VERCOVICIUM
HALTON
ONNUM
RUDCHESTER
VINDOVALA
Newcastle
upon Tyne
BIRDOSWALD
CAMBOGLANNA
BARCOMBE
DOWN
CORBRIDGE
CORSTOPITUM
SOUTH SHIELDS
ARBEIA
CHESTERHOLM
VINDOLANDA
Low
Brunton
CARVORAN
MAGNIS
BENWELL
CONDERCUM
STANEGATE
PEEL
CRAG
POLTROSS
BURN
LIMESTONE
CORNER
CARLISLE
LUGUVALIUM
Irthing
South Tyne
CAWFIELDS
DERE STREET

0   10
MILES

ANTONINE WALL

Loch
Lomond
TENTFIELD
PLANTATION
WATLING
LODGE
Firth of Forth
Bonnybridge
Bridgeness
BAR
HILL
ROUGH
CASTLE
Old
Kilpatrick
HUTCHESON
HILL
BEARSDEN
CROY
HILL
CRAMOND
DUNTOCHER
Firth of Clyde
NEW
KILPATRICK
Clyde

0   10
MILES

Key to symbols used on map

○   Town
▫   Industrial site
♁   Temple or shrine
■   Fort
▲   Site of other Roman relics
•   Other location
⧵⧵   Roman road
     (course certain)
=≡= Roman road
     (course uncertain)
⌁⌁   Continuous fortification

CHAPTER THREE

Towns: a new way of life

Busy streets, theatres, government offices and town houses with piped water and central heating rise from empty landscape as the British take to urban life

Boons of civilisation
Britons took to the conqueror's ways with enthusiasm, not least to his opulent bathing habits, reflected here in the magnificence of Bath. Less popular, perhaps, was the fiscal system that employed tax collectors like this one to ensure that the provincial government got its financial dues.

WHEN BOUDICCA'S TRIBESMEN STRUCK BACK AGAINST THE ROMAN CONQUEROR IN AD 60, IT WAS UPON THE towns that they vented their special fury. Colchester, London and St Albans all went down in bloody, flaming ruin. 'When all else had been ravaged and burnt,' wrote the Roman historian Tacitus about the destruction of Colchester, 'the garrison concentrated itself in the temple. After two days' siege, it fell by storm.' In London, 'those who stayed because they were women, or old, or attached to the place, were slaughtered by the enemy. Verulamium (St Albans) suffered the same fate.'

Modern archaeological discoveries bear out every word of Tacitus's story. Deep beneath the busy streets of the City of London, and under Colchester and St Albans too, there stretches a thick layer of burnt debris. Embedded in the blackened soil are coins and fragments of pottery that confirm the year of Boudicca's assault; and among them are the bones of her victims, crushed beneath their burning homes more than 1,900 years ago.

Lying in and around the fringes of Boudicca's country, Colchester, London and St Albans were especially vulnerable, and were also unfortunate in possessing associations that were particularly detestable to the anti-Roman tribes. Colchester was a *colonia*, or settlement of veterans retired from the army of occupation; London was a Roman seat of government; and St Albans was not only a Roman town, but also the capital of the Catuvellauni, a tribe that had been deadly enemies of the Trinovantes, allies of Boudicca, long before the legions arrived.

The first towns

Perhaps the most remarkable feature of these towns is the fact that they should have existed at all – a mere 17 years after Claudius's invasion. Before the Romans came there were no towns in Britain, and though tribal centres and hill-forts may have fulfilled some of a town's functions, they bore no resemblance to the Roman concept, the very basis of its civilisation, that took root in the new province with such astonishing speed.

Though only 11 years had passed between the foundation of the veterans' settlement at Colchester and Boudicca's revolt, the town already possessed a town hall, a theatre, a temple, and a statue to the goddess of Victory. Among its other amenities was a large granary, shops selling imported pottery, glassware and lamps, and private houses with painted plaster walls and wooden verandas.

Less is known of London at the same period, though Tacitus

In the streets
Shoppers, strolling visitors and off-duty soldiers thronged streets like this in Romano-British towns such as St Albans and Silchester. Sounds of lively banter, argument and revelry

described it as an 'important centre for businessmen and merchandise', and it seems certain that the financial administration of the province was already centred there. Several large timber buildings, some with painted, plastered walls, stood along present-day Fenchurch Street, and a water main had already been laid near by. Imported wine jars and an Italian lamp, abandoned in Boudicca's assault, tell of London's connections with the outside world.

Well before its destruction in AD 60, St Albans boasted a large masonry building, with plastered walls whose decorations included the painting of a lyre. At the centre of the town, there were at least eight shops of almost uniform size, all under a common roof – no doubt the property of a single owner with sufficient commercial acumen to acquire this substantial frontage on the town's main street. He must have been a bargain-spotter of no mean ability, for the timbers he used in his shops were well seasoned and second-hand, probably purchased from the army when the fort at St Albans was demolished in AD 49. The shops were leased to local tradesmen and craftsmen – bronzesmiths, perhaps a restaurateur or two, and possibly a cobbler and an outfitter. St Albans also possessed defences and the beginnings of a properly laid-out street system by the time Boudicca's rebels came storming in over the ramparts.

However, it is important to remember that each of these towns was in its way a special case, not at all typical of the urban development that was taking place in southern Britain at this period. Most Roman towns developed in a much more casual way, simply growing up as adjuncts to the forts; Chichester, Dorchester, Cirencester, Exeter and Wroxeter are examples. Most of the early forts were held by garrisons of around 500 men, all of whom had money to spend and needed somewhere to spend it. Local populations were swift to supply that need, and within a short time, shops, taverns and girls too, could be found only a stroll away from the barrack gates.

There was a garrison at Cirencester for about 30 years, which encouraged the growth of a civilian settlement of timber huts and shops to the north-west. By the time the army finally moved on, the civilian settlement had grown large enough to have developed into a market for the surrounding countryside, gradually eclipsing a native *oppidum* at Bagendon, 3 miles to the north. The fort was no doubt initially built to dominate the *oppidum* and the region around it, a pattern that was often followed in other districts as well. At Canterbury, Silchester, Chichester and St Albans, for example, the remains of major native settlements lie directly beneath the Roman foundations.

There was a strong link, too, between forts, towns and roads.

echoed far into the night from inn and tavern. The well-preserved street above is in Herculaneum, Italy, but its paved road and pavements are typical of those in many Romanised towns.

Most of the major roads of Roman Britain were originally constructed to allow troops to be moved swiftly to wherever they were needed. Garrison towns, therefore, were all served by roads, an important factor in their future development.

From officialdom's viewpoint, the towns had new roles to play when the garrisons moved on, particularly as centres of administration. It was much easier for the government to control and tax townspeople than to track down those spread around the countryside in dozens of isolated farmsteads. Equally, a town could provide services, such as offices and staging posts, as well as a market for local industrial and agricultural produce. There are some towns, however, whose role was neither administrative nor economic. Bath was primarily a spa and a religious centre, with medicinal baths, a temple and perhaps a theatre for religious drama occupying its central area. Wilderspool in Cheshire was an industrial estate, with the workshops of nearly a dozen crafts lining the main street on either side. The main function of Hardham in West Sussex was a relay station for government couriers on Stane Street, while Sea Mills near Bristol was a seaport.

Capital of Britain

The largest of all the administrative and commercial centres was London. There was no major native settlement on the site before the conquest, but in the 17 years before Boudicca's revolt a thriving settlement had grown up on the north bank of the Thames, on the spot which has remained the heart of the City ever since. It has been suggested that before the rebellion, the offices of the governor and the procurator, the military and the financial administrators of the

Golden London
A corner of London and the Thames in AD 300 . . . glimpsed tantalisingly on a superb gold medallion glorifying the Caesar, Constantius Chlorus, shown entering on horseback.

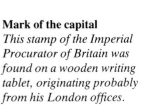

Mark of the capital
This stamp of the Imperial Procurator of Britain was found on a wooden writing tablet, originating probably from his London offices.

province, had been at Colchester. If so, it may have been Boudicca's rising – in which the Trinovantes of Essex joined with the Iceni of northern East Anglia – that persuaded the government to move to London. But with its easy access to the sea and to the network of major military roads that already focused on the lowest bridging-point of the Thames, London was in any case a far better location for a provincial capital.

The tombstone of Classicianus, the first procurator appointed after the rising, was discovered in London, suggesting that he lived there. Confirmation that his department was moved to London is provided by a number of roofing tiles stamped P.P.BR.LON – Procurator of the Province of Britain, London – and by some wooden writing tablets similarly marked. It may well be that the procurator's office lay beneath what is now the south end of Gracechurch Street; there the remains of a vast building were discovered, raised up on the ashes of Boudicca's inferno. At one end was a great hall overlooking a gravelled courtyard, whose three other sides were covered by a veranda, giving access to rows of rooms that look very much like offices.

About the time that Julius Agricola became Governor of Britain in AD 78, a massive palace was constructed in the area now occupied by Cannon Street Station. There can be little doubt that this was the governor's residence; only fragments have survived, but these show that the palace was built around a large central court or formal garden, featuring a 115 ft long pool with a fountain.

Overlooking the garden were staterooms, an 82 ft hall, another great room, and perhaps guest rooms; the governor's own quarters may have been grouped around smaller courtyards further east. Only fragments of mosaics and wall plaster remain of the once splendid interior decoration of the palace, but even so, it is not hard to envisage the receptions that took place here, the gardens and rooms filled with gleaming uniforms, elegant women, and toga-clad administrators – the most brilliant scene in all the province.

The governor's staff included clerks, secretaries, and soldiers on detached duty, some of whom formed his personal guard. After about AD 100, the guard was stationed in a fort at Cripplegate, at the north-western corner of the city. This was eventually incorporated into the city wall, about 2 miles long and of solid stone.

Temples and baths soared among shops and private houses, but the biggest building was the 8 acre combination of forum and basilica – the market square and town hall. Its construction, around AD 80, indicates that by then London had become a *municipium*, an officially self-governing community.

But London's status was proud above titles. Tacitus implies

The great baths at Wroxeter
Great double doors once filled the opening in the centre of this wall. They led into the exercise hall of Wroxeter's public baths, where townspeople could relax and enjoy a good soak, and gossip and gamble away an hour or two. The masonry, now bare, was once richly decorated. The wall remains an imposing monument.

Lines of a Roman town
The grid lines marking the streets of Roman Silchester are still clearly visible from the air. They were laid out at right-angles, but with less regularity than those of more sophisticated Roman-built towns. Trees and hedgerows grow now along the almost-hexagonal line of the town walls. Silchester was the capital of the Atrebates.

that it was a great commercial city and it continued to be so throughout the occupation. Workshops and stalls making and selling all kinds of wares lined the banks of the Walbrook, a tributary of the Thames that now runs underground.

The hustle and haggling along the Walbrook was matched by the bustle on Thames side where coasters, barges and sea-going ships tied up to unload cargoes and discharge passengers. Officials, soldiers, sailors, itinerant scholars, Gallic, Greek and Egyptian merchants – they came to London from all parts of the Empire.

The urban framework

In the period between about AD 75 and AD 90 ten or eleven *civitates* were established by the Romans. Each was based on an earlier tribal territory, each had powers of local self-government, and each had its own administrative capital or principal town. The

rapid development of such towns as Silchester, Chichester, Exeter and many others was deliberately fostered by the imperial government to encourage the Britons to accept Roman ways – or, as Tacitus put it, 'to lead them on to the amenities that make vice agreeable – arcades, baths and sumptuous banquets'. Government assistance probably included the provision of army surveyors to lay out the street systems of the towns.

The framework of a new town was based upon its street system. There were two main roads, laid out at right-angles to each other, and from which side streets ran off at regular intervals to form a grid of rectangular building plots called *insulae* (islands). No town in Roman Britain had a perfectly symmetrical street system, but all the major towns attempted to follow this pattern.

Rome's New Deal

Though coins had been minted in Britain before the invasion, it was the Romans who introduced their widespread use in daily transactions. The Imperial currency consisted of gold aurei, *silver* denarii *and brass* sestertii *and* asses. *These coins circulated throughout the Empire, considerably facilitating international trade. The coinage created a whole new urban class of bankers,*

The streets were 16 to 26 ft wide, depending on their importance, with a gravelled and cambered surface. This surface was frequently repaired, and completely renewed every 25 years or so. At Gloucester, evidence has been found of no fewer than ten re-surfacings, probably demanding frequent rebuilding of the houses in order to keep their thresholds more or less at street level.

Few of the towns founded towards the end of the 1st century had defences, for now that the conquest was complete, the imperial authorities, fearful of civil disturbances, were reluctant to allow unnecessary fortifications. But at some time late in the 2nd century, many of the larger towns were permitted to build earthen ramparts that during the course of the next 100 years were replaced by stone walls. Why this was done is not certain, but it may have had something to do with the Brigantian uprising that took place in the middle of the 2nd century, or the need to secure the towns when the Governor of Britain, Clodius Albinus, withdrew most of the province's troops to support his attempt upon the imperial throne in AD 193–6. Whatever the reason, the towns were glad of their walls during the incursions of Picts, Irish and Saxons in AD 367, which were more serious than any that had come before. It was probably as a result of these 4th-century invasions that projecting bastions, perhaps to carry catapults, were eventually added to the walls.

The Town Hall

The basilica and forum were built at the crossroads at the centre of town, usually as a single complex. The basilica consisted of a great hall, with a row of offices and chambers at the rear. The hall was generally divided into a nave and two aisles by two rows of columns, often as much as 30 ft high. At the end of the hall were tribunals in which magistrates dealt with the petty crime and civil disputes of the district, ranging from theft and adultery to quarrels over property and inheritance. Where punishment was called for, the magistrates would generally impose fines or confiscate the guilty party's property. Imprisonment was not a usual form of punishment in the Roman world, and Romano-British towns did not possess gaols.

The remainder of the basilica was given over to local administration, including a large chamber for the use of the town council. All these monuments to civic pride have long since vanished, but excavations of the basilica at Silchester have given some idea of what it must have looked like in its days of glory.

The interior of the great hall, whose roof stood a full 72 ft high, was partly panelled with Purbeck stone, topped by plaster

clerks, money-lenders and tax collectors who, as can be seen in this relief from Belgrade, spent long hours in accounting offices balancing the books of commerce and Empire.

Similar scenes must have been common in the council offices of Romano-British town halls as clerks and tax men checked cash received against accounts, and jotted their findings down on wax tablets.

panels in red, blue and green. Light from high windows illuminated inscriptions on the walls, and glinted from a life-size bronze statue of an emperor.

The semi-circular tribunals at each end were decorated in red and ochre, made the more sprightly by simulated drapes in green and yellow paint. Facing the main entrance was the shrine containing two statues, one representing the spirit of the community and another a venerated emperor. Clerks, accountants and copyists busied themselves in offices surrounding the council chamber which stood to the far right of the shrine.

Markets and shopkeepers

On market days and holidays the clerkly decorum of Silchester's town hall was shattered by the cries of craftsmen and stallholders whose premises occupied the other three sides of the gravelled square outside. It is known that a jeweller, a butcher, and perhaps a restaurateur carried out their business there, but of the other shopkeepers no trace remains.

Just one lingering glimpse of a Romano-British market has been preserved through an accident that occurred in Wroxeter about 1,800 years ago. One market day a fire started among the shops and swiftly got out of control. Panic followed; stalls were overturned, crates and packages trodden underfoot, their contents scattered and broken. One dealer lost more than 200 expensive Samian vessels imported from Gaul, another a crateful of mixing bowls made by Sennius of Mancetter in Warwickshire, and another, an ironmonger, lost about 100 Buckinghamshire whetstones. The day had been a disaster for everyone, but provided a treasure-trove for modern archaeologists.

Some of the larger towns, including Wroxeter, also possessed a permanent market hall in which traders could lease shops. Like the forum, these halls stood at the very heart of the town; those at Wroxeter and St Albans were built around a central courtyard, flanked on two or three sides by one-room shops, but at Cirencester a single row of shops ran behind an open veranda on one side of a street approaching the forum and basilica.

Each market hall contained ten or a dozen shops, and each hall was probably devoted to a single trade or commodity. At Cirencester, pits containing the remains of butchered animals suggest that this was a meat market, while a building at St Albans may have been a horse-meat sausage factory, to judge by the finely chopped bones discovered on the site.

High Street butcher
From cleaver and chopping-block to hooks and steelyard, this relief captures a Roman butcher's shop that in all essentials differs little from those in British market towns even a few decades ago. Though the Roman shop is open to the pavement, the meats offered for sale are familiar – pork and bacon, mutton and beef. Sausages were popular too; the large basin on the floor was probably used to collect scraps that were later converted into sausages. Open-fronted shops were hardly hygienic, but they added to the colour and bustle of market days.

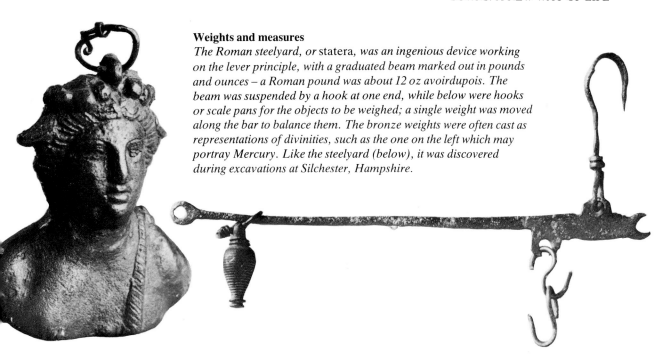

Weights and measures

The Roman steelyard, or statera, *was an ingenious device working on the lever principle, with a graduated beam marked out in pounds and ounces – a Roman pound was about 12 oz avoirdupois. The beam was suspended by a hook at one end, while below were hooks or scale pans for the objects to be weighed; a single weight was moved along the bar to balance them. The bronze weights were often cast as representations of divinities, such as the one on the left which may portray Mercury. Like the steelyard (below), it was discovered during excavations at Silchester, Hampshire.*

St Albans and other towns have yielded shopkeepers' tools and equipment, including butchers' steelyards, often still complete with their attractive bronze weights depicting gods or goddesses. Scale balances, too, have been found, with their lead, disc-shaped weights that seem to be based on units of either the Roman or Celtic pound – 12 oz and 11 oz respectively. The accuracy of these weights fluctuates considerably, though whether through accident or fraud is impossible to say. In either event, they should not have escaped the vigilance of the public weights and measures office, a branch of which may have occupied a room at one end of the market hall at St Albans.

Time stilled

Narrow, open-fronted shops jostle one another along the pavements of Herculaneum, smothered and protected for centuries by the mud that overwhelmed the town during the eruption of Vesuvius in AD 79. The streets of Romano-British towns were built on very similar lines, but most of them disappeared beneath ploughland or rebuilding long ago.

Down the High Street

Along the main streets leading to the forum and market hall, further rows of narrow-fronted shops competed for the best trading positions. The little workshops and showrooms of craftsmen and tradesmen jostled each other along the pavements, each clinging to a few feet of frontage. Some shops were just one-room lock-ups, others had store-rooms and living quarters behind them; and all vividly testify to the vitality of town life in Roman Britain.

Many shops sold food and drink but, of course, little trace of their wares has survived down the centuries. Fruit and vegetables were probably sold in the forum, but the 'High Street' shops would include wine merchants, bakers and restaurants. Large millstones of the type rotated by donkeys have been found at Canterbury and

Street scene

Like costermongers in a thousand present-day British towns, Roman fruit and vegetable sellers used to set up temporary stalls in the streets on market days. This stall-holder in Ostia, near Rome, has piled his wares in opulent heaps on a sturdy trestle table, while he points out the virtues and bargains among his stock to passers-by.

London, suggesting the presence of bakers, as does the heavy iron slice for lifting loaves discovered at St Albans. Neither of these objects belonged in a domestic kitchen. Nor did the 24 lb 'caterer's pack' of honey found in London.

Meat pies may have been baked in the ovens of the little shops across the street from Cirencester's meat market, while St Albans' main street probably had an oyster bar and an eating house. The appetising smells drifting from these establishments would have mingled with the sharp reek from charcoal furnaces of their coppersmith neighbours.

Ovens, crucibles, slag and waste trays beneath work-benches tell of the occupation of these craftsmen, but few of the wares have been discovered in their shops. Probably this was because most items were made to order, and little stock was kept in hand. Not that it matters, for the coppersmith's products are found everywhere

Daily bread
Bread was a staple of the Roman world, and most towns supported several bakers like this one portrayed in a mosaic from Gaul. The baker is using a long-handled slice to remove loaves from the oven; the strongly built foundations of such ovens are often found during excavations, but here the entire domed construction is revealed.

Tools for the job
The Romans used a wide range of tools, many of which – cleavers, chisels, shears, saws – would not be out of place on a modern work-bench. A Roman cutler and his wife (right) display their neatly racked stock on a stall, which has been reconstructed (above) by the Museum of London.

else on Roman sites, from town houses and country villas to other shops and even rubbish dumps and sewers. Pins, rings, bangles, brooches, razors and mirrors were produced by casting and hammering bronze. Hinges and clasps for jewellery boxes, and buckles and studs for clothing were also turned out. Saucepans, jugs, spoons and pastry-cutters were made for the kitchen, and weights, writing styli, ink-pots and rulers for the shopkeeper and the clerk.

The craftsmen

The coppersmith's skills were in such universal demand that the members of the guild of smiths who were able to afford the cost of erecting a temple to Neptune and Minerva at Chichester may well have been workers in bronze. By a remarkable chance, the name of one coppersmith – and those of his customers – has survived on an inscription on a statuette of Mars found in Lincolnshire:

> 'To the god Mars and the Deities of the Emperors
> the Colasuni, Bruccius and Caratius, presented this
> at their own expense at a cost of 100 sesterces; Celatus
> the coppersmith fashioned it, and gave a pound of bronze
> made at the cost of 3 denarii.'

Since 3 denarii were the equivalent of 12 sesterces, Celatus seems to have made a handsome profit from the Colasuni family.

Smith of York
Hammer raised and ready to beat out the iron gripped in his tongs, a Romano-British blacksmith stares proudly from his tombstone, found during excavations in York.

Copper shop
Coppersmiths at work in their shop – seen in a marble relief at Pompeii. One man is decorating a bowl while the others hammer a new vessel from sheet copper. Bowls and buckets already completed hang above them, with scales to weigh the metal.

Beauty from bronze
*Much of the bronzesmith's day was engaged in making
small toiletry articles – razors, tweezers and the like –
and a whole host of other items including weights,
measures and writing implements. He could also turn his
hand to the creation of beautiful objects such as these
found in the Isle of Ely (below). The fine skillet (above)
is signed 'Boduogenus', the name of its maker.*

The blacksmith was as important a figure in Roman Britain as he was to remain for centuries to come. Like the coppersmith he made most of his products to order – a new ploughshare for a farmer, a plane blade or a set of gouges for a carpenter, or a front-door lock for a householder. However, some of them must have kept a stock, since among the belongings of two busy Silchester smiths were discovered some 160 articles including axes, mortise chisels, gouges, ploughshares, mowers' anvils and forks. Farmers and carpenters, it would seem, were their chief customers.

The Silchester ironwork hoards also contained complete blacksmiths' kits. The long-handled tongs, hammers and other gear would be instantly recognisable to a 20th-century blacksmith; indeed, but for his tunic, the bearded British blacksmith who stares out from a York tombstone might easily be a village smith of a century ago.

Shoes to measure

To judge from a carved relief found in France, the shoe-maker of the period sat near the front of his shop bestriding a sturdy bench with a last at one end. Behind him were shelves of ready-made shoes, sandals and boots waiting for customers who did not require a pair made to measure. One enormous shoe found preserved in Walbrook mud suggests either a customer with abnormally large feet or, more likely, that the object was a display sign for some cobbler's shop near the river.

Much of the leather used in shoe-making, and for tunics too, was tanned in the countryside, where the noxious pungent smells

Ingenuity in bone
Bone was to the Romans what plastic is to the modern era – the basic material for the production of hundreds of articles for everyday use. The boneworker was therefore one of the busiest craftsmen in any community; the sheep's shoulder-blade from Silchester shows how bone gaming-counters were made, while the fine double-sided comb from Vindolanda, Northumberland, proclaims its maker's skill. Some comb-makers were so well-known that they signed their products.

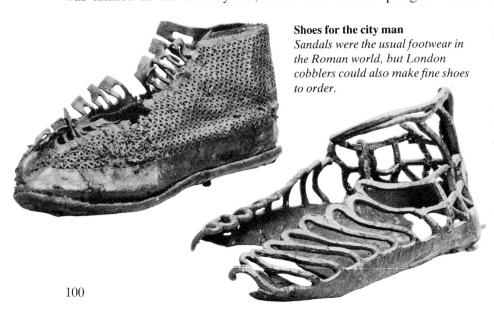

Shoes for the city man
Sandals were the usual footwear in the Roman world, but London cobblers could also make fine shoes to order.

Touch of quality
Romano-British textiles found a ready market in Gaul and the Rhineland, and were exported sufficiently widely for their prices to be fixed in an Empire-wide edict by Emperor Diocletian in AD 301. Cloth merchants and drapers both probably had establishments in the larger British towns, though it is doubtful if either customers or assistants in London or Bath approached the elegance of those depicted in this Italian relief.

inseparable from the process might disperse with the minimum of offence. But Silchester possessed at least one tannery, a big, barn-like building with a 62 ft long clay-lined tank used for steeping the hides of horses and oxen.

Most High Streets featured a draper's and, almost certainly, a bone-worker's establishments where all kinds of useful articles were created from bone, horn and antler. Bone products turned up everywhere in the Roman world. Combs, pins and pendants, gambling dice and counters, spindles, awls and needles, inlays and hinges, whistles and flutes – the list is a long one. Bone was, in short, the plastic of the day, and its products made their way into every British home from the humblest to the highest.

Most town traders in Roman Britain were craftsmen selling their own produce. Middlemen were rare, apart from wine merchants, and the vendors of pottery and glassware. Though there were glass-works at Caistor, Norfolk, glass and pottery were generally made outside the towns. Most kitchenware was made in the area, however, and sold from stalls in the nearest market squares. The attractive pottery and glassware, from Gaul and beyond, was sold by permanent shops. There must have been quite a number of these, since the imported products have been found in large quantities in every British town.

Sights and sounds

There was no Vesuvius in Britain to preserve one of its towns, Pompeii-like, beneath a sealing of ash and mud. Most Roman towns in these islands have to be re-erected in the imagination after painstaking detective work among the foundations. All the same, it is not difficult to envisage the main streets of St Albans or Silchester in, say, the early 2nd century. Creaking carts and pack animals laden with goods weave through the shoppers, plainly dressed slaves and servants crowd the street, smart ladies visit the jeweller's or the draper's, sturdy farm bailiffs pack the wine shops and restaurants. Such scenes, so full of energy, colour and vitality, were convincing proof of the astonishing success of the Romans in persuading the conquered Britons to adopt town life.

This enthusiastic commitment to an entirely new life-style was expressed not only by individuals, but also by the community as a whole. The forum and basilica were the focus of town life, but they were by no means the only public buildings. The town inn, or *mansio*, was not always privately owned; in the capital of every *civitas* there was one run by the local authority whose main function was to provide accommodation and a change of horses for the couriers of the imperial messenger service.

These inns had their own bath-suites that provided privacy, but were dull places indeed compared with the public baths in the town. The public bath was the great social institution of the Roman world, and bathing was only one of its many attractions. Business deals, gambling, exercise, gossip – all were carried on there, producing an echoing babble through the stone chambers and corridors. A lively description of the public baths was written by the Roman statesman-philosopher, Seneca, in the middle of the 1st century AD:

'I have lodgings right over a bathing establishment. So picture to yourself the assortment of sounds, which are obnoxious enough to make me hate my very powers of hearing! When your strenuous gentleman, for example, is exercising himself by flourishing leaden weights; when he is working hard, or else pretends to be working hard, I can hear him grunt; and

Oil and scrape
Since soap was unknown to the Romans, bathers used to take a small flask of oil and a strigil, or scraper, to the baths. Having oiled themselves, they would scrape off oil and dirt in the steam room.

Ladies' day
Mixed bathing was not customary in Roman Britain, and most public baths offered their facilities to women only in the mornings. Even so, they provided a splendid opportunity to combine hygiene with the day's gossip, as can be seen from this lamp-top, now in the British Museum.

103

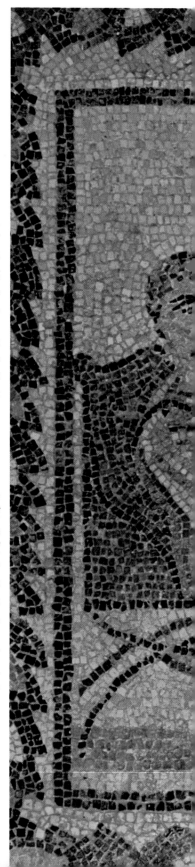

whenever he releases his imprisoned breath, I can hear him panting in wheezy and high-pitched tones. Or perhaps I notice some lazy fellow, content with a cheap rub-down, and hear the crack of the pummelling hand on his shoulder, varying in sound according as the hand is laid on flat or hollow...

Add to this the arrest of an occasional roisterer or pickpocket, the racket of the man who always likes to hear his own voice in the bathroom, or the enthusiast who plunges into the swimming tank with unconscionable noise and splashing ... Then the cake-seller with his varied cries, the sausage-man, the confectioner, and all the vendors of food hawking their wares, each with his own distinctive intonation...'

Though observed in Rome, these sights and sounds would have been equally familiar to the inhabitants of Silchester, Wroxeter or Leicester. The baths themselves were complex affairs, with even more stages than the modern Turkish bath. From the changing room, the bather proceeded to the *frigidarium*, the cold room, beyond which lay the warm room, or *tepidarium*, where he would oil his body, and where steam would begin to open his pores.

Then followed a choice of hot rooms – the *caldarium* – with superheated steam of near-impenetrable density, and the *laconicum*, a very hot, dry-heat chamber. In one or the other he would apply his strigil, a curved bronze blade for scraping off dirt and oil. A hot-water bath would complete the operation.

Gambling at the baths

Hardier bathers would round off with a massage and a lightning dip into the cold plunge, and after dressing, wander off in search of friends or try their luck at one of the endless games of chance in the exercise yard. Dice was popular, as was 'Twelve-lines', a kind of backgammon; but played throughout the Empire, and especially by the army, was a game called 'Soldiers'. This simple war-game was played on a board with eight rows of eight squares, using fifteen pieces in each team or army. A complete set of pieces, white and brown, has been found in a tomb at Lullingstone, Kent.

Gambling was generally a masculine occupation, and in any case mixed bathing was frowned upon; therefore, women bathed in the morning and men in the afternoon and evening. In towns like

The dice players
The Romans were inveterate gamblers – at the amphitheatre and at the chariot races, where the punters cheered on their favourite teams with all the fervour of a modern football crowd. This Tunisian mosaic shows dice players in a tavern.

Chichester, Leicester and Wroxeter in Shropshire, probably as many as 500 people a day used the baths, even if they only visited them once a week. One of the finest suites of public baths in Britain was at Wroxeter, which also included an outdoor swimming pool and a massive exercise hall. One wall of the exercise hall rises over the exposed remains of the baths, to its full original height of 26 ft. In its hey-day, the hall was some 220 ft long by 65 ft wide; this, coupled with the presence of an outdoor and unheated swimming pool in Britain's brisk climate suggests a high standard of robustness in the townsfolk of Wroxeter. But of course, a healthy mind in a healthy body was one of the great precepts of the Roman world.

One snag of having the baths in the town centre was that their furnaces were an ever-present fire hazard. Many towns had municipal fire-brigades equipped with hand-pumps, hoses, buckets and ladders; but they could seldom do more than attempt to contain the blaze. There were also private fire-brigades, who it was darkly hinted, were not averse to encouraging trade by starting fires themselves.

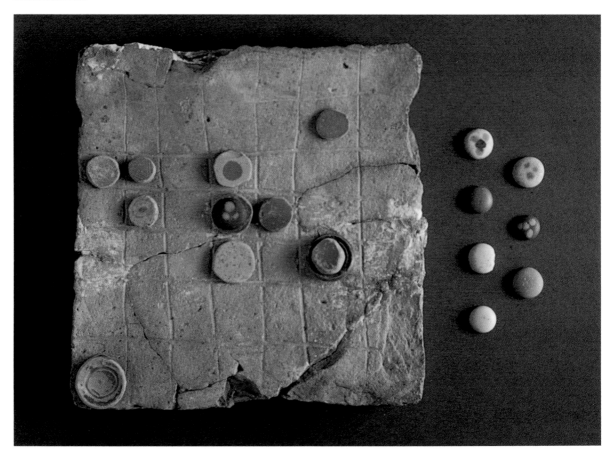

Water and drains

Town baths used enormous quantities of water, though this could be almost equalled by the cumulative demands of inns, restaurants, private houses and public fountains.

Water in most large towns in Britain was supplied by aqueduct – contoured channels dug in the ground and perhaps lined with clay. The most impressive surviving example is the one running into Dorchester; an 8 mile channel, 5 ft wide and more than 3 ft deep.

A similar aqueduct at Wroxeter had the capacity to deliver 2 million gallons of water each day, distributed through the town by a complex system of timber and lead pipes. Mains ran along the principal streets to side channels from which sluices diverted the water into individual buildings. If, during drought, the level of water in the mains dropped below 7 in., then the supply to private houses was automatically cut off. Householders often supplemented their needs with wells, lined with stone or with old topless and bottomless barrels.

Timber-lined drains were constructed in many towns, and substantial stone-built sewers have been found beneath the streets of Roman Colchester and York. Those at York are especially remarkable. Built of 3½ ton blocks of millstone grit, and high enough to walk through, they illustrate the importance that local authorities placed upon sewage disposal. Short side passages lead off to smaller drains from private houses. In one side passage, the upper end of a shaft reveals a Roman lavatory seat, still in position after 1,500 years.

Main sewers collected water from the public baths, and re-cycled it to flush the latrines. These were usually built within the bath-house, though at Wroxeter a very large public latrine next to the baths was flushed by water that had already coursed through another lavatory in the market hall. The original source was rain-water collected from the roof of the market. Sometimes, on market days and public holidays, the demand for latrines may have exceeded the supply. One enterprising shop-owner in St Albans built his own 20-seater, and since he lived on a lane running between the forum and the theatre, business was presumably brisk.

Not all public services were so well established. There were no lights in the streets apart from the blazing torches carried by the hurrying pedestrian or his slave, and there was no regular police force. Soldiers were sometimes called in to supervise market days and other crowded occasions but, generally, there was no deterrent to crime after dark other than the *vigiles*, or town nightwatchmen.

107

Not every town appointed them, and in any case, their main job was to keep an eye open for fires. Nor was there any system of street sweeping or refuse collection; householders made do instead with their own private rubbish pits.

The old saying about cleanliness being next to godliness had a particular application at Caerwent, Leicester and possibly Lincoln where temples were built close by the public baths. The six known temples at St Albans, and the four certain and three possible temple sites at Silchester indicate the importance of religion in the daily life of the Romano-Briton. The official Roman gods, such as Jupiter, Juno and Minerva, demanded constant attention; there were also deified emperors to be worshipped, and local British divinities to be placated. Apart from the ceremonies and rituals performed on the many public holidays in the Roman calendar, the temples also gathered a constant stream of visitors who came to seek help in adversity, or to win the favour of the gods prior to a gambling session in the baths, the taverns or at the amphitheatre.

Bread and circuses

Amphitheatres were built all over Britain in places as far apart as Dorchester, Chichester, Carmarthen and St Albans, indicating the widespread popularity of public sports.

Most amphitheatres consisted of an earthen bank between timber or stone walls enclosing an oval area with seating for several thousand people. At Dorchester, the amphitheatre was constructed on the cheap by adapting the banks of a prehistoric henge monument; here, the location of the amphitheatre was determined by that of the henge, but it was usually constructed beyond the fringes of the town. This helped to minimise the hazards both of over-enthusiastic crowds in belligerent mood, and of escaping wild animals.

Theatres, on the other hand, were built within the towns, but they were few in number in Roman Britain. Their remains, showing traces of semi-circular banks of seats facing a raised stage, have been found at St Albans, Canterbury, at Gosbecks near Colchester, and perhaps at Bath, while the tombstone of the old soldier Marcus Ulpius Januarius records his gift of a stage to his home town of Brough-on-Humber. But these appear to have been the sum total. Music and drama, it seems, did not appeal nearly so much to the robust Britons as wild beast shows and gladiatorial combats. Perhaps they were too far from the cultural heart of the Empire for its subtler influences to take root.

Beneath the streets
One of the great benefits brought to Britain by the Romans was a proper system of town sewers. The one most recently discovered and excavated was a main sewer at York, superbly built of ashlar stone. Side channels from private and public buildings fed into it, and the discharge ran downhill until it passed through gates and emptied finally into the River Foss.

Bringing in the water
Supplies of water on a scale undreamed of before the Romans arrived were needed to service the public baths, fountains, lavatories and sewer systems they introduced. The answer in most cases was to build aqueducts like this, which brought water to the fort at Chesters, on Hadrian's Wall, along a carefully contoured channel from springs outside. Britain's undulating countryside obviated the need for huge aqueducts like those in Italy and North Africa.

Hail, Caesar!

Public convenience
Privacy was not a feature of public lavatories during Roman times. They were sturdy but simple stone buildings with seats along the walls. Several have been found in Britain, but none survives so well as these in Ostia.

Better-off town councils often deemed it prudent to raise an ostentatious monument or two to the glory of the imperial government. Several towns are known to have erected life-size, or larger than life-size, statues of emperors. Lincoln and Gloucester possessed equestrian statues of emperors; the one at Gloucester stood in the forum, where it could be admired by the greatest number of people. London had at least five life-size bronzes, including one to the Emperor Hadrian, while a bronze head of Claudius found in the River Alde in Suffolk was probably once a part of a statue erected to him in Colchester.

The monumental arch was another means of expressing civic pride and imperial loyalty. St Albans built three, all spanning Watling Street, the main road through the town. Two marked the town limits of Claudius's day, and may have been built to commemorate the granting of *municipium* status. Only fragments of these arches remain – little more than a few pieces of marble facing – but the foundations are preserved, and suggest a dual carriageway through a double arch.

Another arch, the Balkerne Gate at Colchester, has survived almost intact. It, too, had a dual carriageway, and was constructed before the end of the 1st century. It was later incorporated into a fine gateway bridging the main road into the *colonia*.

London also had at least one arch, but its discovery was at once an exciting and frustrating event. Though its original appearance is better known than that of any of the other four arches, no one knows where it originally stood. This is because it was dismantled in the 4th century when its stones were re-used to build a defensive wall along London's waterfront.

Originally, it probably had a single span, standing to a height of some 30 ft. Each side was decorated with a frieze, one of which probably depicted the deities of the seven days of the week, while the other showed flying cupids that very likely flanked an inscription commemorating the builder. Elaborate mouldings decorated the inside of the arch, and panels portrayed gods and goddesses, including a club-bearing Hercules and Minerva with her helmet and spear. Obviously, so grand an arch must have stood at some key point in the town – perhaps at the entrance to London's principal baths – and symbolised the commitment of the *municipium* to the Roman government and the Roman way of life.

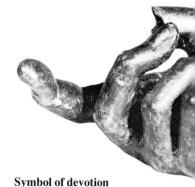

Symbol of devotion
Both wealthy citizens and public authorities were expected to display their loyalty to the emperor in ways that all could see. These symbols of devotion included works such as monumental arches, but were, more commonly, bronze or stone statues. None of these has survived intact in Britain, but fragments like the huge bronze hand above, found in London, give some idea of their impressive size.

Town houses

Nothing demonstrates the readiness of many Britons to embrace Roman ways better than their alacrity in building Roman-style houses. Well within a generation of the conquest, large, timber-framed private houses were being built in the towns, some already standing upon strong foundations of mortared stone.

Nothing like them had ever been seen in Britain before. Late-1st-century houses at St Albans occupy about ten times as much space as the nearby Belgic farmhouses at Park Street and Gorhambury. Instead of one or two communal rooms, the new houses possessed four, five or six, each with its own private entrance off a corridor – a novelty that in itself must have wrought great changes in British family life. The first Romanised decorations appeared – coarse mosaic floors, glazed windows, and plastered, gaudily painted walls, all helping to create much brighter and more comfortable homes than the plain and primitive Belgic hut.

Such houses were very expensive to build, showing that their owners were drawn from the old tribal aristocracy, now fully committed to Roman civilisation. But by the mid-2nd century, still larger, more luxurious and costly private houses were being erected. These possessed finely painted walls and mosaic floors of accomplished workmanship, and some even had their own bath-suites, all constructed either around a central garden or courtyard, or sometimes as a long main building with projecting wings at either end.

Christian emperor
By far the most interesting of the few stone portraits of emperors found in Britain must be this one of Constantine the Great, from York. Apart from his role in making Christianity the religion of the Empire, he had strong associations with York: it was there that he proclaimed himself emperor, on July 25, AD 306.

Builder of the Wall
This great bronze head of Emperor Hadrian – now in the British Museum – is all that is left of a colossal statue of the man whose frontier wall across northern Britain is the most enduring monument remaining of the Roman conquest. The head was found in the River Thames.

There were a number of such houses in most British towns, but of course most people lived much less grandly. Four or five-roomed houses were fairly common, however, and shopkeepers generally reserved two or three rooms of their business premises as living quarters. At Silchester, out of a total of 160 private dwellings, only about 45 could really be described as substantial.

Some houses on the edge of towns may have doubled as farms. One small house by Cirencester's town wall had a barn with a cobbled yard next door, and debris found on the site suggests an agricultural rather than an urban way of life. However, as the secure years of the occupation advanced, the point at which town ended and country began becomes less and less easy to define. Suburbs stretched along the main roads, some devoted to potteries and other industries, as at Wroxeter or St Albans, while others developed into fashionable residential areas. At Bath, houses with mosaic floors lie well beyond the defences, and Gloucester's suburbs appear to cover a larger area than the Roman town itself.

Facts and figures

Amphitheatres might give a rough idea of a town's population. The one at Silchester had room for about 3,000 spectators, so allowing for children, the total population may have been between 5,000 and 6,000. But since the management probably also hoped to entice folk from the surrounding countryside, this may not be a true reflection of the population of the town.

A more accurate assessment might be achieved by comparing the towns of Roman Britain with their medieval successors. Since the latter were often encompassed within the same boundaries, and the people who lived in them followed much the same occupations, the populations may also have been similar. Towards the end of the 14th century, Canterbury held 3,800 people, Exeter, 2,300 and Winchester, 2,100. Add some hundreds to allow for the fact that most of these towns had not yet recovered from the carnage of the Black Death, and it is possible to think of their Roman counterparts housing populations of between 3,000 and 5,000 people apiece. The larger towns in the Roman period, of course, held proportionately more; London may well have had a population of 20,000.

These figures are hardly spectacular by modern standards, but other Romano-British towns were much smaller with populations that ranged from a few hundred up to perhaps 1,500 – towns like Alcester in Warwickshire, Kenchester in Hereford and Worcester, and Malton in North Yorkshire, whose chief purpose was to provide

Town centre on market day
Crowds throng the centre of Silchester on a midsummer market day early in the 4th century AD, in the reconstruction on pages 114–15. In the shade of the basilica (1), which houses the town hall and law courts, rows of stalls have been set up in the forum, or market square (2). Shoppers haggle for bargains among the pots and pans, jewellery and trinkets, fruit and vegetables offered for sale. In the colonnades around the forum (3), permanent lock-up shops are also doing good business, while beggars and pedlars cluster around the entrance to the forum (4) beneath an inscription carved on Purbeck marble recording the construction of the building. Meanwhile estate managers, villa owners and farmers gather around the open market in the foreground (5) where cattle are to be sold 'on the hoof', and horses auctioned. On the right, work is in hand on a new building, and the solid timbers needed to support the heavy clay roof tiles can clearly be seen (6). New tiles will certainly be needed soon for the private house on the left (7), which has caught fire. Residents and the local fire-brigade strive

shops, taverns and, above all, a market for the people of the surrounding countryside.

Though these little towns possessed few public buildings, they seemed to have thrived as market centres. Timber shops and warehouses, and the remains of a leatherworker's and blacksmiths' shops have been found at Alcester, Kenchester and Great Chesterford. A hint of sophistication in these provincial backwaters appears in an inscription from Malton which reads: 'Good wishes to the spirit of this place. Prosper, young slave, in your employment in this goldsmith's shop.'

Other little towns owed their growth, or origins, to the combination of a major crossroads, a relay station of the imperial messenger service and an inn. Travellers foregathered there, attracting shops, taverns and baths, and so the nucleus of a town grew. Though these little settlements lacked the great public buildings and administrative importance of the major urban centres, they played an important part in the Romanisation of the British. Alcester or Great Chesterford might have been tiny, but they were just as much a part of town life in Roman Britain as were Cirencester or Chichester.

frantically to save what they can of the building. Further along the street are more narrow-fronted shops shaded by a covered veranda (8), and behind them, fashionable houses belonging to well-to-do families (9). In the distance (10) is the battlemented wall that encircles and protects the town.

THE RULING CLASS

Conquest accomplished, Rome governed its new province with the co-operation of the conquered

By granting self-government to many of the British tribes, the Romans managed to shift much of the burden of local administration – law-enforcement, tax-collecting and public works – on to the shoulders of the natives. Far-off, the province was ordered by the governor and procurator, respectively its military and political, and fiscal rulers, whose offices passed on directives and demands to the councils of *colonia*, *municipia* and *civitates*. The most important of these bodies were the councils of the *civitates*, tribal authorities administering large areas of tribal territory. Each consisted of 100 members – *decuriones* – from whose ranks were elected two senior and two junior magistrates. The first administered civil law and tried minor criminal cases. The second were charged with the everyday affairs of the community and the maintenance of roads and public buildings.

Writing on the wall
Magistrates were elected by local townsfolk – and elections were as rumbustious and hotly contested then as they are today. Slogans and graffiti appeared on walls urging

Law of Rome comes to Britain
Roman law became the law in Britain after the conquest. As the new rulers took over, life in the province became governed by a vast and complicated legal system – further complicated as time passed by many new edicts of the senate, the emperor and magistrates. The system created something of a lawyers' paradise, with talented advocates and jurists in great demand, and earning very large fees for their skills. Offences such as theft and fraud, now under criminal jurisdiction, were in those days tried as civil cases in the magistrates' court. Justice was dispensed in the hall of the town's basilica, *which was also the seat of local government. The carved stone relief pictured on the right is believed to show such a civil case in the process of being tried by a magistrate. Clerks of the court are busy recording the proceedings, and the magistrate – or possibly an advocate – appears receiving the plaudits of interested parties for a wise verdict or speech.*

voters to back this or that candidate. *The wall writing above is in the Street of Abundance, Pompeii, but similar slogans must have been painted in Romano-British streets.*

Through the ranks
A man had to be at least 25 years old before he could qualify to seek election as a magistrate. Senior holders of the office – like this Roman of the 1st century AD – were usually older men who had risen through the ranks of junior magistrates.

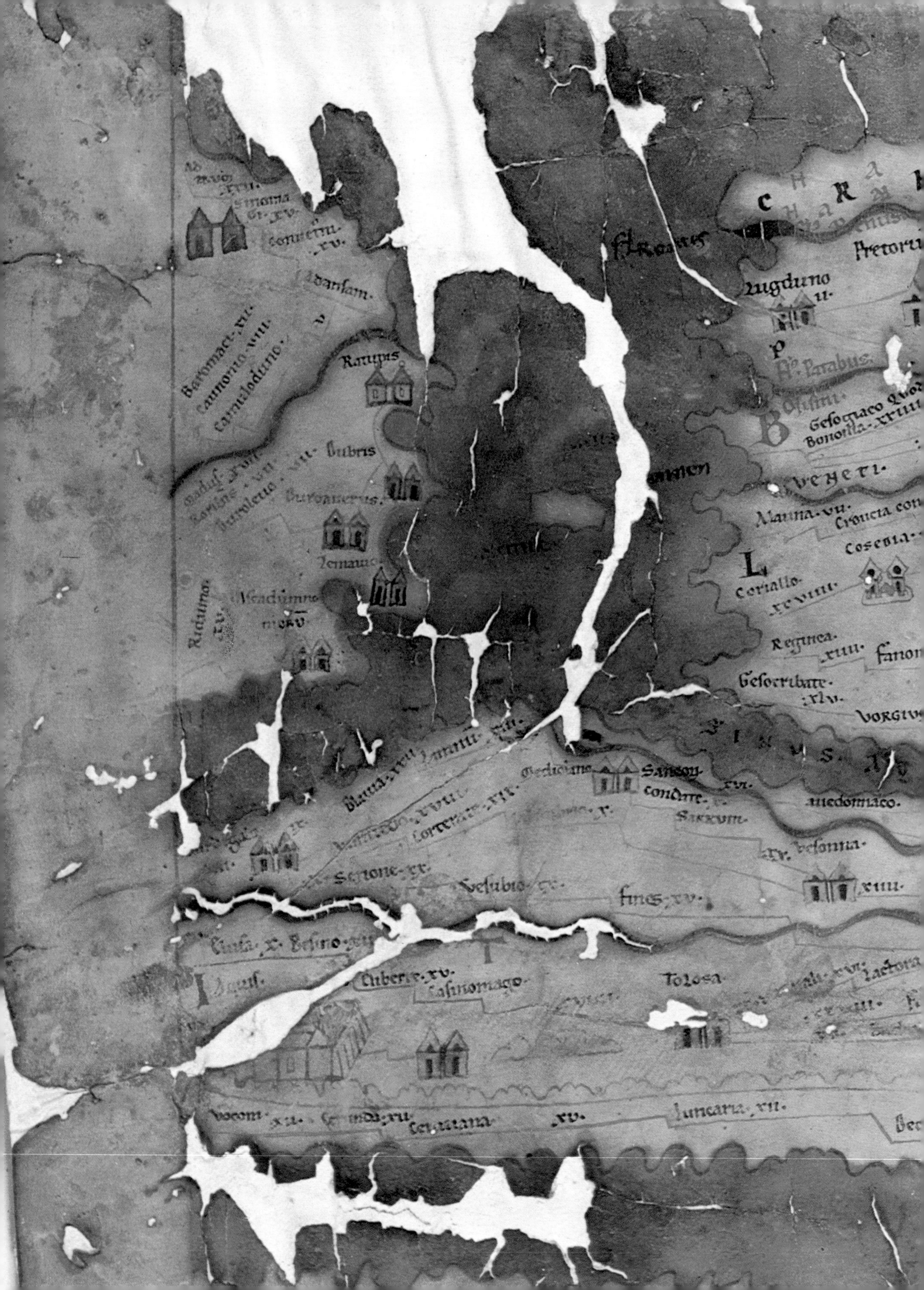
Ratupis
bubris
Burdaneus
Lugduno
Pretoriu
Gesogiaco Quod
Bononia
VEHETI
Nauna
Croucia
Coseria
L
Coriallo
Reginca
Fanom
Gesocribate
Vorgiu
Sarrum
Besonna
Tolosa
Fines
Lactora
Luncaria

CHAPTER FOUR

Traders and travellers

A brand-new communications network draws the province into a 'common market' where silver and hunting dogs, wine and oysters, pots and pans unite British, Germans, Gauls and Greeks

Edge of the world
This 12th-century copy of a 4th-century road map shows Britain on the western edge of the known world. Yet by road, river and seaway this most remote of provinces was linked to the whole of the Empire, including Gaul, from whence came Roman-style luxuries like this fine samian bowl.

ONE OF THE MOST REMARKABLE EXISTING RECORDS OF ANCIENT TIMES IS THE PEUTINGER TABLE, ORIGINALLY published in the mid-4th century AD and surviving as a 12th-century copy. Once owned by a German, Konrad Peutinger, the Table is nothing less than a guide book and map of the Roman Empire – and beyond. The 22 ft long scroll shows all the main roads and routes from Hadrian's Wall to Ceylon; more than 500 towns and relay stations for couriers and other official travellers along the roads are named, with symbols to indicate the type of accommodation offered. Neither is the tourist element neglected. Notable sights along the way, such as the Black Forest and the harbour at Ostia near Rome, are shown, and for some towns, there are even instructions on how to find the inn.

The Table was designed for the imperial courier service and for high officials travelling on imperial business; it was probably not available to the public. Unfortunately, the surviving copy has just one section missing, and that is the one covering most of the province of Britain. Only eastern England is shown, with the positions of Richborough, Dover, Lympne, Canterbury and Caistor all clearly marked.

Some of the missing information, however, appears in another document, the Antonine Itinerary, probably so called because it was compiled in the reign of Emperor Caracalla (AD 211–17), one of whose names was Antoninus. The Itinerary is not a map but a route book, listing the routes used by couriers in the 3rd century AD. Fifteen routes in Britain are described, and more than 100 towns and relay stations. The document is pure gold to historians and archaeologists, who through it have been able to identify not only the Roman names of modern British towns and villages, but also the capitals of tribal areas. For instance, the route called Itinerary 14 shows that Bath was *Aquae Sulis* and Caerleon was *Isca*, while *Calleva Atrebatum* and *Venta Silurum* – Silchester and Caerwent – were administrative capitals of self-governing tribes, the Atrebates and the Silures.

By studying the Antonine Itinerary and other ancient documents, and backed by a great deal of field work, archaeologists have been able to trace more than 6,000 miles of major Roman roads in Britain, as well as many more miles of minor roads and local trackways. Yet before the Roman conquest there were no roads in the modern sense in Britain at all. In some marshy areas, especially in Somerset, log causeways were built from about 3000 BC, connecting one settlement with another across a few miles of bogland; but these were the only artificial ways in the country.

Rivers were the main trade arteries of pre-Roman Britain –

A rolling British road
Apart from one or two timbered causeways in marshy areas, there were no paved or surfaced roads in Britain before the Romans came. There were, however, a number of 'trackways' or routes that had been followed for 2,000 years and more by wandering traders and seasonal migrants. Such tracks tended – like this section of the Icknield

these, and the trackways followed by men and animals over the high chalk escarpments of the south. After the Roman conquest some of these routes, like the Icknield Way which runs from the Wash to Salisbury Plain, were gravelled in places and used as secondary roads. For the most part, though, Roman roads broke new ground and provided the base of a comprehensive transport system whose efficiency must have surprised the British.

Lifelines for the army

Originally, all the main roads of Roman Britain were built to carry military traffic. They were the supply routes that provided the garrison forts with corn, beef and leather, the lifelines for armies on campaign, a nervous system for the swift transmission of messages

Way in Buckinghamshire – to hug the line of the chalk and limestone escarpments, and no doubt local people continued to use them throughout the Roman period. In this case, the Romans at least partially surfaced the lower course of the Icknield Way. It served as a link between the villa estates in the Vale of Aylesbury and Watling Street.

from the governor or a field commander to forts or to units on the march. Probably the earliest main roads were the three that followed the lines of Claudius's invading legions, and the road which crossed them to supply the chain of forts between the Severn and the Humber.

The first of the invader's roads, Watling Street, runs from Richborough via Canterbury to the crossing of the Thames at London. It then heads north-westwards through St Albans, Dunstable, Towcester, and Mancetter in Warwickshire to cross the Severn at Wroxeter. The second, Ermine Street, heads more directly northwards from London, through Godmanchester, to cross the River Nene at Water Newton. Later, it cuts through Lincoln on its way to the Humber, then swings north-westwards to York. From there the road was eventually pushed on to Scotland, enabling the governor in London to keep in touch with his legions, more than 400 miles away.

The third road, the principal route to the south-west, crossed the Thames at Staines and swung westwards to Silchester, before heading south-westwards to Salisbury. From there it ran to Dorchester, then turned westwards again to Seaton, where it met the Fosse Way, perhaps the most picturesque of Roman roads in Britain. From Seaton, the Fosse Way strikes north-eastwards to

Lincoln, never deviating more than 6 miles from a straight line over the whole of its 200 mile length. For the most part, it lies along the top of the limestone ridge that runs from south-west to north-east across England, traversing valleys by angling down one slope and up the other, always shunning the low, damp ground. Nearing Lincoln, it soars up a one-in-six gradient, and eventually joins Ermine Street.

In AD 47, the frontier lay a little to the north-west of the Fosse Way. The road was therefore the major link between the frontier forts and the military ports of Exeter, Sea Mills near Bristol, and – via Ermine Street – Winteringham on the Humber. Later, as the frontier moved north, the Fosse Way became a vital trade route, a role it was to maintain for centuries after.

As well as the many other roads of military origin, there were some that from their beginnings were intended for civilian traffic. They were built to link as yet unconnected towns or tribal capitals with one another. Even these roads, however, had their courses plotted by army surveyors, and their construction overseen by army engineers.

Local needs – local materials

The width of Roman roads, and their surfaces too, varied greatly from one area to another. The original width of most main roads seems to have been about 20–23 ft, but as time went on and traffic increased, this could almost double. When the Godmanchester section of Ermine Street was laid around AD 50, it was 20 ft wide and surfaced with gravel laid directly on the sub-soil. But by AD 120, the road had grown to a width of 43 ft, and its surface had been firmly laid on a solid foundation.

The road-building materials used depended upon whatever was available in the vicinity. Limestone foundations occur through-out the north and west, while in southern England chalk and flints were normally used. Gravel was the preferred surfacing, but where none could be found, the engineers made do with broken flints, crushed stone and even slag from iron foundries. One kind of surface that did not appear on the main roads of Britain was the huge flat paving slabs of the kind that surfaced Roman roads in North Africa, Italy and other parts of the Empire. There were a few paved roads in Britain, but these were minor routes of only local importance. The best-known example, at Blackstone Edge on the Pennine moors, may originally have been part of the army's communications system for controlling the central Pennines, though some scholars dispute its origins.

The trail-blazers
Rome expanded along the line of roads built by the skill and muscle-power of its legionaries. A relief from Trajan's Column shows a pioneer detail clearing trees and undergrowth ahead of the main column.

Rome's way
One of the first roads in Britain was the Fosse Way, which sliced across the country from Exeter to Lincoln. On stretches like this one near Ilchester, modern motorists still owe a debt of gratitude to the legionaries who laid the road's original line.

Lonely road

The road on Blackstone Edge, 16 ft wide, stone-paved and flanked by kerbstones, still soars grandly over the high, exposed moors. On its steepest section there is a central groove in the paving, possibly to hold the brake-poles of carts as their sweating, cursing drivers strove against the slope and the eternal moorland wind.

Such solid construction is unusual in second-class roads; more typical, perhaps, is the road between Towcester in Northamptonshire and Alchester in Oxfordshire whose surface consisted of no more than 6 in. of gravel laid directly on the sub-soil. Minor roads wandering off this were gravelled even more thinly; presumably they led to local hamlets and farmsteads. There must have been hundreds of these minor roads and tracks in southern Britain, for every estate had its links to a major road. One of these estate tracks, 13 ft wide and made of gravel on a limestone foundation, was found in Warwickshire, where it linked the villa at Radford Semele to the Fosse Way, about 1½ miles off. These were private roads, constructed and maintained by local landowners. Once a region was pacified and had passed out of military control, all the roads in it became the responsibility of local authorities, who were expected to keep them in good repair, without any further aid.

Milestones of history

Local authorities were also responsible for setting up milestones along the main roads. Almost 100 of these survive with carved legible inscriptions, and many others whose painted directions have long worn away. Their size and shape made them ideal building stones, and many were uprooted for this purpose; however, some of those found in their original positions still reveal the accuracy of the Roman surveyors, and occasionally the year in which the stone was erected. One, found just over 2 miles from the gates of Roman Leicester, *Ratae Coritanorum*, reads: 'The Emperor Caesar Trajan Hadrian Augustus, son of the deified Nerva, father of his country, in the fourth year of tribunician power, thrice consul. From Ratae, 2 miles' – a Roman mile was 1,620 yds.

Proof that *civitates* – local authorities – erected milestones is provided by examples from Kenchester in Hereford and Worcester inscribed R.P.C.D. (*Respublica Civitatis Dobunnorum* – the Dobunni), and from Old Penrith and Brougham, that both refer to the *civitas* of the Carvetti, based on Carlisle.

Central reservation
The paved road over the moor at Blackstone Edge near Rochdale has a central guttering at its steepest sections. Some authorities believe that this was designed to hold the brake-poles of Roman carts.

Emperor's bounty
Repair and resurfacing of major roads was usually undertaken by the local council, who were expected to furnish the labour, materials and finance for such work. However, this milestone found at Chesterton, Cambridgeshire, draws attention to the works apparently ordered by Victorinus, a Gallic usurper, around AD 270.

In addition to the cost of maintaining roads and erecting milestones, local authorities had to bear that of constructing and maintaining bridges and fords, though the earliest examples, dating from the years of the conquest, were built by the legions.

Bridges over narrow streams were simple affairs of wooden beams supported by stone and gravel abutments. But wider rivers were spanned by beautifully engineered structures like the bridge at Aldwincle in Northamptonshire, built to carry the Leicester-Colchester road for 80 ft across the River Nene. Timber abutments and iron-shod piles 20 in. square bore a timber bridge which probably had stout side-rails and heavy deck planking overlaid with gravel. Sometimes bridges were built entirely of stone, to judge by the voussoirs, or wedge-shaped masonry blocks, that have been discovered in the River Tyne near Chesters, on Hadrian's Wall.

Many smaller rivers, and even some of the larger ones, were crossed by paved fords; some that may be Roman have been found at Benenden in Kent, at Littleborough crossing the Trent, and across the River Yeo at Ilchester. Great rivers like the Humber and the Severn were too wide to be easily bridged, and were served by ferries instead. There was one over the Humber between Winteringham and Brough, and travellers to Caerwent or Caerleon who had to cross the Severn, could either take a ferry from Sea Mills at the mouth of the Avon, or make a long detour via Gloucester. With the kind of transport available in Roman Britain, such a detour could mean an extra day on the road.

On the road
This lively study of travellers, from the Arch of Constantine, shows the two most important means of conveyance in the Roman world – the four-wheeled cart and the mule.

Ox power

Moving goods around Roman Britain was a slow business. As can be seen from the few pieces of harness that survive – snaffles, curb-bits, and rein-rings – horses were used either for riding or for pulling very light carriages. The Romans did not have harnesses suitable for draught horses, and heavy wagons were usually pulled by oxen, or occasionally by mules. The lightest vehicles in general use were two-wheeled mule carts with a pair of seats perched high up – a favourite form of transport with important government officials. Heavy loads were hauled by oxen in four-wheeled, low-sided wagons.

Late in the 2nd century, the Roman traffic laws that banned most vehicles from the streets during the hours of daylight were extended to all other cities and towns of the Empire. From that time, the streets of Britain at night became just as hideous as those of Rome, with the squeals of ungreased axles and the exasperated yells of drivers as their wagons locked together in the dark.

Official dispatches

Slip-on shoe
The exact purpose of this iron shoe is uncertain, but it may be a 'hippo-sandal' – a temporary, removable horse-shoe that could be slipped on to the feet of animals not normally shod, when they were taken on to the hard surface of a paved road.

One group of travellers unaffected by traffic regulations were the couriers of the *Cursus Publicus*, the imperial communications service. Founded in the days of the Emperor Augustus, the service spanned the Empire with a system of post houses and inns (*mansiones*) along all its major routes. A change of horses could be obtained at the post houses, usually set about 10–15 miles apart, and at the end of the day the weary courier could find a meal and a night's lodging at one of the inns that lay at 20–30 mile intervals along the road. He probably needed both; carrying a heavy bag of dispatches, he might easily have ridden 50 miles since dawn.

A courier stationed in Britain rode through a landscape that differed enormously from today's. Villages and houses were few and far between, and for much of his journey his only companions were great forests and the wild, lonely hills. All the same, in some quiet places, and where the modern road follows the old Roman line, it is still possible to capture a fleeting glimpse of the world he knew.

One such journey is outlined in the 14th section of the Antonine Itinerary; and with this outline it is possible to follow the route taken by an imperial courier bearing dispatches from the Governor in London to the legionary commander at Caerleon. Leaving London and the first glimmer of dawn behind him, he galloped west, crossed the Thames at Staines, and having picked up a fresh horse, sped on to reach Silchester in the late afternoon. There, unless the dispatches were particularly urgent, he would spend the night at the large *mansio* on the southern outskirts of the town.

The Silchester *mansio* offered everything the weary rider needed; stalling for his horse, a good dinner, a bath-house and the opportunity to meet friends – fellow-soldiers perhaps, or government inspectors of highways or taxes. His evening ended either with an hour in the tavern, or perhaps a quiet stroll about the enclosed garden of the *mansio* before going to bed.

In the chill of the early morning, the courier's horse stood ready, groomed, fed and watered for the first part of the next gruelling stage of the journey – 65 miles to Bath before nightfall. Hooves ringing beneath the double arch of the west gate woke Silchester's townsmen, but almost before they were out of bed, the courier was out along the valley of the Kennet to Speen. Beyond, on the road to Mildenhall and a change of horses, the downs reeled back on either hand, the way punctuated by the odd farm cart and an encroaching pattern of estate fields and pastures.

With a fresh horse under him, the courier began the 20 mile slog to Sandy Lane, up over the head of the Kennet Valley where the landscape was dotted with rectangular timber huts set among patchwork fields. On the skyline rose the humps of ancient burial mounds; then, as he crossed the line of the ancient Berkshire Ridgeway, there loomed ahead the vast, mysterious bulk of Silbury Hill, built by unknown hands, long before the Romans came.

The rider followed the left swing of the road past the great mound and began the climb up Morgan's Hill, beyond whose crest lay an easy downhill canter to the post house at Sandy Lane.

The fresh mount he found there made easy work of the stretch from the Avon ford south of Lacock to the point where the road joined the Fosse Way just short of Bath. Fashionable suburban houses announced the approach to the town, whose centre was overhung by a haze of smoke from the fires that heated the great baths themselves.

Neither the waters nor the brilliant society of the town could delay the courier long. Next morning he was once more in the saddle, riding by the foot of Lansdown, close to the river, until he had passed the post house at Bitton. Now the road climbed above the river and ran across Durdham Down, to descend the hill to the harbour at Sea Mills.

There might be some delay in waiting for the ferry, but once it had arrived, and the passengers for Caerwent embarked, it took them down the Avon to the Severn, then crossed northwards to dock somewhere near present-day Sudbrook. Having picked up a last remount at the ferry, the courier pressed on along the last

ITINERARY 14

Silchester to Caerleon
Courier's course

Calleva Atrebatum (Silchester)	
to Spinis (possibly Speen)	15
to Cunetio (Mildenhall)	15
to Verlucio (Sandy Lane)	20
to Aquae Sulis (Bath)	15
to Traiectus (possibly Bitton)	6
to Abonae (Sea Mills)	9
to Venta Silurum (Caerwent)	14
to Isca (Caerleon)	9
Roman miles	103

The bridge-builders

The Romans were skilled bridge-builders, and enough fragments have been found to show that they bridged many of Britain's rivers in the course of pushing their military roads across the country. No bridge of Roman times survives intact in Britain, but coins provide a good deal of information about the design of Roman bridges. This gold coin shows a bridge over the River Danube built by Emperor Trajan during his campaign in Dacia, present-day Romania.

The Vaison stage

As well as the light, speedy two-wheeled carts, there were also many types of heavier, more ponderous four-wheeled vehicles. Some of these were used for freight, but others, like this one seen in a relief from Vaison in France, carried a number of passengers. Behind the driver, with his three-strand whip, sits an official and his servant, no doubt on some government errand, while other passengers travel inside.

129

9 miles to the gaunt grey walls of Caerleon. Beyond, high, wooded hills crowded down to the bridge over the Usk, on whose other side he could see his destination – the proud, clean-cut lines of the legionary fortress. Gaining the sentry's permission to pass the gate, he rode straight to the headquarters building and delivered his dispatches. Only then could he afford to relax over a well-earned cup of Falernian wine.

From roadside inn to township

So much vital traffic flowing up and down the highways, as well as the need for a meeting place for merchants and tradesmen, made the public inn a very important feature of the towns. The *mansio* at Silchester was vast, but even the smaller ones were designed along the same luxurious lines with the accommodation grouped around a central yard or garden. This is true even of the tiny *mansio* found at Wall, near Lichfield, where the courtyard is only 23 ft square. Indeed the bath-house at Wall, which is separated from the inn by a gravelled path, is larger than the inn itself; as well as having a small suite of bathing rooms, it also possessed a sizeable exercise hall – much appreciated, no doubt, by saddle-stiff couriers.

   The combination in one spot of a major road and a relay station sometimes led to the development of a small town. At

Soldiers' road
The road from the Severn ferry at Sudbrook to the legionary fortress at Caerleon ran straight through the town of Caerwent, capital of the Silures. The same road is still the high street of the modern village, whose houses are still almost entirely surrounded by its Roman walls.

Chelmsford, the erection of the first timber *mansio* in the late 1st century was followed by the building of two-roomed and three-roomed timber shops, including a bakery and perhaps a dye works, which lined the main road through the town, and probably there were other taverns as well. Towards the river was a wooden temple, rebuilt in the 4th century, while in the opposite direction, towards London, there were pottery kilns and a smithy. The whole settlement covered little more than 20 acres.

Quite a large number of present-day towns and villages owe their beginnings to Roman roadside inns. Braughing in Hertfordshire is a quiet enough place nowadays, but in Roman times it was an important settlement on the crossroads of Ermine Street and Stane Street. Narrow-fronted shops along Ermine Street sold articles of iron, bronze and bone, and there was a bath-house, an inn with a courtyard and possibly a market place as well.

Deuce or trey?
Gambling was a feature of the many wayside inns along the roads of the Empire. However, the merry camaraderie of a game of dice seems to be wearing a little thin in this tavern scene from Pompeii; one of the players claims he has thrown a winning three, while his opponent is certain he has thrown only a two.

Thirty miles further north along Ermine Street, another small town grew up at Godmanchester in Cambridgeshire. Originally a farming village built on the site of a Roman fort, by the 2nd century it possessed an inn, bath-house, and a number of timber-built shops and smithies. Just to the west of the inn was a small temple dedicated to the native god Abandinus. Godmanchester's increasing prosperity is signalled by a small 3rd-century building that may have been a basilica, and by an extensive gravelled market place. To match its growing status, Godmanchester was permitted to surround its 27 acres with town walls, complete with gate-house and guard room in the late 3rd century. But by then, the town's most important feature, its fine *mansio*, had been long established.

A merchant travelling up Ermine Street to Lincoln, and wishing to put up for the night, could turn his wagons off the main road and down a 65 yd gravelled lane that led directly to the inn. Just beyond the main gateway were the stables and wagon sheds where the mules were unhitched, fed and watered and the carts put under cover. Everything settled, the merchant made his way along the main corridor, which ran round a large enclosed garden.

The main reception room and dining hall lay in the south wing; both rooms had mosaic floors, and plastered, painted walls. In the south-east corner of the building was the kitchen, with rubbish pits outside, while the bedrooms were situated in two rows down the long sides of the building, and perhaps on an upper floor too. Baths, which had separate facilities for men and women, were provided in a separate building to the rear of the inn.

By a wall of the tiny plunge-bath a rich discovery was made – coins, a gold pendant, bone pins, silver and bronze finger-rings, a glass necklace, a shale bracelet and a bronze brooch. Almost certainly, they were hastily buried there by a visitor when the *mansio* was burnt to the ground in AD 296, perhaps during the course of a Saxon attack. It was at this period that Saxon raiders drove inland, taking advantage of the chaos attending the fall of the British usurper Allectus, and the reconquest of the island by Roman forces under Constantius Chlorus.

The vital waterways

The most important centre of communication on Ermine Street was Lincoln, the meeting place not only of the Fosse Way and Ermine Street, but also of the River Witham and the Car Dyke as well. The Car Dyke was part of a chain of natural and man-made waterways which enabled bulk cargoes to be moved swiftly and easily from the southern Fens to as far north as York. At the southern end of this system, the River Cam was linked to the River Ouse by an 8 mile canal, beyond which further stretches of canal and river carried barges to the River Nene. Between the Nene and Lincoln, the system was almost entirely artificial, and some of it still survives in stretches 50 ft wide and 23 ft deep, arguing the existence of large and commodious river craft.

These northern waterways coincided with extensive drainage and land-reclamation projects undertaken by the Romans in the Fens and may well have been approved, if not initiated, by Emperor Hadrian himself during his inspection of the province in AD 122. The waterway was no doubt valuable as a secure supply route for the legionary garrison at York and for the auxiliaries manning the forts on the eastern flank of the Pennines. Pottery from Nene Valley

Manpower
The barrelled wines of France and the Rhineland were hauled in barges to the ports where they were trans-shipped to sea-going vessels. This relief is from Avignon, but similar barges plied the waterways of Britain.

The shipwright
A Ravenna shipwright trims a timber for a great ship that looks almost ready to go down the slip. He is using an adze, a tool of shipwrights from Roman days until the building of the last wooden ships.

Fenland artery
The remains of Car Dyke, a Roman-built canal, snake across the fenland landscape near modern Peterborough. The Romans were the first to build canals in Britain, and they used them both for transport and as a means of draining marshy, low-lying country. The most important system was in the Fens and the east Midlands, where navigable rivers were connected by stretches of canal, permitting the transport of large quantities of goods between East Anglia and York.

133

kilns, as well as grain, beef and hides from the Fens could have been easily transported by the great barges which, from their curved bows to their raised sterns, measured some 115 ft overall.

On their southern journey, these vessels may have carried stone from Yorkshire and Lincolnshire, and from the quarries at Barnack in Cambridgeshire and Ketton in Leicestershire. Then there was north Midland iron to be picked up, and woollen cloth from York. Odd spaces could be filled with small packages of jet trinkets produced by craftsmen in and around the city.

On the western side of the Pennines, the legion at Chester and its neighbouring civilian settlement were both served by water transport centred upon nearby Heronbridge, where there were storehouses and quays for barges on the Dee. The vessels drew into the quays and unloaded their bales and crates on to wagons for the last 2 miles to Chester. Further south, Wroxeter was the terminus for boats and barges working up the River Severn, bringing iron from the Forest of Dean, corn from the west country estates, and oil and wine from overseas.

Londinium's river

In south-east England, the Thames conveyed an unceasing flow of traffic. Heavily laden boats bearing pots from the Oxford kilns could pull in and unload crates at points where major roads crossed the river. From Hedsor, goods could be speeded to St Albans or Silchester, while Staines was another point at which freight for Silchester could be off-loaded.

As the pottery boats moved downstream, the river grew

End of the voyage
Preserved in Thames mud for nearly 2,000 years, this barge (below left) once carried pottery and other goods up and down river from the docks of Roman London. To judge from better-preserved examples found in the Low Countries, these vessels could be up to 115 ft long.

Corn for Rome
Grain was imported to Italy from many different parts of the Empire. Here, in a painting from Ostia, a grain ship is being loaded with its cargo.

Dockers remembered
These tools were lost by dockers on the London wharves some 1,800 years ago. Yet the use of baling hook, grappling hook and crow-bar would be perfectly familiar to their modern counterparts.

steadily more busy until eventually the waterfront of Roman London came in sight. There, dozens of boats laden with pottery, tiles and farm produce from the villas in the Thames valley, jostled for space by the wharves that stretched along the north shore. Bales and sacks, crates and barrels were piled high alongside tableware, glass, wine and oil waiting to be loaded for the return journey.

Among the river boats were berthed sea-going ships, with dockers heaving at their cargoes with crow-bars and hooks. Clerks and keen-eyed merchants inspected the goods amid a babble of Latin, Celtic, Greek and tongues from the uttermost parts of the Empire and beyond. Occasionally, a badly handled crate or bale would drop into the Thames ooze – where it would remain until rediscovered by archaeologists nearly 2,000 years later.

The north bank of London's river still provides a glorious insight into the workings of Romano-British trade. Traces of timber wharfing stretch for 500 yds along the waterfront, where dockers' tools, styli and writing tablets, imported pottery and figurines, have all been found by the Roman harbour, and the remains of at least two large Roman vessels have been discovered, preserved in the mud of the river bed.

Gateways to Britain

Though London was Britain's principal port, at least a dozen others served the province as well. Many of them, including Fishbourne in West Sussex, Hamworthy in Dorset and Sea Mills in Avon, were originally founded as supply bases for the army and navy, though Fishbourne also had a short but active life as a civilian port. Between AD 55 and 75, its timber wharves and jetties were busy with boats from Cornwall, the Channel Islands and probably Brittany, as well as coastal traffic from Dorset, Sussex and other south coast harbours.

Further west, Hamworthy benefited from the growth of the great pottery industry around Poole Harbour, where the port stood. The pottery was shipped round most of the province, and in great quantities, especially to the garrisons of the north. Coastal shipping must have been constantly moving in and out of the bay in order to meet the demand for Poole's black cooking pots and dishes.

At Sea Mills, a town of about 6 acres, timber and stone-built shops and taverns clustered near the mouth of the Avon at its meeting-point with the Trym. Apart from handling military supplies and passengers for South Wales, Sea Mills also appears to have been the port through which Mendip lead was exported.

The legionary fortresses and civilian settlements at Chester and York had a secondary role as ports. Alongside the Dee at Chester are the remains of the Roman harbour wall, a timber wharf and solidly built warehouses, and though York may seem a long way inland to be a port, in Roman times the Ouse was tidal above the town, and navigable by barges and sea-going ships. A massive stone quay, with the base of a derrick still in place, indicates the amount of traffic that tied up at York, and tablets set up by foreign merchants have been found there. The presence of sea-going ships is confirmed by an altar set up by Marcus Audens, who described himself as a *gubernator* – a pilot – attached to the Sixth Legion. Audens would have been responsible for guiding ships down the Ouse to the Humber, and thence along the Humber to the sea.

The merchant venturers

Many of the ships sailing along the Humber and the Ouse were loaded with goods moving between York and the Rhineland, and often carried merchants with them. One named Fufidius, whose tombstone was found on the Rhine at Mainz, probably exported

Harbour lights
The Romans built two lighthouses to mark the entrance of Dover harbour, an important naval base and port throughout the occupation. An imposing 50 ft of one of them still stands; originally, it rose to about 80 ft and was crowned by a roofed lantern chamber, or by a platform bearing beacons.

Heading for port
This lively mosaic from Ostia, the seaport of Rome, shows a ship from Narbonne, steering oars and sails straining, running up to the lighthouse and into harbour. The depth of the vessel proclaims it to be a transport ship rather than a man-o'-war.

pottery from eastern Gaul to Britain. Marcus Silvanus was another pottery merchant, according to a tablet he set up near the mouth of the Rhine asking for divine protection on a forthcoming voyage – very likely to York. The most successful of these pottery exporters seems to have been Viducius Placidus of Rouen, who in AD 221 erected an arch and a shrine at York dedicated to Jupiter and to the cult of the emperors.

Other North Sea traders dealt in fish sauce, salt fish and wine. Not all York's wine came from the Rhineland, however, for two merchants who established businesses in York traded with Aquitania in southern Gaul, through the port of Bordeaux. One of them, Marcus Diogenes, was a native of Aquitania, married to a Sardinian woman called Julia Fortunata. The other was Marcus Aurelius Lunaris, who set up an altar at Bordeaux in AD 237 as a thank-offering, having successfully completed a voyage from York. Since the altar is of gritstone, brought all the way from Yorkshire, round the coast of Brittany and down the shore of the Bay of Biscay, he must have been confident indeed of his journey's outcome.

Several of these foreign merchants made their homes in York, and became influential members of local society. Placidus, Diogenes and Lunaris were all appointed *seviri*, in charge of ceremonies at York connected with the cult of the emperors. Though the post carried considerable prestige, it also involved the holder in a good deal of expense, since he was expected to contribute to the cost of the ceremonies he arranged; Lunaris, it seems, was rich enough to have held office in both York and Lincoln. Whether Placidus and Lunaris settled permanently at York or eventually returned to their homelands is not known, but Diogenes and his Sardinian wife made York their home and died there, buried next to one another in fine stone coffins.

Among other foreign visitors who came to Britain were natives of Metz, Trier and Chartres, according to the inscriptions set up at Bath. Priscus of Chartres was a stonemason; he may have settled at Bath to work the local sandstone. At least two foreign merchants shipped wine to Silchester; their names, Sualinos and Herm(ogenes), are inscribed on wine barrels found in a well there. Sualinos was a Gaul, to judge by his name, and Hermogenes a Greek. The Greeks were highly successful merchants, and there is evidence of their activities in London, where a ruler was found, marked not only in Roman inches but also in Greek *digiti*, units of one-sixteenth of a foot. An Athenian, Aufidius Olussa, who died in London at the age of 70, may well have been a merchant, and a sandal inscribed *Ektori* – 'for Hector' – may have belonged to the child of a Greek in business in London. The commodities such men dealt in were most likely the products of the eastern Mediterranean, such as olives, wine and oil.

Product of Gaul
In the years just before and after the Roman invasion, south-east Britain was flooded with Gallic bronze, glass and pottery. This lead-glazed flagon, found in Colchester, was made in France in the 1st century AD.

Pots for sale

Though trade in exotic foodstuffs was extensive, their value was completely outweighed by that of imported pottery, for even before the Roman conquest, the people of south-eastern Britain had imported large quantities of pottery from the Continent. With the conquest, the business boomed. A wide variety of wares from continental Europe found their way to Britain; one rubbish pit at York, for example, contained four different types of imported pottery, made in four different areas of Roman Gaul. Most popular of all, however, were the products of the Gaulish potteries making samian ware – so called because early archaeologists believed that it was pottery from the island of Samos in the Aegean Sea.

The scale of operations at the major centres producing samian ware was staggering. From the workshop of a single firm at La Graufesenque in southern France, 20 surviving tally lists record that

Decorative mythology
Scenes from mythology, in continuous friezes or in panels, were popular themes for the decorative moulds on bowls and vases – as on this example found at Silchester. The widespread use of moulds often permits even fragments of pottery to be traced back to particular workshops.

Top import
Between the 1st and early 3rd centuries the quantity of samian ware brought into Britain exceeded that of any other import. This glossy red pottery, made in different parts of Gaul, found its way into thousands of Romano-British homes, and was especially renowned for its fine decoration moulded in low relief. There was a wide range of designs, but this pot, found in Felixstowe, is remarkable both for form and fine workmanship.

Trade mark
Tracing samian ware to its factories of origin is a fascinating study, facilitated here by the potter's stamp. Sextima worked at Lezoux, in Gaul, around AD 150.

139

over an unknown period – probably several months – 34 workmen produced more than 400,000 pots. Samian ware was exported to Britain in crate-loads, which have been found at every stage of the journey from factory to market stall – in a Roman shipwreck on Pudding Pan Rock in the mouth of the Thames, by London quaysides, and among the debris in Wroxeter market square. From the markets, the vessels found their way into the kitchens and living-rooms, and eventually the rubbish pits, of every Roman town house and country villa, and into many a native hut in the remotest corners of Wales, the Pennines and Scotland.

Everyone, it seems, was expected to have a samian table-service. But fashion and status apart, samian was – and still is – very attractive. Produced in a very fine red clay with a rich, glossy red surface, it was good to look at and good to touch. The vessels were mainly dishes, bowls and cups; most were pleasing, some even elegant. The plainness of the cups and dishes in a table-service was often relieved by the elaborate moulding on the bowls – decorations that included scrolls, plants, medallions and abstract motifs, as well as human and animal figures. The human figures were sometimes mythological, but appeared just as frequently in hunting and gladiatorial scenes.

Pottery from the Rhineland was never as popular as samian ware, but in the later 2nd and 3rd centuries it was shipped to Britain in quantities large enough to enrich merchants like Silvanus and Placidus. Indeed, it did possess a dark, metallic lustre that contrasted well with the brilliant red of samian ware; by far the greatest sale was for bulbous mugs that bore brief, white-painted injunctions such as *Bibe* – 'Drink'.

Rough pottery amphorae containing wine, oil or sauces, were imported in their thousands as were clay lamps from Gaul, Italy and Africa. These were the ancillary lighting of the Roman world – useful for lighting the way to bed, or along a dark corridor, but insufficient for the job of illuminating a dining-room.

Dining in style

Wealthier Britons swiftly acquired bronze candlesticks or the even more handsome standing candelabras from Italy or Gaul. They also yearned for saucepans, bowls, flagons and jugs of Italian and Gaulish bronze, while the most spendthrift indulged in silverware from the Mediterranean. The stupendous treasure found at Mildenhall in Suffolk, and now in the British Museum, reflects the extravagance to which a few rich British families could rise.

Aristocratic preference
Even before the conquest, the rich Belgic aristocracy of south-east Britain had acquired a taste for Roman wine, tableware, glass and silver. Goods found in graves in the vicinity of Welwyn, Hertfordshire, especially reflect the Romanisation of British chieftains. One of them was accompanied into the next world by five amphorae of Italian wine.

Lights for the home
The guttering glow of oil-lamps illuminated the corridors, kitchens and bedchambers of Romano-British town and country houses. Yet these simple and effective articles hardly seem to have been manufactured in Britain at all, but rather imported from Gaul, Italy, and even Africa.

Copied in Britain
*Glossy black cups and flasks were a
speciality of the Rhineland that
inspired local imitations in Britain.
Apart from simple decoration like this,
Rhenish ware often bore such exhortations
as* Bibe *('Drink!') and* Vita *('Life!').*

The dining table of a fashionable British house was a
testimony to the extent and wealth of the Empire. Samian bowls
piled with fruit gave a warm glow to the table, a dash of colour to be
set against the sparkle of silver and the dull lustre of bronze.

Some of the food and most of the drink consumed during the
course of the evening would have come from far-distant shores.
Olives, figs, mulberries and raisins were all imported, as were the
fish sauces and pickled fish brought from Spain and Italy packed in
special amphorae, whose fragments have been found as far apart as
Colchester, London, St Albans, Gloucester and Leicester. The very
oil for cooking came from estates in Spain, Italy or Greece.

Massive though these imports were, they were small indeed

compared with those of wine. In the early days of the province, most came from Spain, Italy and Greece, but by the 3rd and 4th centuries the fine wines of Bordeaux and Moselle found increasing allegiance in Britain. Barges laden with barrels of wine travelled down the Garonne, the Moselle and the Rhine to off-load their cargoes into sea-going vessels that carried them to York, London and Chichester. There they crammed the quaysides together with tall, buff amphorae containing the wines of the Mediterranean.

Extra space on the wine-ships was filled with lesser imports such as glass from the western provinces, and from Syria and Egypt. The fine ribbed bowls and cut-glass vessels produced in the East were always in great demand, and though few of these reached the smaller towns, bottles, bowls and flagons from Italy, Gaul and the Rhine seem to have been plentiful in the larger centres. Moulded trademarks such as *CCA* on glass from *Colonia Claudia Agrippinensis* – Cologne – make it possible to identify the place, or even the workshop, where the glass was manufactured.

From the Rhineland, too, came millstones of Andernach lava, which were sufficiently superior to the native product to make the cost of transport worth while. This was also true of fine marble. Though Purbeck stone from Dorset was widely used for friezes and inscriptions, a certain amount of true Italian and Aegean marble was imported for fine embellishment; it is found in major towns, and in wealthy country houses. Marble statues were also imported, to be set up in market squares, town halls, temples and family shrines.

The export drive

Large-scale imports seem to indicate a regular, organised trade between Britain and the rest of the western Empire that could only be carried on if Britain had goods of her own to exchange in the international market. But, in fact, a lot less is known about Britain's exports at that period than about her imports. This is because most of the exports were commodities that rarely, if ever, survive in recognisable form today. Martial, a Spanish poet who lived in Rome late in the 1st century, refers to British exports of hunting dogs and basketry. In AD 301 Emperor Diocletian issued an edict on prices and incomes, designed to combat the runaway inflation then afflicting the Empire. In this, two types of woollen British cloaks were thought to be sufficiently in demand to have their maximum prices fixed by law. Yorkshire linen, too, probably found a good market in western Europe, and trinkets of Whitby jet were popular in the Rhineland.

Britain's only contribution to the tables of the Empire may have been oysters. British oysters are referred to by Pliny and Juvenal, writing in the late 1st and early 2nd centuries; both appear to have considered them something of a delicacy.

More valuable than any of these were Britain's mineral exports. Before the conquest, writers such as the Greek Strabo had drawn attention to Britain's mineral wealth, and the Romans expended considerable effort in extracting lead, silver, gold and perhaps tin from the island. The imperial coinage devoured gold and silver, and there can be little doubt that most, if not all, of the British output was exported to the mints in Italy and Gaul.

Lead ingots, each weighing around 200 lb, have been found in or near the ports at Brough-on-Humber, Sea Mills, Chester and Bitterne, and lead from the Mendip mines has been found in France and even further afield. Analysis of the lead in Pompeiian drain-pipes suggests that some of it came from the Mendips.

It seems likely that Britain's balance of payments was permanently in the red during the Roman period, particularly in the 1st and 2nd centuries, before British craftsmen had developed the skills to compete with imported manufactured goods. But the British economy did not depend on exports to the extent that it does today, since local manufacturers found a good market for their products at home. Some of the purchasing power that the British required to buy imports may have been generated by the sale of goods and services to the Roman army, whose representatives in Britain were considerably more numerous than in many other provinces of the Empire. Every soldier had money in his pocket, and he spent it largely on locally produced goods. There was some advantage in this, since imports from other parts of the Empire were subject to duty of about 2½ per cent when they entered a British port.

When British goods were exported beyond the frontiers of the Empire, a 25 per cent levy was imposed on them by the Romans. But the demand among the outer barbarians for the status symbols of civilisation easily overcame price resistance, as is shown by the abundance of Romano-British pottery, trinkets and other manufactured articles exported beyond Hadrian's Wall.

In spite of its imbalance of trade with the rest of the Empire, by the 3rd century the province of Britain was part of a 'common market' which stretched from the Tyne to the Nile. The trackways and roads, the canals and navigable rivers, the relay stations and ports of Roman Britain were integral parts of a vast communications and trading network. Within it moved manufactured goods, foodstuffs and raw materials bought and sold through a common coinage, under a common law, and for a common price.

THE MILDENHALL TREASURE

Lost for 1,600 years, a hoard of imported silver recalls the last tragic years of Roman Britain

In 1942, a ploughman working at Mildenhall, Suffolk, turned up a number of blackened, oxidised objects; his employer put them into a cupboard and forgot about them.

However, an inquest in 1946 revealed that the objects comprised one of the most important groups of Roman works of art ever discovered in Britain. Now in the British Museum, the treasure consists of 34 bowls, dishes, spoons and chalices in ornamented silver, while the *Chi-Rho* monogram on some of the pieces indicates that the later owners were Christians. Nothing else is known about them. Probably they were a rich family of East Anglian landowners who, in the troubled years of the mid-4th century, buried their most precious possessions, hoping to come back for them one day. But they never did.

Elegant silverware
Though the Mildenhall treasure is sometimes called a dinner-service, the pieces are really too diverse to merit this description. While it contains as many as six dishes and seven spoons, there are only two platters and a pair of silver chalices. The elegance of the latter, however, with their openwork stems, is remarkable.

Glory from Gaul
The Mildenhall hoard is one of the richest collections of Roman silverware to have survived in the western provinces of the Empire. Some of the pieces may have been made in Gaul, like this exquisite covered dish, whose principal frieze depicts fighting groups of centaurs, boars and lions, each group separated by a human mask. A little of the fine decoration on the flange is also visible.

Bacchus triumphant

The finest of all the 34 pieces in the Mildenhall treasure is this superb silver dish. Weighing more than 18 lb, it was made in southern Europe, quite possibly in Rome, in the 4th century. The theme of its joyous and magnificently moulded decoration is the victory of Bacchus, god of wine, over Hercules. Bacchus stands proudly with his foot on a panther, while the hero, overcome by the god's hospitality, is supported by satyrs. The sea god Oceanus glares from the centre of the plate upon the revellers, led by a pipe-playing Pan.

CHAPTER FIVE

Gracious living in the country

*New market towns, new
implements and new attitudes
towards farming bring greater
prosperity to the tribal aristocracy
of Britain, and herald the elegant
world of the country estate*

Bright new world
*The great majority of British villas were the centres of working, profit-making farms.
Nevertheless, their owners insisted upon a high degree of comfort and upon pleasant
interiors whose mosaics mirrored as far as possible those found in towns like St
Albans (below), and even those in the magnificent palace of Fishbourne (left).*

I N APRIL OF 1806, AN ADVERTISEMENT IN A LOCAL NEWSPAPER DESCRIBED A HOUSE TO BE AUCTIONED IN THE BULL'S HEAD INN at Fishbourne, near Chichester. The auctioneers drew attention to the 'pleasing views of the harbour' it commanded, and mentioned that the property included a 'curious Roman pavement, thirteen feet square'. Neither the auctioneers nor the man who finally bought it could have known that beneath the house and gardens lay the remains of the largest, most luxurious private residence built in Britain during the Roman occupation.

Despite the 'curious pavement' clue, those remains stayed hidden for more than 150 years until, one day in 1960, a workman cutting a trench for a water main turned up traces of Roman pottery. Excavations that followed revealed the staggering size of the workman's chance discovery: the mansion had covered a vast area about 500 ft square – about the same as that occupied by the main building of Buckingham Palace today.

Fishbourne, indeed, *was* a palace. Though built only 40 years after the Roman invasion, its size, design and lavish decoration proclaim it as no ordinary house, but the show-place of a ruler who lived and entertained on a spectacular scale. The four main wings formed a hollow square around a formal garden, with lawns, flower beds, shrubs and trees. Piped water fed fountains lining broad gravel paths. Visitors entered through the main gate in the east wing, crossing the garden to the great reception hall in the raised west wing. As they stepped from the entrance hall into the sunlit garden, a scene of carefully contrived magnificence met their eyes. A 30 ft wide path was flanked by shrubs trimmed into semi-circular and rectangular recesses, in some of which stood fountains with bowls made of grey-blue, marble-like Purbeck stone, and statues in fine marble from the Mediterranean.

The monumental entrance to the reception hall, towering 40 ft, was approached by broad steps. Beyond the four massive columns of the porch was an audience chamber, its floor paved wall to wall with finest mosaic. The ceiling was vaulted and covered with plaster painted blue, purple and red. To either side of the chamber were suites for distinguished guests, of four or five rooms, with black-and-white geometric patterns on the mosaic floors. The north wing, too, was divided into suites around two smaller courtyards. These rooms also had mosaic floors and plastered walls, the walls of one room being inlaid with marble from France, the Pyrenees, Turkey and the Aegean.

A great assembly hall in the north-east corner was 80 ft long. Its roof must have weighed around 100 tons and was supported by eight massive piers forming a central nave with aisles on each side.

Grand façade
A fresco from Pompeii gives some idea of the kind of villa architecture that the Roman world admired. The high-pedimented porch and the long colonnaded verandas overlooking a formal garden are remarkably close in spirit and design to those at the palace of Fishbourne, in faraway West Sussex.

Six of the piers had statues at their feet. In the east wing were ten small rooms facing two courtyards. They were not elaborately furnished with mosaics or marbles, and were probably intended simply to put up messengers and other humbler visitors.

But the most imposing part of Fishbourne must have been the south wing, where, adjacent to his bath-house, the owner almost certainly had his private apartments. These were set between two colonnaded verandas, one overlooking the central garden of the palace, the other facing southwards towards Chichester harbour. This southern aspect, in contrast to the symmetry and formality of the central garden, was landscaped with random shrubs and trees, a stream, a pond and a quay for boats and barges.

The Briton who loved Rome

The expense and effort spent in building this enormous palace and its gardens were immense: some 40,000 cu. yds of earth had to be excavated. Building the palace walls and gutters alone called for quarrying, transporting and working thousands of tons of sandstone and limestone. Add the tons of lime-mortar, iron nails, clay tiles and timber needed, and the wealth, authority and organising power of the man who built Fishbourne become evident.

Inside, the palace was equally impressive. Beside the imported marbles and statues, 160 Cotswold or Gallic stone columns surrounded the gardens and fronted the porches of the entrance hall, audience chamber and assembly hall.

Unobtrusive formality
Charming enclosed gardens, like this one at Pompeii, found distant echoes in the small villas of Britain. Protected by colonnades, and full of marble seats and fountains, such gardens would encourage after-dinner conversation or a quiet stroll among the neat shrubs.

149

There may have been as many as 50 mosaic floors, laid by craftsmen from Italy, where black-and-white geometric mosaics were then in fashion. Other continental craftsmen may have executed the plasterwork, and only a Roman architect could have contrived the visual effects repeated throughout the palace.

Few men in Britain would have had the drive, wealth and authority for such a project. One was the Roman governor, but nothing found suggests that Fishbourne had anything to do with him. And its position, far from the hub of administration at London, also makes this doubtful.

The more likely candidate is Cogidubnus, king of the Regni, a branch of the Atrebates, on whose territory Fishbourne stood. Pottery and coins found on the site can be dated from his time. He seems to have succeeded Verica, the king whose plea for aid against the rival Catuvellauni first drew Claudius into the conquest of Britain. Claudius granted Roman citizenship to Cogidubnus, let him keep his throne, and gave him new lands. This favoured treatment seems to have continued under Claudius's successor Nero and emperors who followed.

In return, Cogidubnus proved a firm friend of Rome. He allowed the Romans to use Fishbourne harbour during their conquest of the south-west, and stayed loyal during Boudicca's revolt of AD 60–61. Tacitus, who was not born until AD 55, writes that Cogidubnus 'maintained his unswerving loyalty down to our own times'. He may have had in mind also the king's attitude during the Roman civil wars of AD 69.

Cogidubnus would surely have refused to take advantage of Rome's internal strife to stage another rebellion like that of Boudicca, and may even have offered his support to Vespasian, a contender for the throne. The two men may have become acquainted some 25 years earlier, when Vespasian had commanded the Second Legion in this area. When Vespasian emerged triumphant as emperor in AD 69, he may have bestowed new privileges on Cogidubnus, and he is even more likely to have rewarded his loyalty with cash gifts, which the British king could have used to build his new palace.

Birth of the country house

Many architectural features of Fishbourne were echoed, on a less-spectacular scale, in scores of country houses built by well-to-do Britons. Most of them stood at the heart of estates run as businesses, self-supporting entities designed to provide the owner

Running repairs
Wear, tear and changing tastes could affect even mosaic floors in the end. Here in a corner of Fishbourne palace, a 1st-century mosaic in a black-and-white geometrical pattern has been overlaid by an early 2nd-century polychrome floor of lesser quality.

Stucco decoration
Painted plaster was about as far as most British villa-owners went in the way of wall decoration, but occasionally an example of stucco work is uncovered. This piece, with a recurring motif of birds and a fruit basket, was part of a cornice in a room at Fishbourne. Considering that the walls of the room extended for 100 ft, and the wooden die was only 3 in. long, the plasterer must have been a painstaking craftsman.

A likely heir to Fishbourne
Cogidubnus, king of the Regni of Sussex and a staunch ally of Rome in the early years of the occupation, is the most likely builder of the magnificent palace of Fishbourne, near Chichester. Destroyed by fire late in the 3rd century, little remains of its former grandeur or of the many statues that once adorned its rooms and gardens. However, this sensitive sculpture of a boy has survived; obviously, it is a portrait taken from life, and it has been suggested that it may represent one of Cogidubnus's sons.

with a good living from the land. Romans called the whole complex of buildings involved in this type of farming – including the owner's house – a 'villa'. Farming was, indeed, the mainstay of Roman Britain's economy, and the 'villa' played an important part in the nation's life for more than 300 years of Roman rule.

But the villa house itself evolved gradually. Some of the earliest ones, often replacing timber hut farmhouses, were built in the hills around St Albans between AD 75 and 100 at Lockleys, Park Street and Gorhambury. Early villas were usually a simple rectangular block of five or six rooms with a veranda or corridor along the front. The roof was tiled and the floors were plain cement, though some were made of attractive pink concrete or laid with a coarse mosaic of tile cubes to add colour and interest.

In time they became more sophisticated, since many of their occupants also owned town houses, where they lived while undertaking civic duties as councillors or magistrates. So when they built in the country they wanted to maintain their accustomed style, surrounding themselves with as many of the comforts and conveniences of urban life as possible.

There were separate rooms for eating, sleeping, entertaining, bathing and cooking – each with its own door from a corridor running around the villa. At least one or two rooms were heated during winter – a previously unheard-of luxury – and many villas had either a bath-suite or an outside bath-house.

All this was in startling contrast to the old-time British hut-house – two or three all-purpose rooms, with the inner ones reached only through the outer ones. But as the British began to adopt Roman ways, their craftsmen learned the skills of building in masonry, plastering walls, laying mosaic floors, and building drainage and under-floor heating systems.

By the 2nd century a typical villa had a central suite of rooms linked by a corridor or corridors, from which a room or suite projected at either end to form wings. Some, like those at Spoonley Wood and Witcombe, in Gloucestershire, had wings projecting far enough forward to create a courtyard, enclosed by the building on three sides. Baths, under-floor heating and mosaic floors became increasingly common.

But the most impressive spate of villa building came in the 3rd and 4th centuries. In some of these later mansions the wings were linked either by a wall or by a fourth wing to create a completely secluded central courtyard or garden. One at Keynsham, in Avon, and another at Woodchester in Gloucestershire, were fashionable country houses of this sort, with dozens of rooms, including heated suites, baths and many mosaics.

Villa bath-house
All the Roman villas in Britain have long been reduced to their foundations, and what remains is often little more than a shadow on the turf. But the little bath-house of the villa at Dicket Mead, Welwyn, still survives, complete with its furnace room, from which an arched flue led into the hot room beyond.

Stately home in the Cotswolds

Chedworth, in Gloucestershire, is a particularly well-preserved example of this later, luxurious style of villa, set at the heart of a Cotswold country estate. One wing alone had not only a row of four bedrooms, but also a sauna-bath-suite: hot, dry heat was available in two small sweating chambers, with a cold plunge alongside. In the adjacent wing was a further bath-suite of the more usual steam-heat variety, and beyond it a reception chamber and a superb dining-room with a heated mosaic floor. The kitchen was in the south wing, and beyond it a series of small, rather plain rooms were probably for servants.

It is possible from discoveries made at Chedworth and at other villas to describe fairly accurately the scene in that elegant dining-room on a chill night in autumn or early spring. . .

As the last evening light filters through the green-tinged glass

A choice of baths
No villa of any pretensions was without a bath-house, and the grander ones might possess one or more bathing suites. The villa at Chedworth in the Cotswolds, for example, had a 'turkish' bath, incorporating a mosaic-floored warm room and a hot room; the floor of the hot room has collapsed, revealing the pillars of tile that supported it. To the right is a semi-circular apse that once contained the hot plunge. Bathers at Chedworth could also avail themselves of a second bath-suite of the sauna, or dry-heat, variety.

of windows set high in the walls, a servant lights the fine bronze candelabra, illuminating the reclining figures of the family on their couches, and low tables upon which food is laid.

The diners are gathered around three sides of a square at the south end of the room, where a mosaic with a central geometric design in red, white and blue covers the floor. The rest of the room is largely free of furniture, so that the diners can enjoy the scenes of revelry shown at the centre of another mosaic panel in the floor at the north end. There is Bacchus, god of wine, with his maenads and satyrs dancing around him, seeming almost to move in the flickering candlelight. In the corners are small figures of the Four Seasons, each an appropriately clad Cupid – Winter, for example, wears a hooded cloak, and carries a bare twig and a dead hare; Spring is all but naked, holding a basket of flowers.

The plainer wall panels are painted with straight-line patterns of red, blue and yellow, in imitation of veneers and recessed

Joyous Spring
One of the most popular themes used to fill the corners of Romano-British mosaics was the personification of the Four Seasons. At Chedworth villa they are represented by small figures in the corners of the dining-room. Here, lightly attired Spring gambols over the meadows with a bird on one hand and a basket in the other.

The mosaic as a status symbol
Since it was very expensive to install, a mosaic floor at once indicated to visitors to a villa that its owner was a man of substance, while the choice of motif for the mosaic could delicately suggest the extent to which he was Romanised, and the degree of his acquaintance with classical mythology and literature. For this reason, elaborate mythological scenes were very usual in dining-room mosaics, though somewhere in the design there often appeared a hospitable two-handled cup or chalice. Less showy designs, like this one from St Albans, took the cup, symbol of generosity and good fellowship, as the central motif.

A stag at bay
Sporting scenes rivalled mythology in popularity as themes for mosaics. Chariot racing, gladiatorial combat and scenes from the chase appear in many villas, though this 2nd-century mosaic from St Albans, depicting a lion attacking a stag, is more unusual. In general, such elaborate designs are more often found in town houses and villas of the 4th century.

panelling. As the evening wears on, braziers are brought in, the red glow of burning charcoal lending a new warmth to the coloured walls, and encouraging the diners to talk late over their wine.

Scenes like this must have been common in villas throughout southern Britain in the 3rd and 4th centuries, as their owners put in mosaics and had walls replastered and painted. Dining and reception rooms had floor designs showing Venus and Neptune, Orpheus charming the animals or Bellerophon slaying the Chimaera. A frequent motif in the dining-room was the chalice or wine cup, and hunting scenes were common enough to suggest that stories of the chase were popular at the table.

Wall decoration imitated that of fashionable Italian houses, like those at Herculaneum and Pompeii. Around the room above floor level ran a dado or skirting, painted on to the wall, often about 20 in. deep and imitating marble or wood panelling. Above, the wall was divided into large panels separated by painted-on stone columns. Sometimes, human figures or plants were painted in the centre of a panel, and – judging by fragments of plaster showing flowers, berries, shrubs and birds – whole gardens as well.

Statues for decoration were usually standing figures of classical gods and goddesses in fine limestone or imported marble – at least two adorned the Chedworth villa. Occasionally, sculptures

Gracious living
The uncluttered elegance of a Romano-British living-room is brought to life in this reconstruction in the Museum of London. The restrained decoration on the wall panels is set off by the simple couch, the basketry chair and the small tables. Such rooms would have been typical of town house and villa alike.

Painted interior
Well-off Romans and Romano-British decorated their town and country houses in precisely the same way. This wall is in St Albans, but its counterpart could well have been found in a nearby country villa. Panels painted with a 'candelabra' motif were highly popular, as was the simulated veneer of the surround.

Landed gentry
Stylised likenesses on tombstones abound, but it is rare indeed to discover true portraits of Romano-Britons. The villa at Lullingstone, Kent, has yielded two, both of which had been carefully stored, and there is no reason to doubt that the busts represent successive owners of the villa. Both were sculpted in the 2nd century, but a number of years apart; the figure on the left is the earlier, and the second may portray his son or grandson.

carved in relief and sculptured portrait busts were used, and two busts found at Lullingstone villa in Kent allow a unique opportunity to gaze into the faces of a British villa owner and his son, the former solemn but benevolent, the latter more businesslike. The originals are in the British Museum, but casts can be seen at the villa.

How farming was made to pay

A Roman ran his farm to make money, like any other business activity. Villa-building British farmers shared this attitude, and were helped by innovations brought by the Romans, such as intensive breeding of animals to produce hardy livestock, and specialisation, so that many farms emphasised the production of one crop or another. Many more new ideas about the management of land, plants, animals and farmworkers followed rapidly.

New implements helped to make these new ideas work: heavier, more-efficient ploughs and large, two-handled scythes not only made ploughing and hay-making easier, but also freed more land for cultivation. Solidly built granaries and byres improved storage for crops and sheltered animals in winter. New vegetables, fruits and herbs extended the scope of market-gardening.

All the new ideas and technology, however, could not have made farming profitable without two other features of Romanised life in Britain: the growth of towns – new population centres where farm produce was in demand – and the road building that made it possible to get produce quickly to market. These were the foundations on which estates large and small were able to profit and prosper.

Estates great and small

Some idea of the size of estates can be gained from the distribution of their villas, their likely natural boundaries, and the amount of land they had under the plough. To the east of the Chiltern Hills, for example, villas such as Gadebridge Park, Boxmoor and Latimer are so evenly divided that each estate probably had 450–600 acres of pasture and arable land, as well as woodland. By contrast the villa at Bignor, West Sussex, was much larger and more luxurious, and its estate probably covered 2,000–3,000 acres.

Then, as now, estates had bailiffs, who managed them in the owner's absence. There might also be other workers living in, for whom room had to be found. At Sparsholt villa in Hampshire there was a solidly made building with aisles formed by rows of pillars down each side – almost certainly communal living quarters for estate labourers.

On some large estates the tenants may themselves have lived in villas – a small villa at Somerdale, in Avon, may well have housed a tenant of the wealthy man who owned a more sumptuous house at Keynsham, near by. Other tenants may have lived in farmsteads and huts little different from those of pre-Roman Britain, like those at Butcombe, not far from Bath, which were probably connected with the villa at Lye Hole. But such buildings may have housed labourers and slaves, as well as tenants.

Macabre relics of slavery

Slaves were commonplace in the Roman world. They did much of the work on farms in Italy, and there is macabre evidence of slaves on British estates, too. Where a large number of graves of new-born children have been found – more than can be accounted for by normal infant mortality – these probably belonged to the children of slaves. At Hambleden villa, on the Thames near Henley, nearly 100 of these burials have been found; many were baby girls, a sad reminder that women slaves were less in demand than men.

Most farm slaves would have been unskilled labourers, cheap to buy, cheap to keep and expendable. They may have lived in aisled buildings such as that at Sparsholt, though the Roman author Columella suggested that slave quarters should be below ground – and not necessarily well-lit as long as they were reasonably healthy. But then the Romans lived in constant fear of slave revolts. Debris found in the cellar of a villa at Chalk, in Kent, included pieces of what may have been shackles. This cellar was 40 ft long and 13 ft wide, and its only natural light came from a single small doorway and one small window. Beneath the rubbish that had accumulated were three shallow pits, one hidden under the stairs, in which were three skeletons of infants. A dozen slaves may have lived in that squalid cellar, squatting to eat their meals of scraggy beef or mutton from pottery bowls. Small lamps in niches in the east wall would cast a flickering light, but there was one corner where daylight could penetrate, at the foot of the stairs. There, perhaps, sat an elderly slave no longer able to work in the fields, who earned his keep with other skills. Around him were bits of antler from which he carved pins, some of which also lay on the floor beside him, with his knife and whetstone, and his pewter plate and spoon.

Most slaves lived and died without leaving a trace of their

Time for reflection
Roman wit often tended towards the bawdy, expressed here in an oil-flask shaped as a young slave squatting on a bucket in one of the few free moments of his day. However, his cheery expression seems to suggest that he was not badly treated; in fact, young house slaves were often regarded as members of the family.

Servile chains
Slavery in Britain was not a Roman innovation. Indeed, it had played a large role in the Celtic economy, and years before the Roman invasion slaves had been noted as a British export. These shackles, which probably held a member of a chain-gang, were found in a Celtic hill-fort at Bigbury.

A slave who died free
This elegant figure depicted on a tombstone in South Shields (above) was not a prominent member of Romano-British society but a former Moorish slave named Victor. According to the inscription, Numerianus, his master, not only freed him but paid for his funeral when he died at the age of 20. The tombstone alone must have cost a considerable sum.

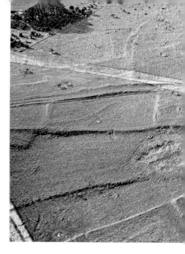

passing, but one seems to have left his name, if no more, in this Kentish cellar. Among the debris on its floor were the remains of a pottery vessel on which had been inscribed, in Greek letters, the name Felix. Ironically, the name means 'happy'.

Grain to feed the troops

Most estates grew a range of crops and reared several species of animals, as well as keeping geese, hens and ducks and growing fruit and vegetables, but the owner would concentrate on what was best suited to the local soil and climate, and what was most in demand.

However, the provincial government put heavy pressure on farmers to grow grain to feed the army, and arable farming prospered. The heavy Roman plough had a vertical blade in front of the ploughshare to help to cut the soil, and may also have had a mould-board to turn the furrow. As a result heavy ground, on which the less-efficient British ploughs made slow progress, came increasingly under cultivation, and existing arable land could be more efficiently ploughed, so improving its yield. But the plough was difficult to turn at the end of a furrow, and in order to reduce the number of turns the land was cultivated in longer, narrower strips than in the older British fields.

Wheat became the favoured crop over much of southern Britain – particularly spelt, a hardy wheat suited to damp climates.

The year's round
Reliefs on a Roman sarcophagus tell the story of the seasons' work on a great estate. At upper left, oxen plough the earth, which is then cultivated by hand. To the right of the central figure, reapers cut the corn with sickles, and below them, a heavy ox-drawn farm wagon brings the harvest home. At bottom left, the corn is ground in an upright mill, before being made into bread by the baker, who can be seen stacking bread into his oven.

Barley was the next most popular cereal crop, and both were hand-harvested with reaping hooks. Other crops included beans, peas, vetch and clover – possibly for animal fodder, but also useful in crop-rotation schemes.

Corn was part-dried in ovens – a new feature in Britain – and then threshed. Most of the corn was taken to the nearest town for milling but some estates did their own, and many stored grain in specially constructed granaries.

Agrarian revolution
The adoption of a larger, heavier plough, together with steady improvements in the use of land, led to the introduction of a longer, narrower field pattern on estates and government farms in southern Britain. The pattern can still be clearly seen on Overton Down.

Daily bread
This upright mill (left) found in London was probably used in a bakery serving a large number of customers. Country estates usually ground their flour with a much simpler hand-mill.

Looking after the animals

After harvesting, the straw remaining in the fields was gathered for animal bedding, and the stubble left behind for cattle or sheep to graze. Apart from providing cheap fodder, this also ensured that the fields were manured. Mostly cattle and sheep were reared, but pigs, goats and horses were sometimes bred for profit, too.

Cattle byres usually had aisles down each side, divided into stalls; they were solid, specialised buildings unknown in pre-Roman Britain. About 20 or 30 cattle were probably kept through the winter, fed mostly on hay. Harvesting hay was speeded up and production boosted by the great Roman two-handed scythe, much more efficient than the British reaping-hook, which was then used only for harvesting cereal crops. Roman scythes have been found in the remains of a blacksmith's workshop at Great Chesterford,

Essex, and at Barnsley Park villa in Gloucestershire.

The most popular cattle were little Celtic short-horns – the Dexter is today's closest equivalent – kept mainly for beef and hides. Traces have been found of a larger breed probably used to pull ploughs and farm wagons.

Wool, too, was important – valued enough for two kinds of British woollen cloak to have had their prices fixed by the Emperor Diocletian in AD 301. Then, as now, the South Downs, the Mendips and the Cotswolds were thriving areas of sheep farming. A walled enclosure at Bignor, on the South Downs, was almost certainly a sheep-pen large enough to take 200 animals; sheep were raised for wool at the Mendip villas of Star and Chew Park; and in a shed at Frocester Court villa, below the Cotswolds, fuller's earth and traces of other wool-processing techniques such as felt-making have been found

Horses were neither reared nor used to any great extent, except for riding or pulling chariots or light carriages – wagons and ploughs were drawn by oxen. Most farms kept just a few horses for riding, but those with large herds of cattle, like Hambleden and Downton, had more – probably ridden by Romano-British 'cowboys' to herd and protect the animals on their wide ranges, and drive them to new pastures when necessary. At Frocester Court, however, horse-breeding may have been a profitable part of the villa's economy.

Rustic pleasures

The energy with which estate owners pursued profit did not prevent them from pursuing the pleasures of country life with equal enthusiasm, especially in spring and early summer. Those were the seasons when their fields and ample woodlands blossomed. They could ride through their meadows or hunt the fierce wild boars in the woods, where wolves also roamed.

Far from the strains and stresses of the town, the landowner and his family could relax on their open veranda, or stroll along paths lined with shrubs and herbs, through fragrant and colourful gardens, and orchards where the last blossoms clung still to the trees and where bees droned among their pottery hives as ducks and geese waddled by a pond or stream.

In the damp bottoms of wells at some villas have been preserved the pips, seeds and shells of the fruits and nuts grown – cherries, apples, pears, plums, walnuts and hazelnuts.

The remains of vegetables are more scarce, but cabbages,

Blades for the harvest
Throughout the occupation, many British farmers continued to use the old-fashioned short-bladed sickles to harvest their crops. On larger estates, landowners and workers alike swiftly adapted to the more efficient scythes, like these found at the fort at Newstead in Scotland.

The vast quantities of grain consumed by townspeople and the army had to be transported from the corn-growing estates by ox wagon. Sure but very slow, they must have created considerable traffic problems on the roads around harvest time. In this relief from the Museum of London, a pair of oxen, urged on by their driver's goad, strain to haul a heavily laden cart. The sturdy wheels appear to be constructed of four heavy planks held together by cross-pieces.

carrots, parsnips and celery were all grown in Roman Britain; so was a wide range of herbs, including fennel, dill and coriander. Pruning knives, saws and the iron blades of spades, all discovered on villa estates, show that gardening was an accepted part of villa life. Fruit and vegetable plots were not new to Britain, but plums, pears, carrots and celery were cultivated for the first time.

A few of the more enterprising farmers experimented with vines: wine was the Empire's favourite drink, and vines were being grown successfully in France and Germany. Seeds, skins and other tell-tale evidence found at Gloucester show that wine was pressed in at least one vineyard near the town. Vine stems are also said to have been found close to the villa site at Boxmoor.

Perhaps more suited to Britain's climate was breeding fish in tanks. When the Roman author Varro was discussing the merits of various continental estates he was able to cite the examples of a villa fishpond and an aviary, both extremely profitable. At Shakenoak villa, in Oxfordshire, two large, shallow tanks, each containing a silt deposit, have been identified as fish-tanks, successful enough to have been worked for nearly a century.

Country crafts and industry

A widespread way of making extra profit was for estates to take up small-scale crafts or industries. At Park Street villa, for example, a large kiln was built early in the 4th century to make tiles for nearby St Albans during a great spate of rebuilding in the city. Kilns on the Netherwild villa, further south, made tiles for roofing and heating systems for several decades in the 2nd century.

Every villa probably had a smithy for its own needs, but the mass of cinders from iron-working found at the Great Weldon house in Northamptonshire includes lumps weighing up to 77 lb, and may be evidence that local iron ores were smelted there in some quantity. Lansdown villa, on the hills above Bath, produced pewter ware, which probably found a ready market among the visitors thronging the famous spa town.

One villa owner seems even to have tried to emulate the success of Bath by developing his villa as a spa: at Gadebridge Park, in the early 4th century, he built a great open-air swimming pool, 66 ft by 40 ft – almost as big as the central pool at Bath, and far larger than any other swimming pool known in Roman Britain.

Portrait of a great estate

If there was no such thing as a 'typical' villa farm, it is possible to piece together a picture of one that includes all its more important aspects.

When the Bristol–Exeter railway was being laid in 1838, a deep cutting was dug at Gatcombe, near Bristol. The digging uncovered extensive foundations, the capitals of stone columns, coins, pieces of pottery and other remnants. Part of a mosaic floor, tiles from the heating system and other fragments came to light later. There can be little doubt that the railway works almost totally destroyed a fine villa. But though the house was lost, archaeological attention was drawn to the vast enclosed farmyard and the estate beyond, whose outlines have survived.

A rider approaching from the north some time in the 4th century, at the peak of its prosperity, would have gazed upon an extraordinary panorama of activity...

Behind him, as he pauses at the edge of the Failand Ridge, are great tracts of pasture where cattle graze, watched over by mounted herdsmen. Dotted over the high pastureland across which he had just ridden are small settlements, with enclosures and a few cornfields around them, where the herdsmen and their families live. Immediately below, fields of wheat and barley stretch along the slopes of the Failand Ridge in either direction, while the floor of the valley is green with pastures and hay meadows. At the bottom of the slope stands the villa, ideally placed for the heavy wagon-loads rolling down from the fields.

Seen from above, the villa settlement might easily be mistaken for a small town, encircled by a massive wall enclosing nearly 20 acres. Inside are a couple of dozen large buildings with stone-tiled

Autumn gold
Apples and cherries are probably native to Britain, but plums, pears and walnuts were all introduced by the Romans – to judge from pips, stones and shells found on villa sites.
The presence of pruning knives and saws indicates a degree of expertise in fruit farming, and the chances are that orchards

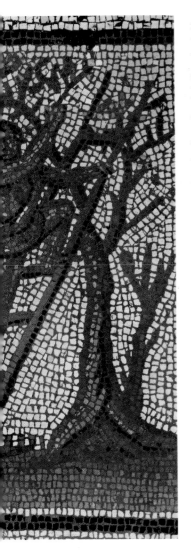

roofs. The farm's working buildings cluster in the northern half of the enclosure, while at the southern end, in the valley bottom, lies a broad sweep of garden and beyond that the main villa house. South of the settlement, the ground rises again to rough grazing on Backwell Hill and Broadfield Down, where large flocks of sheep graze under the eyes of shepherds, whose huts stand in the pastures.

Riding down the slope to the north entrance of Gatcombe villa, the visitor crosses fields running right up to the walls. Inside the gate is a row of buildings along a terrace cut in the hillside. From his right comes the din and acrid smoke of metal-working from the smithy, an iron-smelting shed, and a small workshop for lead and pewter craftsmen. On his left stand pottery stores and a slaughter-house – a wide building with a cobbled yard where the animals are killed, and a platform where carcases are loaded on to wagons. Most of the meat is beef, but pigs and sheep are also killed to vary the workers' diet. Along the terrace is an underground cold-store, carved from the solid rock and paved with closely fitting stone flags, where food can be kept cool even in the heat of summer.

On the next terrace below are more workshops and stores, and a bath-house for labourers and their families; beyond the workshops is an open space for threshing, surrounded by another group of buildings. The two most solidly constructed of these are stores or granaries, while next to them are two bakeries, where large stone ovens bake bread for the whole work-force. There is also a mill, its millstones cut from sandstone outcrops on the estate.

At the very bottom of the slope, a stream separates the working area from the main villa residence and gardens. More farm buildings are strung out on each side of the stream outside the enclosure wall.

Wealth from trade

were established in walled enclosures close by the main villa buildings and the vegetable gardens. Here, a mosaic from Gaul shows the apple harvest in full swing on a villa estate. Fruit that was not used or stored for home consumption would have been sold in the nearest forum.

Gatcombe's prosperity came mainly from wheat, beef and the wool of sheep. But many other products like mutton, pork, dairy produce, barley, fruit and vegetables, hides, flour, millstones, and possibly iron and pewter all played a part. They found a ready market at the town and port of Sea Mills on the Avon, 4 miles away, or upstream at Bath – an even larger and wealthier market.

The wagons and boats that carried it all did not return empty. They brought back food and wine, oil, oysters, salt and imported sauces. They also brought raw materials such as Cornish tin, for alloying with local lead to make pewter; coal to fire furnaces and ovens; and sometimes best-quality iron from the Forest of Dean on

167

CENTRAL HEATING

A simple invention that transformed the lives of the British upper classes

It seems extraordinary that once having experienced the benefits of central heating the world should have largely forgotten them for almost 1,500 years. Though it had its drawbacks, Roman central heating offered hitherto unimagined luxury to the wealthier classes of the Empire, especially to those living in its more northerly climes, and credit for its invention is generally awarded to a Roman businessman, C. Sergius Orata. It is believed that he developed the hypocaust system as a means of heating his oyster tanks.

The principle is simple. A furnace, fired by charcoal, wood or even coal, pumps hot air through channels beneath the floor of a room; both heat and gases eventually escape by means of flues behind the wall plaster. Thus warmed from below and on every side, it is thought that Romano-British rooms probably reached a temperature of about 70°F (21°C).

The disadvantages were that the system worked only on the ground floor, and that each suite of rooms required a separate furnace, involving considerable expenditure on both labour and fuel. However, the wealthier British probably accepted the charges cheerfully, just as they no doubt also accepted the risk of fire; in any case, the open braziers that provided the only alternative to the hypocaust system were at least equally hazardous.

Box-tile flue
In a villa's heating system, the flues served a double purpose – to carry off the smoke and fumes and to heat the walls at the same time. They were constructed from box tiles, like this one from Gadebridge Park villa in Hertfordshire, cemented end to end.

Untried innovation
Roman under-floor central-heating systems were generally constructed in one of two ways. Either the floor was supported by a series of tile columns, or upon solid piers of masonry, with the heating flues running in channels between them. Both had advantages; the stonework of the channelled floor retained the heat longer, but a pillared floor permitted a higher and more even temperature. In this room at Fishbourne there was an attempt to combine both systems, but work was abandoned before completion.

the other side of the Severn. Finally there were the valuables – jewellery of bronze, shale and jet, British and imported glassware, clothing and, occasionally, a new statue to stand in the villa's dining or reception rooms.

Bulkiest loads on the creaking wagons would be crates of pottery – Dorset cooking pots, storage jars from kilns at Congresbury, and tableware made in the New Forest and in the kilns around Oxford. At least one loaded wagon came to grief on the track to the villa pottery store: perhaps a wheel broke or a shaft on the wagon snapped, but whatever the cause, some crates fell off and more·than 300 brand-new pots were smashed. The fragments were swept up and shovelled into the nearest rubbish dump, below the slaughterhouse loading platform. There they remained until they were dug up nearly 1,700 years later, as bright and fresh-looking as when they were buried.

The discovery of these pots, together with evidence of other commodities brought from towns, played an important part in unravelling the story of Gatcombe villa. Both economically and socially, villas were closely tied to the towns, for it was there that the owners marketed their produce, purchased luxuries, and spent much of their time in performing civic duties or attending functions. It was the commercial and social amenities of the towns that made the existence of the Romanised house in the country possible.

Country life – Roman style

The landed gentry of Roman Britain – like their modern counterparts – often combined business with pleasure on their country estates. The reconstruction overleaf shows the villa at Latimer, Buckinghamshire, in the early 4th century AD. The main wing (1) is the family's quarters, with bedrooms and both heated and unheated reception rooms. The kitchen is in the north wing (2) where the servants also live, while the south wing (3) has more bedrooms, with mosaic floors and hypocaust heating. The integral bath-suite is to the rear of this wing. A small formal garden is laid out between the wings, fringed by trimmed hedges and trees (4), which divide it from the market-garden area beyond. Meadows for grazing cattle (5) surround the villa enclosure, and in the distance woodland covers the south-east facing slopes (6). The trees are mostly beech, providing food for pigs – and a happy hunting ground for the owner and his friends. A hunting party is indeed about to set off on this idyllic day in late spring. The owner of the villa and a friend (7 and 8) are talking to four young horsemen (9) armed with light lances, who are about to set off in search of game. They are, perhaps, the two men's sons, with companions from neighbouring farms. One of the villa farm-hands (10) looks on while awaiting further orders from his master.

CHAPTER SIX

Enter a middle class

The Roman occupation made little difference to the grinding daily round of Britain's peasantry. But a whole new life opened up for the tribal aristocracy, and a powerful third force joined them in the scramble up the ladder of prestige and wealth: a new middle class was born

The new society
The better-off British took to the ways of the conqueror with ease. This portrait of a Yorkshire matron closely resembles similar reliefs in Rome. Even the Celtic charioteer abandoned his ancient fighting role, and starred in chariot races.

Father and son
A picture of tender devotion, a Roman father gazes fondly at his small son. However, a father played little part in his son's education in the boy's early years – this being generally the mother's responsibility. Childhood was short: at the age of seven the boy began learning about his father's business affairs. To what extent the British adopted Roman family customs is not certain.

THE UPPER-CLASS BRITISH TOOK TO ROMAN WAYS WITH ENTHUSIASM, AND THE GROWTH OF TRADE AND INDUSTRY gave more and more Britons the chance to acquire wealth and status. This was particularly so in towns, where Roman fashions and behaviour were adopted by a new and expanding section of society – a British middle class.

The fashionable house of just such a wealthy family has been unearthed at St Albans. It was built in the 2nd century and discoveries made in it, added to what is known of everyday life in other parts of the Roman Empire, allow a fairly detailed picture to be drawn of the way this couple lived.

Scratched on two pot fragments found at St Albans are the names Paternus and Sabina, which could well have been the names of the couple. Paternus must have been quite well off to afford such a place – perhaps with an income from a farm-estate or town property. His status would have carried with it an obligation to undertake civic duties as a magistrate or councillor.

His house had a central suite of rooms with short projecting wings at each end, enclosing a small yard or garden. Along the front of the central suite ran a broad corridor, with a door into each room. Next to the principal dining-room was a furnace for the hypocaust heating which warmed the dining-room and the bath suite. The baths, in the south wing, were reached by the front corridor or a second, more private, one behind the bedrooms and dining-room. This rear corridor was probably used also by servants passing to and from the baths or carrying food from the kitchens, which were in the other wing.

Perhaps a dozen people lived in the house, six or seven of them servants. The middle or upper-class family in Roman Britain seems to have had only two or three children; and with an average life expectancy of around 40 years, not many parents lived long enough to share a house with their children when they grew up and had families of their own.

Their day starts at sunrise

The daily routine of the house begins at sunrise in the servants' quarters – two small, square rooms next to the kitchen. Before the family rises, the servants fuel and stoke the heating furnace and draw water from the well.

Paternus and Sabina sleep on long, low couches, each with a head-rest and cushions. Beside each bed stands a small table.

An hour or so after the servants, Paternus rises, washes in a

Small families

Couples were encouraged by the State to raise large families, but few succeeded. Childbirth was hazardous as well as painful, and infant mortality was high; rarely did more than two or three children survive infancy. For wealthy Romans like Cornelius and his wife, seen above on his sarcophagus with their only child, the size of the family may well have been limited more by these factors than by the methods of birth control and abortion.

bowl of cold water, combs his hair and dresses. The simple tunic in which he has been sleeping is used as an undergarment, and what he wears over it depends on how he is to spend the day. If he is due at a council meeting or the law courts, it will be a toga: according to Tacitus, writing about AD 80, Roman dress was soon adopted by the British upper classes on official business.

If Paternus is to spend the day with friends, doing some shopping and perhaps visiting the theatre, he will put on a longer over-tunic or robe, worn without a girdle and covered partially by a light cloak. For a ride into the country he will be in knee breeches with a warm cloak pinned at the shoulder, and thick-soled shoes.

In town a full boot was fashionable, while at home and at the public baths sandals were worn. Dozens of shoes from the Roman period have survived, especially shoes from London and the tannery at Lullingstone villa, in Kent. Most Roman footwear left parts of the foot bare – socks or stockings were seldom worn.

While Paternus dresses, Sabina is also preparing to face the day, helped by one or two maids. She sits in a wickerwork chair with sides and a rounded back. On her bedside table, beside a polished bronze mirror and a bone hair comb, lie a variety of beauty aids. A set of bronze instruments includes a pair of small tweezers for removing facial hair, a pointed rod for loosening wax in the ears and a tiny scoop with which to remove it. Other bronze scoops and spatulas are used for spooning perfumes and oils from cosmetic pots and slender glass flasks. On a small marble palette, Sabina mixes her chosen shade of make-up from an array of cosmetics – chalk or white lead, red ochre and fine ash for eye-shadow. While she sees to her make-up, the maids fix her hair. Hair styles vary, depending on current Roman fashion gathered from coins bearing portraits of the empress.

Similar waves, curls and plaits can be seen still, adorning the heads of wealthy Romano-British ladies on tombstones and busts, and miraculously preserved in the auburn ringlets of a woman buried at York. These may not, however, have been her own: wigs were used widely in society circles. Indeed, like many of today's beauties, the Romano-British temptress may not have been all she appeared to be: the Roman poet Martial, writing as long ago as the 1st century, made a cynical comment on the subject:

> 'Your tresses, Galla, are manufactured far away, you lay aside your teeth at night just as you do your silk dresses, and you lie stored away in a hundred caskets.'

In search of perfection
Preparing a Roman matron for a dinner party required the services of a number of maids and young girl slaves. This relief from Trier, in France, shows a lady at her toilette, attended by a maid of

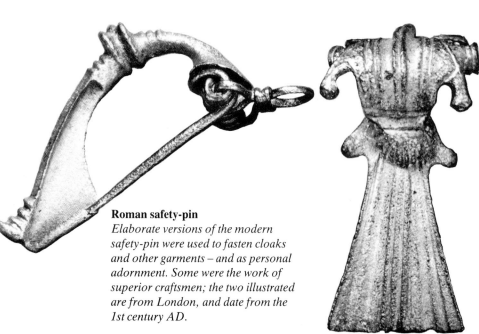

Roman safety-pin
Elaborate versions of the modern safety-pin were used to fasten cloaks and other garments – and as personal adornment. Some were the work of superior craftsmen; the two illustrated are from London, and date from the 1st century AD.

Although a fragment of Chinese silk has been found in York, dresses such as Galla's must have been rare in Roman Britain. Women's clothes, like men's, were mostly of wool or linen. A woman's tunic was much longer than a man's, reaching to her ankles. During the day she wore it beneath a shorter, more colourful, over-tunic ornamented with embroidery or perhaps a fringe, and gathered at the waist with a girdle. A wrap or shawl, worn over the head in public, sheltered her from wind and showers, and her shoes were more brightly decorated than men's. One shoe discovered in a burial mound at Southfleet, in Kent, was of purple

sufficient expertise to be permitted to insert the pins in her mistress's hair. The lady critically views the result in a polished metal mirror, while two more maids, carrying flasks of scented oils, look on admiringly.

leather with a bright pattern of hexagons and decorative gilding.

When Sabina has completed her make-up, she opens her jewellery casket and chooses from her brooches, pins and rings those that take her fancy for the day. Meanwhile, another servant has roused the children in their bedrooms, and helped them to dress in clothes very similar to those of their parents.

And so to work

The family seldom meets for breakfast – not an important meal in the Roman day. After a quick snack of bread and fruit, eaten alone, Paternus gives his servants their orders, gathers up any documents he may need, and goes off to work. This will probably be private or public business with friends or fellow-councillors, or perhaps an inspection of property he owns and leases.

If he is sitting as a magistrate, his duties will take him to the town hall to judge cases of civil law. Most of these cases will be concerned with theft – a civil rather than a criminal offence, the victim of a robbery obtaining justice against a thief only by bringing a private prosecution against him.

If theft is proved, and the thief cannot make restitution, the magistrate can order him to sell himself into slavery to pay off the sum concerned, or impose fines, or sentence the offender to labour in the state mines or on the imperial estates.

While Paternus is out, Sabina is overseeing the servants, ordering the day's meals, and perhaps spinning some wool thread. Later she may visit friends or entertain them in her own house, or go to the shops or market-hall, with a servant in attendance.

She will usually find some time to spend with her children, particularly if they are very young. But if she is occupied, they will play with toys and games that will change little in 2,000 years.

For very young children there were hollow clay animals with rattling pebbles inside. A relief sculpture from Rome shows a baby pushing a low-sided toy cart with four wheels and an upright handle at one end – almost identical to the modern trolley used to help toddlers to walk. Older children had a wide choice of toys, including dolls and models of animals.

Bronze dogs from Carrawburgh, on Hadrian's Wall, and Kirkby Thore in Cumbria, and a bronze mouse found in a child's grave at York, are probably toys. In another grave at Colchester a collection of pipe-clay figurines was discovered. Some of them were animals, but others were remarkable human figures showing men reclining, sitting, reading, or posed as if talking among friends.

A girl's toilette
Expensive perfume is poured carefully from its jar into a small flask. A few drops from the flask, delicately applied, will complete the toilette of this elegant young Roman girl. Maids have combed and curled her hair and bound it back into a tight bun, to emphasise the classic beauty of her face and neck. Her eyebrows have been discreetly lined and her hands manicured to perfection. She has shown sophisticated restraint in her choice of jewellery – just a small pair of ear-rings and a slim bangle on each arm. Her robe is light and sleeveless, made perhaps of cotton or even of silk, which was rarely seen in Britain. This fine painting is from Rome.

Followers of fashion

Women's hair styles changed more often than men's, as fashionable ladies throughout the Roman Empire swiftly copied the empress's latest coiffure. *News of her styles travelled quickly to outlying provinces such as Britain, as they were often shown on new coins. The two women shown here are late 2nd century AD: the carefully contrived simplicity of their hair styles is typical of the times. Of the two men, one is of the 1st century AD (centre) and one of the 3rd century AD (below).*

Although there is little doubt that they are toys, there is a grotesque air about these figures of bent old men, with their staring eyes and wicked grins. In the same grave were three feeding bottles of clay.

A small wooden box in a boy's grave at St Albans held a selection of everyday articles which, because of their location, were presumably his collection of favourite belongings. They included a miniature baton made of shale beads mounted on a hollow iron rod, some purple and green beads, a bronze handle – possibly from a fan – an amulet, and two sea-shells. An urn at Gatcombe holding the cremated remains of a young boy contained also a pottery beaker

Learning to walk
A Roman toddler takes his first unsteady steps as he trundles a four-wheel trolley that looks

Chariot for a child
Roman enthusiasm for all things to do with chariot-racing penetrated even into the play-world of children, as this toy chariot and charioteer show. The steed, however, with its long ears and curved nose, seems more suggestive of a donkey than a racehorse.

180

astonishingly like a modern 'baby-walker'. Few children's toys of the period have survived, but babies' rattles in animal shapes have been found. The older child in this delightful carving from Rome seems to be feeding a pet goose.

and five small stones. One stone was a barbed and tanged arrowhead made by a prehistoric flintworker some 2,000 years before the child was born; the other four were unworked, but seem to have been chosen carefully, because they were all shaped like pyramids or arrowheads. This little collection of real and 'pretend' arrowheads was probably this peasant boy's only possession. The life style of lower-class children – and indeed of adults – was very different from that of their better-off Romanised contemporaries. To these poorer families, the Roman occupation brought few benefits.

Wall-paintings show that Roman children played games like leap-frog, hide-and-seek, and hop-scotch. Clay discs found on British town house and villa sites may have been used in such games. Children also kept pets – several tombstones show a bird perched on a child's knee or on a table near by. Dogs and cats appear, less frequently, on other tombs. Cat skeletons have been found at Gadebridge Park and Latimer villas, and one skeleton of a kitten at Caerwent.

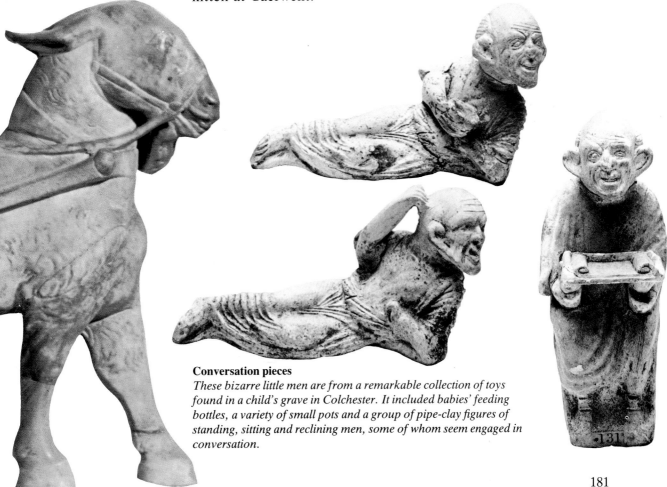

Conversation pieces
These bizarre little men are from a remarkable collection of toys found in a child's grave in Colchester. It included babies' feeding bottles, a variety of small pots and a group of pipe-clay figures of standing, sitting and reclining men, some of whom seem engaged in conversation.

181

Pupils and teachers

Ink . . . and yet more ink
Ink was used by the gallon in the Roman world. Books were made by the laborious process of copying each page by hand, and lengthy documents, reports and letters were written in ink on parchment or papyrus. Any copies needed were also hand-written. The ink was made with lamp black and kept usually in a pottery inkwell like that above, which often had a non-spill device under the rim. Pens were of bronze or split reed. Thin sheets of wood were sometimes used as 'paper'.

Orator in the making
At the tender age of 11 or 12 a boy of a good family would be set on the road to public office. Secondary education was demanding, and he would have lessons in the Latin language and literature. He would be expected to learn poetry and the works of famous authors by heart, and repeat them to his teacher. This is probably what the boy in the carved relief is doing. However, he was also required to compose speeches, and from his histrionic stance he could be reciting one.

Playtime ended, however – at least for children of the well-to-do or ambitious British families – at the age of seven. Quite early in the Roman occupation, a formal education became regarded as a necessity. Tacitus tells how in the winter of AD 79 the Governor Julius Agricola 'trained the sons of the chiefs in the liberal arts and expressed a preference for British native ability over the trained skills of the Gauls. The result was that in place of a distaste for the Latin language came a passion to command it.'

Elementary education consisted mainly of the 'three Rs', taught by private tutors who, early in the 4th century, were paid 50 denarii a month for each pupil – a poor wage. A tutor would have needed 15 pupils a month to earn as much as a farm labourer, and 30 to bring his income up to that of a carpenter. To make ends meet, the tutor had to cram as many pupils as possible into each day, teaching each one for only an hour or two, and then not every day.

Writing exercises were usually inscribed on the same waxed wooden tablets used for letters, the words written with a sharp

A message in wax

Wooden writing tablets coated on one side with wax were used as an alternative to parchment and papyrus, and many examples of them have been gleaned from all over the Empire. Obviously, they were the general-purpose notebooks of the Roman world, used by court reporters, tax-gatherers, clerks and businessmen alike. Characters were inscribed on the wax with an instrument called a stylus, pointed at one end for writing and flattened at the other. The flattened end was used to erase mistakes by running it across the offending words, and to clear the whole surface of the tablet so that it could be used over and over again. These tablets were, of course, especially useful for teaching purposes, and both stylus and tablet are illustrated perfectly in the picture above, of a young girl from Pompeii in the throes of composition. The tile on the right, from Silchester, records a more informal spelling exercise.

183

bronze or iron stylus; the other end of the stylus was flattened and could be used to erase mistakes or clear the tablet. Poorer children, and perhaps adults too, scratched their lessons on pieces of tile. Some survive, one showing how a young Briton at Caves Inn, Warwickshire, carefully copied the alphabet, and another at Silchester making out a word list, and ending with part of a quotation from the Roman poet Virgil.

After four or five years of elementary schooling, children whose parents could afford the fees passed on to secondary education. These fees totalled about five times as much as those for elementary schooling, but the syllabus embraced advanced Latin grammar, Latin literature and poetry, Roman history, philosophy and the arts. Sound Latin was essential for people seeking public office in a tribal or local council, and it was an obvious advantage in commerce and dealings with the government or the law.

Many metal styli have been found, but writing tablets are rare, surviving only in damp, airless conditions; and only the writing of the heavy-handed can be read, their styli cutting right through the wax to leave the words incised in the wood beneath. Part of a letter of this sort has been found in London. Addressed to a senior servant, it reads:

> 'Rufus, son of Callisunus, greetings to Epillicus and all his fellows. I believe you know that I am very well. If you have made the list, please send. Be sure that you look after everything carefully. See that you turn the slave girl into cash. . .'

Other letters were written in ink, with pens of reed or bronze, and usually on animal-skin parchment, or papyrus made from the leaves of the papyrus plant. One letter, again found in London, was written by somebody worried about a slave who had run away with goods entrusted to him.

Off to the theatre

Personal and business correspondence may well occupy Paternus's morning before he returns home for a light lunch with his family – bread and perhaps a salad, with either cheese or hard-boiled eggs served in a juice made of fish sauce, oil and wine. Fresh fruit – local apples, plums and cherries, or imported grapes and figs – round off the meal. Paternus might then spend a pleasant hour or two at the baths in the early afternoon, refreshing himself, exercising and chatting with his friends.

Later in the afternoon the family might decide to take in a

Arena of death
Gladiators fought and died amid cheers for the brave and jeers for the less fortunate in this amphitheatre at Caerleon, well-preserved today. The crowd sat on wooden seats in tiers on the earth banks. Main entrances were at each end of the oval arena, with boxes for honoured visitors built above waiting rooms for performers and combatants in the centre on each side of the oval.

At the pantomime
Theatregoers in towns like St Albans or Canterbury would probably find a pantomime on the programme, with players like those on the right wearing masks to act out a well-known story from mythology. Behind them is seen the ornamental façade which was a permanent fixture at the back of the stage, and which would serve as a backdrop for the performance.

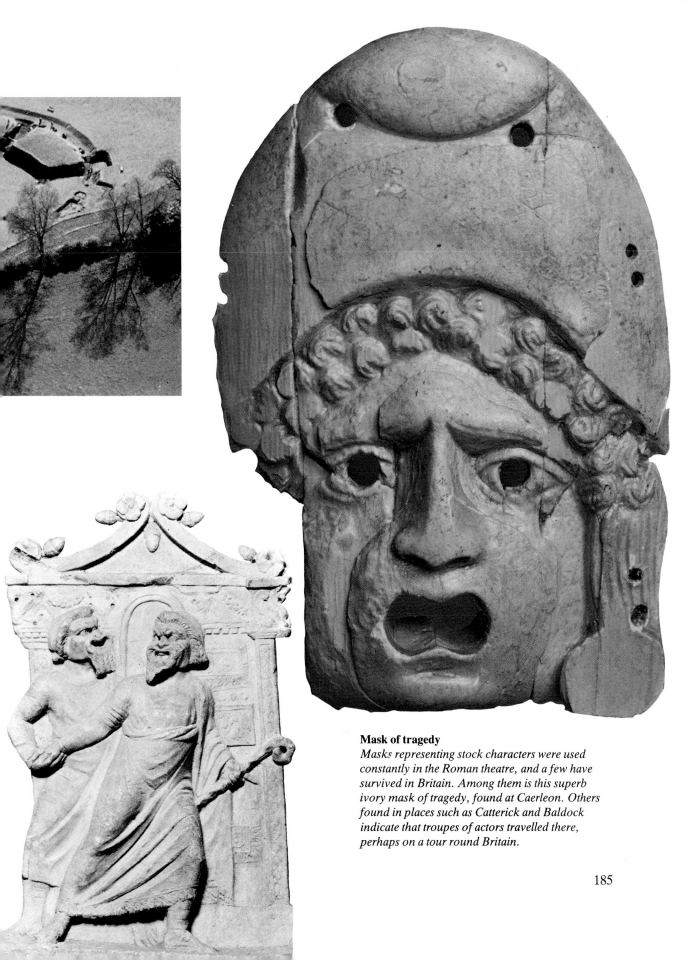

Mask of tragedy
Masks representing stock characters were used constantly in the Roman theatre, and a few have survived in Britain. Among them is this superb ivory mask of tragedy, found at Caerleon. Others found in places such as Catterick and Baldock indicate that troupes of actors travelled there, perhaps on a tour round Britain.

show at the theatre or amphitheatre. Enough remains of the St Albans theatre, with rows of seats set on earth banks, to allow an informed impression of such an occasion...

Climbing the wooden stairs on the outside wall, Paternus and Sabina emerge high at the back of the auditorium, where they can spot any vacant places. Rows of seats open to the sky descend in tiers below, sweeping in a great arc from one side of the stage to the other. On a fine, warm day, and with a good programme advertised, almost 2,000 people will be packed in, some overflowing into extra seats in the orchestra – the flat, oval space in front of the stage – though the view from these seats is not so good.

The show might open with a pantomime – a mixture of music and dancing in which masked artists act out a tragedy based on a story from mythology. To liven things up, this might be followed by a mime, with a group of stock characters cavorting in a ribald topical sketch, to roars of laughter, shouted comments and loud applause from the audience. All the action takes place on a rectangular stage backed by an elaborate monumental façade, beside which is a store for stage props, with a changing room near by.

Townspeople built the theatre and seats are free, the shows being paid for by senior magistrates or other benefactors. The actors are probably a touring company, travelling from town to town and even playing rural theatres. Masks of tragedy discovered at Caerleon, Catterick and Baldock must have belonged to guilds of actors touring in this way.

But popular though the theatre is, even more popular are the blood-thirsty spectacles of the amphitheatre...

Blood on the sand

The amphitheatre is perhaps 100 yds in length, surrounded by tiers of seats on earth banks supported by timber or stone walls. Thousands will crowd in to watch the often horrifying 'entertainments', though the show usually opens with something less sadistic or bloody, such as acrobats and wrestlers. Boxers may also be in action – but their 'boxing gloves' are metal-studded thongs wrapped around their wrists, and they present a foretaste of more gory sights to follow.

Much of the blood-letting in British arenas may have involved animals, rather than humans – cockfighting, bear-baiting and mock hunts, in which well-equipped hunters slaughtered wild animals released into the arena. At a later stage gladiators were pitted against wild boars, bulls and wolves. Finally came the ultimate

The gladiator
This beautifully realised figure of a gladiator holding his shield, his right arm and left leg heavily armoured, was once the ivory handle of a Roman clasp-knife. Now it is in a Newcastle upon Tyne museum.

The boxer

Boxing was a brutal sport in Roman times. The fighters wore no protection, and instead of gloves they had metal-studded leather thongs bound around their wrists. These vicious weapons can be seen clearly on the sculptor Apollonius's magnificent figure of a boxer, below. The face is pitted and scarred, and the tragic, hunched figure is half slumped forward. However, his 'sport' was considerably less horrific than some of the spectacles that stained the arenas with blood.

Fighting to the death

Just how often gladiators fought to the death in Britain is not certain. But scenes like the fierce encounter in the mosaic above, in which one man has lost his shield – and may well be about to lose his life – are repeated on floors in two British villas. Glass and pottery drinking cups showing scenes of gladiatorial combat were popular in the province. The helmet below was found at Hawkedon, in Suffolk, and is typically gladiatorial in pattern – heavy and made of bronze, with a broad plate to protect the neck. Originally it would have had a visor to guard the man's face, like the one pictured in the mosaic. The remainder of his equipment might consist of a short sword and armour from shoulder to wrist, or a net and a trident.

degradation of people watching other people stabbing, spearing and hacking each other to pieces with a variety of weapons, or being torn to pieces by wild animals.

There is little doubt that gladiators fought and died in British amphitheatres, as they did in Rome and other parts of the Empire. A bronze gladiator's helmet with a broad neck-guard was found at Hawkeden in Suffolk, and gladiatorial combats can be seen on drinking cups made in Colchester. Glass cups showing and naming gladiators have been found elsewhere in Britain, and bronze and ivory statuettes of them in London and Colchester. Battling gladiators decorate mosaics in villas at Brading, on the Isle of Wight, and Bignor, West Sussex. A graffito at Leicester names a gladiator as 'Lucius', and a tomb sculpture in York shows another armed with his net and trident.

Gladiators were drawn from the ranks of slaves, prisoners of war and petty criminals, to all of whom the dangers of the arena might have been preferable to alternative fates that awaited them elsewhere. People convicted of offences against the state were often executed publicly in the amphitheatre. This was the fate intended for the Christian martyr Alban, from whom St Albans derives its name. Eventually, however, Alban was beheaded by the sword outside the town, in AD 209. Other criminals – including numerous Christians, who were regarded as undermining imperial authority – were condemned *ad bestias*, 'to the beasts'. These unfortunates were left tied to a stake, or as an extra refinement were pushed naked and weaponless into the arena, then wild and half-starved animals were turned loose on them.

More wholesome, if hardly less dangerous, was chariot-racing. There are no remains in Britain of a circus – or arena – where races could have been held, but any flat stretch would have served, so long as it had a slope to one side on which an audience could sit. There are, moreover, many signs that the British were great enthusiasts for the sport. Gladiator cups are outnumbered by similar ones showing chariot-racing scenes, and fragments of a beaker from St Albans have *Celer* – Latin for 'Speedy' – scratched on them, alongside a charioteer's picture.

Sculptures of charioteers have come to light in Lincoln and Bedford Purlieus, and at Chedworth villa the single word *Prasina* was inscribed on a stone. The significance of this is that *Prasina Factio* – 'the Green Company' – was one of the four traditional chariot team names in the Roman circus, and the inscription is no doubt the work of some local fan. Mosaic floors at Rudston and Horkstow, in Humberside, show a head-on view of a four-horse chariot, and an action picture of a race.

Thrills and spills
The British passion for the Turf goes back a long way, to judge from the large number of racing relics that have been unearthed from sites up and down the country. Both horses and chariot races seem to be depicted on the mosaic (below) found in a villa at Horkstow, Lincolnshire. This shows how chariot races were run around a central barrier, and shows, too, some of the hazards of the sport – a lost wheel and a wild swerve as one of the horses stumbles. No formal circus, or race track, has ever been found in Britain; nothing that reflects, say, the great Circus Maximus in Rome. So presumably the races must have taken place on areas of flat ground outside the major towns, preferably with a hillside near by as a vantage point for spectators.

Winner's enclosure
Successful charioteers were idolised by the punters, and it may be that the mosaic (left) from a villa at Rudston, Humberside, immortalises a spectacular win by a favourite of the time. The charioteer, who bears a victor's crown, is a member of the 'Reds', the same team as the leading chariot in the Horkstow mosaic, though the numbers of horses pulling the vehicles are different. Four-horse chariots were by no means unusual, and in some of the great circuses of the Empire the drivers rode even six-in-hand. One of the greatest charioteers on record was the Spaniard Diocles, who won more than one-third of the 4,200 races he contested. The name of the Rudston winner can never be known.

189

Wining and dining at home

By the time Paternus and his wife return home from their afternoon's entertainment, the servants are busy preparing the main meal of the day – dinner. Three or four of them are at work in the large oblong kitchen in the north wing. On a raised hearth is a grid-iron over a charcoal fire, on which small dishes are bubbling; large joints sizzle on a spit above a long pit, or sunken hearth.

Around the walls stand storage jars, some sunk into the floor. Words are scratched or painted on several of them to label their contents – corn, oil, peas, apples. Against one wall are stone-built bread ovens. A bench is littered with iron knives and cleavers, bronze pastry-cutters and spoons, while pie-dishes, stew-pots, bowls, colanders and mortars and pestles are stacked around.

The meal will be ready by early evening with three courses: hors d'oeuvres, main course and dessert, all liberally washed down with wine. In the dining-room, couches are arranged around three sides of a square, within which are low, oblong tables.

The servants have arranged place-settings and other tableware – one place-setting found at Winchester consisted of a tray made of Kimmeridge shale, a samian pottery cup and dish, two iron knives and a bronze spoon – the Romans did not have forks. Also decorating Paternus's table are glass and samian-ware bowls of fruit, bronze jugs and wine strainers, a bronze ewer, and a bowl for washing hands. Glass or pottery beakers are decorated with painted mottoes such as *Nolite sitire* – 'Don't be thirsty'.

Wine was the popular drink at the upper-class dining table, and a wide variety of wines were enjoyed in Britain, including the much-admired red Falernian vintage of Campania in Southern Italy, and others from Spain, Bordeaux and vineyards along the Moselle. Less Romanised or poorer families drank Celtic beer, brewed from barley; this was popular enough to have its price fixed in Emperor Diocletian's price edict of AD 301. Mead, a brew of fermented honey and water flavoured with a variety of herbs was also popular.

A fashionable dinner party

With Paternus, Sabina and their guests seated, the hors d'oeuvres are brought in, and the first beakers of wine poured. The first course might be eggs and green salad, or shell-fish; oysters were the favourite dish, but mussels, cockles, whelks and winkles were also popular, and were shipped to inland markets in barrels of brine.

Food and gossip
An evening meal at a friend's house was one of the pillars of the Roman social scene. Course followed lavish course, and the chief entertainment was the exchange of gossip, opinions and business 'shop'. This Pompeiian wall-painting shows the later stages of a dinner party – the host and his guests recline on couches while servants see to their comfort. One guest, it seems, has already dined rather too well.

Place setting
Services of silver, pewter or bronze appeared on Romano-British tables on special occasions, but the attractive russet samian ware was considered adequate for everyday use. Forks were not yet invented; however, polite society made do perfectly well with knives, spoons and fingers.

190

There was an elaborate Roman dressing for oysters, made of pepper, the herb lovage, egg yolk, vinegar, oil and wine.

Among other popular first courses was fish. This included not only freshwater fish but a number of sea fish such as smelt, haddock, grey mullet, herring, sea-bream and mackerel. These were normally boiled and served with a sauce heavily flavoured with herbs, sweetened with honey and wine, and thickened with wheat starch; sauces, in general, tended to be robust.

Fish sauce, called liquamen, was important in the preparation of a Roman meal. It was made by mashing small fish such as sprats and anchovies with the entrails of larger fish. This mixture was put in a vessel and left to mature in the sun, then the concentrated juice, or sauce, was strained off. It was used constantly in cooking the main course for dinner. Beef or veal would be roasted, then a sauce made of liquamen, pepper and oil was poured over before it was served – probably accompanied by leeks and onions. Another sauce made with pepper, lovage, caraway, honey, vinegar, liquamen and oil, all pounded, mixed together and thickened, was used with venison. The meat would be first boiled, then lightly roasted, and the sauce ladled over when it was ready for the table.

Many Romans have written about the pleasures of wining and dining, but the best-known recipes are from the books of Marcus Gavius Apicius, a gourmet who lived early in the 1st century. Seneca tells how Apicius calculated that he had spent in his lifetime 100 million sesterces on food for himself and his guests – enough to pay a legion's wages for 50 years. Apicius then counted what he had left, found it totalled only 10 million sesterces, and then resignedly poisoned himself rather than face the appalling prospect of what he regarded as a starvation diet.

To round off Paternus's evening meal there will be fruit, or perhaps stuffed and fried dates. But the dessert could also be pastry, and its popularity led to a marked increase in tooth decay, clearly apparent when teeth found in British graves of the Roman period are compared with those found in pre-Roman ones. Some cakes were simply bread enriched with milk, eggs and butter, perhaps fried in oil and served with honey poured over. Other cakes were more like biscuits, cut into portions, fried in oil, and served with honey and pepper. A more unusual pastry, described by the statesman Cato the Elder, was flavoured with aniseed, cheese and the grated bark of a laurel twig, then baked on a bay leaf. Stomach upsets were not infrequent, and it was also Cato who advised: 'If you want to drink a lot and eat freely at a dinner party, eat some raw cabbage soused in vinegar before and after.'

Kitchen ware
The well-equipped kitchens of both villas and town houses would have looked much like this reconstruction of a middle-class Romano-British kitchen (right) in Cirencester Museum. A rotary quern for grinding corn sits on the floor near the utensil-littered table, while behind is the raised hearth with its grid-iron and pot-hanger.

Dinner postponed
Most of what is known about Roman cuisine is contained in the works of the 1st-century gourmet M. Gavius Apicius but, very occasionally, prepared foods survive by chance. This selection – eggs, a round loaf, beans, peas and fruit – was preserved by the eruption of Vesuvius in AD 79.

Profits of the chase
Most of the meat that appeared on the tables of Romano-British town houses and country villas was obtained from domesticated animals. However, gentlemen of the period had a passion for hunting, fishing and wildfowling, and the results of a day's sport could make a welcome addition to the menu.

Post-prandial joys
Like many succeeding generations, Romano-British hosts and guests looked to one another to provide after-dinner entertainment – music or recitations. This charming bronze in Reading Museum depicts a girl about to perform on the tibia, *a wind instrument.*

After-dinner conversation

There was, however, more to the evening meal-time than eating and drinking. A simple family dinner was still a social event, but often there would be friends or other guests to entertain. While they ate, a slave might play on the pan-pipes; but most of all it was a time for conversation. Some of the talk was little more than idle chatter, but Britons who followed the Roman custom of several courses served with wine could hold their own in the kind of discussion expected around a Roman table.

High on the list of popular subjects were poetry and literature, and the classics were sometimes read aloud. Although the manuscripts have long since decayed, their existence is remembered in mosaic portraits in British villas. A mosaic portraying the birth of Bacchus found at East Coker, Somerset, may have been inspired by a similar illustration in a manuscript of Ovid's *Metamorphoses*. An inscription built into a mosaic at Lullingstone must have been composed by someone familiar with both Ovid's verse and Virgil's *Aeneid*. Virgil's epic poem, in particular, seems to have been widely read among educated Romano-Britons. It is the source of a mosaic scene at Frampton villa, Dorset, and is briefly quoted on a wall-painting at Otford villa, in Kent. A superb mosaic at Low Ham, Somerset, illustrates Virgil's account of the love of Dido, founder of Carthage, for Aeneas, prince of Troy.

Eventually, when the table talk begins to flag and yawning becomes contagious, servants or slaves are called with their torches to light the guests home. By 10 o'clock, oil lamps flicker in the corridors as Paternus and Sabina make their way to bed.

A slave about the house

The comfortable living style of a couple like Paternus and Sabina depended largely on their team of servants, who, if they worked well and did not expect too much, could themselves live quite comfortably. Some were undoubtedly slaves, but domestic slaves were well clothed, fed and housed, and often were cherished members of the household. However, their fate was very much in their master's hands: they were his property, he could buy or sell them, and he was legally entitled to kill them. Runaway slaves were hunted down, and any found posing as citizens could be executed. If a slave murdered his master, every slave in the household was liable to be executed with him.

Talking points

Many Britons, businessmen or landowners, who had made their mark under the new regime, decorated their villas with Roman-style wall-paintings and mosaics that no doubt helped to stimulate after-dinner conversation. Themes might be taken from literature, as in the Dido and Aeneas mosaic from Low Ham villa, whose central panel (left) shows Venus, goddess of love, flanked by two Cupids; other panels tell of Aeneas's arrival in Africa and of the lovers' introduction to one another by Venus. Other villa owners preferred to illustrate their dining-room floors with scenes from classical mythology, such as the Rape of Europa (below), discovered at Lullingstone villa. The superscription is thought to have been inspired by the works of Ovid, and it may be that other mosaic designs, too, were based upon illustrations or texts in books long vanished.

Yet slaves had certain rights: they could take a concubine, rent land, lease a shop, or even own slaves themselves. They could own and save money earned by selling some of their food rations or by using their skills as craftsmen. They earned a commission, agreed with their master, on the sale of the articles they made. Finally they could buy their freedom, if their master did not give it to them first. These freedmen became citizens and often grew rich by using their skills and talents. One of them, Gaius Nipius Ascanius, became an imperial official at the Mendip lead mines; then, with this experience behind him, he took a lease on part of the Clwyd lead mines and worked them for his own profit. Quite often, however, a slave who had been freed would carry on living and working in his former master's household.

A wedding in the family

Weddings were just as much occasions for celebration in Romano-British households as they are now, even though a couple's courtship and the ceremony itself were quite different. To begin with, the bride was usually chosen by the bridegroom's parents – who often took the advice of friends. If a betrothal was arranged, the bride's dowry would be discussed and gifts exchanged – perhaps accompanied by betrothal medallions or rings.

On the wedding day itself, the bridegroom walked in procession to the bride's home, where she waited in a chaste tunic of white wool, with a short veil and a crown of the aromatic herb marjoram. In a brief ceremony, her bridesmaid handed her over to her new husband, a contract was signed ... and the feasting began. The revels usually lasted until evening, when the couple would be escorted to their new home to begin married life.

It was at this stage, unfortunately, that troubles also began. For the Roman custom was to marry young and start a family as soon as possible: marriages were arranged when a boy was about 16 and a girl 13 or 14. Until that time a girl led a sheltered life, so she was abruptly plunged not only into the physical and emotional strains of marriage, but also the responsibilities of running a household, followed by parenthood. In Rome itself divorce was common – particularly on the ground of adultery.

Emperor Augustus had started this trend towards teenage marriages, and encouraged them by imposing irksome penalties on men who remained single – for instance, they were not allowed to attend public games. He also encouraged larger families by awarding privileges to couples rearing several children. But the primitive

One of the family
The existence of slaves on imperial estates or in the mines was generally nasty, brutish and short; on the other hand,

196

household slaves were often cherished and well looked after by their owners. In fact, it was not unusual for young boys, like the slave portrayed here in a mosaic in Pompeii, to be given their freedom and adopted into the family. Though no one could ever quite rid himself of the stigma of having been born a slave, there is no doubt that many freedmen – ex-slaves – became prosperous and even influential. Some were renowned craftsmen; others made fortunes as merchants. Not a few sat on town councils, and one or two, astonishingly, became valued advisers to emperors.

maternity care available acted as a powerful deterrent: Roman cervical forceps are fearsome objects, and relief sculptures showing women in childbirth, sitting upright in a chair tightly grasping the hand-grips on either side, suggest that it was a painful experience not willingly suffered twice.

Various forms of contraception were in use, including doses of alum, vinegar or brine. Unwanted pregnancies were terminated by abortion. Such measures, together with the killing of unwanted babies – particularly weak or deformed ones – combined with a high rate of infant mortality to keep down the size of families.

Celtic weddings in the country

In the less sophisticated homes of British villagers and country farmers the different and far more ancient customs of the Celtic wedding remained fairly common. Not only did Celts wed later, they took marriage rather more seriously. Caesar wrote that the continental Celts – of the same stock as the British – had a very stern attitude towards the permanence of marriage, and strongly opposed adultery, divorce, bigamy, contraception and infanticide.

Tacitus noted that they married several years later than Romans, and that during the wedding ceremony the bride was reminded that she was to share in her husband's dangers and difficulties, and be a partner in all his sufferings and adventures. Her husband, instead of getting a dowry with his bride, had to take one to her parents. This would be made up not of cash or precious metals, but oxen, horses and other goods.

Indeed the whole life-style of country folk differed markedly from urban ways, though they would make a trip to town for a theatre show that attracted them or some new spectacle at the amphitheatre. But the countryside had its own entertainments.

A villa owner, visiting his country estate to talk business with his bailiff, might well spend an afternoon hunting or fishing. The 4th-century Gallic poet Ausonius, who had a villa on the Moselle, painted an almost idyllic picture of fishermen:

> 'This man, far out in midstream, trails his dripping nets and sweeps up the shoals, ensnared by their knotty folds; this man, when the river glides with peaceful flow, draws his seine-nets, floating with the aid of cork markers; while over yonder on the rocks another leans over the water that flows underneath, and lets down the curved end of his pliant rod, casting hooks baited with deadly food.'

Another Roman writer says that the lure might be an artificial

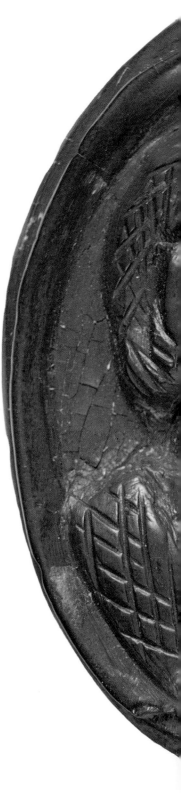

The betrothal

Roman law and custom encouraged marriage and the raising of a large family, even to the point of awarding privileges to couples who had more than three children, and mild penalties to those who had none. That marriage was the norm in the Roman world is perhaps emphasised by the fact that there is no word for 'spinster' in Latin.

The minimum age for marriage was 12 for girls and 14 for boys, and in Italy many marriages were made at these ages; most girls, especially, were married by their early teens. How far this custom was followed in the provinces, including Britain, is uncertain, but it is quite possible that it prevailed among the wealthier classes in the larger towns and in the coloniae.

Matches were arranged by parents, or sometimes by friends of the family, who would also settle such matters as the bride's dowry. It was probably at this point that gifts such as the betrothal medallion shown here were exchanged. One side of the medallion shows the engaged couple who, from their dress and hair styles, belong to the Romanised class, while the other carries the motif of a pair of clasped hands. A number of such trinkets have been found in Britain, carved from the jet that occurs along the beaches near Whitby, North Yorkshire.

fly made of wool and small feathers. The catch varied: British rivers were probably well stocked with trout and salmon, and the bones of dace, perch and pike have been unearthed at Silchester. Whether fly-fishing with rod and line or using a net, the British fisherman could hope for a good catch and a tasty meal later.

Hunting seems to have been popular throughout Britain: rubbish deposits on villa estates usually include the bones of deer, hare and wildfowl. In the south-west, hunting seems to have been especially favoured – there are altars to Diana, goddess of the chase, and stone reliefs showing boar and hare being carried home and hunting dogs straining at the leash. A mosaic from the villa at East Coker shows two men carrying a doe, slung by the legs from a pole.

The pursuit of deer and hare called simply for stealth, speed and fast Celtic hounds. But, according to the Greek writer Xenophon, hunting fierce wild boar demanded a certain amount of tackle, such as strong netting in which the boar could be slowed or enmeshed, and a combination of cunning, strength and courage. A charging boar could pose a serious threat to life or limb.

Going to the doctor

Injuries sustained in hunting or at work, and all the other ailments that plagued the population of Roman Britain, could be treated by doctors – if the family were sufficiently rich to afford them.

Skeletons from cemeteries at York and Cirencester show that citizens there suffered badly from arthritis and rheumatism: at Cirencester almost half the population seems to have endured some form of arthritis. Other afflictions included tuberculosis, scurvy and similar diseases arising from vitamin deficiency.

The prevalence of ailments such as asthma and stomach ulcers is known from the records of Roman doctors' attempts to cure them. The writer Pliny recommended garlic in milk to counter asthma, and a mustard gargle for stomach upsets. Chilblains, which Roman footwear must have encouraged, were treated with hot turnips. As for scurvy, one British remedy known as *radix Britannica* – 'the British root' – seems to have won an international reputation, for a small ointment box found in the Roman fortress at Haltern, in West Germany, was inscribed with the name. It seems to have been made from dock plants, and many other wild and cultivated herbs figured in the doctor's medicine chest.

Eye infections were common, and oculists left behind them small stamps with which they made impressions in the surface of their patent ointments. On these stamps can be read the names of

The apothecary
Rather than hire the expensive services of a doctor, most people with aches or pains would first try to find a suitable cure at their local chemist's shop. Pharmacists like the one in this Roman relief, surrounded by the vats in which he mixes his potions, would have been found in all the larger towns of Roman Britain. Their cures were culled from the Egyptians and the Greeks, and Celtic potions in which wild herbs were important ingredients.

The eye-doctor
Eye troubles must have been endemic in the Roman Empire, to judge from the large number of oculists' ointment moulds that have survived. Many towns had an oculist's establishment, like this one, where patients could purchase a wide range of herb-based salves and ointments; how efficacious these remedies were is uncertain.

the eye-specialists concerned, and details of the preparations. One oculist named Silvius Tetricus practised in London and another, Vidacus Ariovistus, in Kenchester, near Hereford. In Chester, Julius Martinus had among his ointments a 'saffron salve for soreness'. A St Albans doctor, Julius Juvenis, offered a more elaborate salve for inflamed eyes, made from myrrh, opobalsam – an antiseptic balm – and egg. The most impressive armoury of cures, however, must have been that of Gaius Valerius Amandus, who at Sandy in Bedfordshire prescribed 'poppy ointment for inflammation of the eyes', 'drops for dim sight' and 'vinegar lotion for runny eyes'.

Oculists probably had their own shops, and a relief from France shows a woman patient seated while the doctor holds her forehead with his left hand and pulls down her lower eye-lid with his right. His expression suggests that the complaint was serious.

Skills of the surgeon

Of course some complaints required surgery, and instruments found suggest that most large towns in Britain had surgeons. Scalpels, probes and spatulas have been discovered in London and at Silchester, where a finely made pair of artery forceps was also found. A grave at Wroxeter held a set of instruments that were probably buried with the surgeon who owned them. Syringes, scissors, bone saws and a variety of forceps, all found on the Continent, were doubtless available also to British surgeons.

Much of their routine work would have been with broken bones and wounds. Minor cuts and abrasions were treated with vinegar-soaked compresses, but major surgery included trepanning, in which a small disc of bone was cut from the skull to relieve pressure on the brain and as a way of treating severe headaches and depressed skull fractures. Most of the trepanned skulls found in Britain show new growth of bone after the operation, indicating at least partial success. A man buried at Cirencester had a head wound that had caused a large piece of his skull to press upon the brain, certainly resulting in headaches and possibly fits. His trepanning operation was doubtless intended to bring him some relief.

But despite all that doctors could do, people in Britain could not normally look forward to a long and happy old age. Nearly 300 skeletons examined at Cirencester suggest a life-span of 41 years for a man and 37 for a woman. The problems of old age are exemplified by an elderly lady buried outside St Albans. She suffered from deafness, arthritis, dental disease and probably scurvy. Her last years were endured rather than enjoyed.

Brink of life
With large families encouraged by both State and the social climate, childbirth may have occurred fairly frequently in the life of a Roman matron, though considering the fearful rate of infant mortality, perhaps no more than two or three of her children might survive into adolescence. Childbirth itself seems to have called for the most stoic qualities, to judge from the scene above, in which the pregnant woman is braced against the back of a chair by a servant while the midwife feels for the head of the child. Perhaps it was the repetition of such experiences, added to financial considerations once the family had been established, that led couples to experiment with contraception. But the agents suggested – alum, vinegar or brine – were of dubious value.

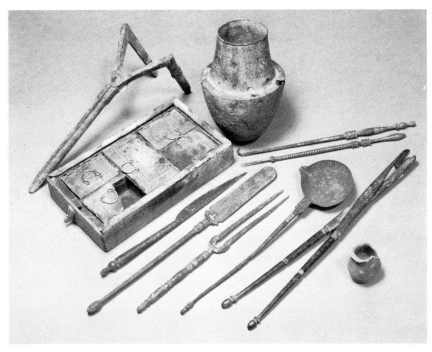

Surgeon's kit
Roman surgeons carried out a wide range of operations, from tonsilectomies to trepanning to amputations, with instruments such as these. Anaesthetics, however, were in their infancy; though poppy juice was administered to dull the patient's pain, it cannot have been very effective, since surgeons were specially exhorted to ignore the cries from the table.

The physician
In this relief from Rome, the doctor is probably prescribing one of the hundreds of pills, potions or plasters in his pharmacopoeia. Remedies were mostly of herbal origin; mustard, belladonna, wormwood, crocus, henbane, linseed and mallow were all highly favoured, and some of the recipes were still in use until relatively modern times.

203

JEWELS FOR A LADY

Women of the Celtic aristocracy happily combined new Roman fashions with traditional materials

A Romano-British lady of means – even one of only modest social ambitions – would include among her status symbols a fairly comprehensive collection of personal jewellery. Her collection would inevitably include a number of the brooches that were essential fastenings for the cloaks, loose gowns and tunics used for everyday wear. Some of these brooches would be elegant but practical, others were finely worked and bejewelled, to be worn on formal occasions. However, she would also have collected a number of finger rings, bronze – or even silver – bracelets and bangles, strings of beads and necklaces set with semi-precious stones.

Utility with beauty
Roman ladies' dresses were held in their soft, graceful folds by strategically placed brooches. The type in widest use was the fibula, *which operated rather in the manner of the safety-pin, though plate and disc shapes were also highly popular. Bronze brooches, bearing enamelled motifs of hares, horses, dolphins, and even of such exotic creatures as tortoises, have frequently been found in Britain, while other women seem to have preferred the old Celtic abstract designs of whorls and scrolls. Costume jewellery of the day is represented by very thinly gilded bronze brooches with glass or paste imitation precious stones at their centres. But fine cameos like this one in Indian sardonyx, now in the Museum of Antiquities at Newcastle, would have been worn only on very special occasions indeed.*

Ring for a finger

While the lower orders had to be content with simple rings of bronze, the wives and daughters of the upper classes decked themselves with rings of silver, jet, or of fine gold, like this one in Reading Museum.

Amber beads for a necklace

The last memento of some Romano-British lady, this necklace, consisting of 70 beads of Baltic amber still strung together on their original flaxen string, now lies in the Museum of London. That necklaces were a favourite form of female adornment is apparent from tombstone portraits found up and down the country, and from the large number of beads that turn up in dozens of archaeological digs. Poorer women, it seems, wore necklaces of glass, bone or pottery, while their richer sisters sported coral and amber, or even gold chains with pendants of the kind that have been found in Cheshire and Northumberland.

CHAPTER SEVEN

Village and farm

The old ways and the old gods lived on in Britain's high places, but the winds of change blew in the seeds of a new prosperity

Pastoral life
The idyllic impression of peasant life given by this relief belies a grimmer reality. The life of the shepherd or of a herdsman raising Celtic shorthorn cattle was a hard one. This shorthorn skull is one of a number found in a Roman well at Rothwell. A high proportion of farm produce was taken as tax in kind.

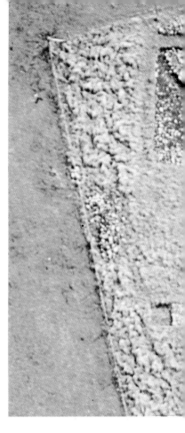

EVEN WHEN THE VILLA WAS AT THE PEAK OF ITS POPULARITY IN BRITAIN, ONLY A PRIVILEGED FEW WERE ABLE TO ENJOY the civilised style of life it provided: the vast majority of country folk lived in a very different way – many in conditions scarcely touched by the coming of the Romans.

Perhaps no more than 20,000 people lived in villas – and apart from owners and their families they included household servants and slaves. Many more people – possibly up to a million – lived directly off the land: peasant farmers, tenants and labourers, either slave or free. Some worked on estates belonging to villas or the government, and some led the independent lives of their ancestors in scattered farmsteads and hamlets.

The extent to which they became affected by Roman ways depended mainly on how far they lived from a road, villa, market town or fort.

Village at the crossroads

Some of the more Romanised settlements owed their very existence to Roman roads and relay stations. Traces of one of these villages have been found at Scole in Norfolk, where the road from Colchester to Caistor crossed the River Waveney.

Scole was a village of peasant farmers and their families, either landowners or tenants of some villa-owning landlord. Crafts-men and shopkeepers were there too, making a living from the farmers and travellers on the busy road. Some of the timber-built houses and workshops were Romanised to the extent of having stone foundations, but most had only clay or chalk floors. They stood beside the main road or in cobbled lanes running off it at right-angles. The houses were well spaced out, possibly each with its own plot of land, cess-pit and sometimes a timber-lined well.

Remains of furnaces, iron ore and slag show that smiths plied their trade at Scole, but most villagers worked in the fields and meadows around. Their meat was mostly local beef, but sheep were also raised for lamb and mutton. Chickens, ducks and pigs were probably reared on a household's private plot for variety. On the higher and drier land, the peasants grew wheat, barley and oats.

Their life would be monotonous and at times hard. Leather shoes found preserved in the wells of two households are mostly cheap, badly worn, and in some cases patched. Yet these humble folk could save enough to buy typical Roman trinkets such as bronze brooches, bracelets, rings and pins. Though meals were usually cooked in and eaten from coarse local pottery, tableware also

Cottage industry
Wool played a major part in the economy of many peasant farms in upland areas of Britain, especially in the Cotswolds and in the Mendip Hills. Iron shears such as these were used to clip the wool before it was carded and prepared for spinning. The wool was spun at home by hand. Spindle whorls, which weighted the bone spindles, are found in most peasant houses during the course of excavation. The scarcity of loomweights, however, suggests that weaving, although a traditional Celtic craft, was no longer done at home. Perhaps the wool, once it was spun, was sent away to weaving mills in the towns.

included bowls and dishes of samian ware, and jugs, bowls and flasks of bronze and glass.

Styli, inkwells and wooden writing tablets have also been found there, so some villagers could write – probably they worked at the government inn or relay station, where records of travellers passing through would be kept by minor officials.

A smattering of Roman habits and luxuries has been detected in other settlements such as that just north of Berkhamsted, in Hertfordshire, and another at Neatham, in Hampshire. Some Neatham houses even had their walls plastered and painted in bright colours. None of these settlements had amphitheatres or theatres, so the villagers doubtless spent some of their hard-won spare time in local taverns, where they could quaff Celtic beer and gamble a little. Gaming pieces were found at Berkhamsted, and a fine set of nine bone counters was discovered in a hamlet at Ewell in Surrey.

With the farmhands

Labourers on villa estates often had communal quarters within aisled buildings on one side of the farmyard, but others lived in villages and hamlets on a corner of the estate.

In West Country fields it is still possible to see humps and bumps marking the remains of some of these hamlets; two lie within about 500 yds of each other on a plateau south of Bath. At one of them, Butcombe, the first 250 years of Roman rule brought little change. But small rectangular buildings gradually replaced its circular huts, and larger flocks of sheep were reared for wool. Plenty of beef was raised too, judging from the ox bones found, though the bones also reveal that most of the better joints went elsewhere – to market or as tax in kind to the Roman army.

Then, at the end of the 3rd century, a villa was laid out in the valley below at Lye Hole. It brought dramatic changes to the villagers of Butcombe, whose land was probably incorporated into the estate. A dozen new enclosures were built, with drystone walls. In one stood a large oblong wooden building with a roof of sandstone tiles, drystone foundations, and a floor of rough flag-stones. Cattle would have been sheltered in part of it, but the rest housed peasants working on the land – some of their spindle weights, a bronze finger ring, a few coins and a grindstone have been found. Their beds would have been simply blankets spread on straw. But with stout doors to keep out wind and rain, this barn-like building was at least a warm place in which to eat supper and lay their heads when the long day's work was done.

Their few leisure hours were spent in much the same way as those of the roadside villagers. They drank and gambled a little – but they could also go hunting for hares and birds, which not only gave them sport, but varied their dull diet of tough meat and bread.

A villa at Bricket Wood, near St Albans, was among some that provided small bath-houses for workers who lived some distance from the villa. There the labourers could gather, a few at a time, to refresh themselves – perhaps taking a drink as well as bathing, if fragments of beakers and a pewter cup can be counted as evidence. However, among items mislaid at the Bricket Wood bath-house were a bone comb, some bronze bracelets and a silver ring, suggesting that the workers were not entirely poverty-stricken. Coins also found there may have been lost while men gambled.

Life on the imperial payroll

The lot of a peasant on a privately owned villa estate was often a good deal easier than that of a man on a government-owned estate. Workers on these imperial properties included criminals con-demned to slavery and tough tenant farmers who paid rent. These tenant farmers not only worked their rented plots, but also laboured in the estate fields at certain times.

The most extensive of these imperial estates that has been

Paying the rent
Peasant farmers who were tenants of an estate might be required to pay their rent in a variety of ways. In this relief the landlord or his bailiff is shown receiving payment in kind – a hare, fish, a lamb, chickens and a basket of fruit. The peasants might also be expected to pay a sum of money, and to work in the owner's fields at busy times such as ploughing or harvesting time.

Off to market

The beasts of burden on Roman farms were often donkeys, like the one being fed in this mosaic. With panniers attached to either flank, they could be used to carry produce from the gardens and orchards to market. Several Roman writers, including the poet Virgil who wrote his four Georgics *on the subject of farming, talked about the animals and their drivers. Virgil describes how a donkey might be loaded with 'cheap fruit' for the outward journey, and return laden with some useful object for the farm, such as a quernstone for milling.*

Beasts of burden
The burly peasant driver shown goading his team of toiling oxen in this relief may be following the advice of Columella, a successful Roman farmer and author of 12 books on agriculture. His technique for training a young bullock for the plough or wagon was to yoke it with the most docile beast in the existing team. In this way, he explains, 'only a few blows' are needed to make the animal work hard.

identified was on Salisbury Plain and the downland to the west of it. This was good farming land but with few villas; instead the landscape was dotted with farmsteads and villages surrounded by hundreds of acres of Celtic and Roman fields. Roman farmsteads here differed little from those that preceded them. Roughly circular enclosures surrounded a single dwelling hut, small granaries and drying racks, and storage pits cut into the chalk.

However, a comparison of storage space on these farms before and after the Roman conquest suggests that the government may have been requisitioning almost half of their corn, leaving the peasants little reward for a lot of hard work. They left few traces of wealth in their homes, and scant remains of personal belongings.

But even this slave-like existence had its occasional good times: a long village street at Chisenbury Warren, in Wiltshire, ended in a half acre of land, surrounded by a ditch, that may well have been a village green. After a good harvest, the villagers could gather there for a festival and fair. Traders and craftsmen would set up stalls, and travelling entertainers danced and sang, while the locals kept up a steady flow of home-brewed beer and food. Small knots of men would gather around the fringes of the green to gamble or shout encouragement at fighting cocks, while the young village bloods pitted their strength against each other in wrestling or boxing.

By and large though, a peasant's life in lowland Britain was grindingly hard, whoever he worked for. He laboured seven days a week, except for major public holidays, and faced an old age racked by rheumatism and arthritis from a lifetime spent in the fields.

Even so, because he lived near flourishing towns and villas, and his masters, whether Roman officials or British landowners, lived Romanised lives, he too gradually adopted the trappings of culture. His everyday clothes had changed little – a belted woollen knee-length tunic, leggings and short leather boots tied at the ankles. But adorning and fastening his garments, and the very similar clothing of his womenfolk, were Roman-style brooches, pins and jewellery. His household's coarse pottery was still British made, but was now mass-produced, and alongside it would be a few imported vessels.

His money and his gods

Some of his religious festivals, his gods and the spirits he worshipped were Celtic. But other festivals were Roman, and the native gods were usually identified with Roman deities who performed the same functions: Sulis, Celtic goddess of the springs at Bath, was linked with Minerva, Roman goddess of good health. Many peasants had Roman or Latinised names, and some learned how to write them, how to count in Latin and how to write the names of items in common use. They bartered among themselves, but they also used money; in villages like Scole, travellers constantly needed goods and services, so money was essential.

Most peasants earned their money by honest toil, but as in every age there were those looking for easier ways ... There were, for example, a number of forgers at work turning out counterfeit coins. They were metal-workers and there is widespread evidence of their counterfeiting operations in Somerset, where coin moulds and metal-working tools have been found at several sites.

They usually worked in out-of-the-way villages and hamlets, and one of their more secret hideouts has been discovered – a small cavern in the Mendips called White Woman's Hole. In it were found 100 fake coins of the late 3rd and early 4th centuries.

Other illegal activities seem also to have flourished, to judge

The heavy wagon was an important piece of equipment on the Roman farm, used for carrying hay, grain and manure, or for transporting slaves and labourers. Few peasants, however, were able to take the advice offered by the writer Cato to fellow-farmers – to sell their wagons once they were worn out. Many peasants were poor and could perhaps afford only run-down wagons sold off by villa owners.

by large hoards of genuine coins unearthed in caves and remote rural spots like Wookey Hole and Shapwick. It is hardly likely that villa owners would have hidden their personal fortunes so far from their homes, so some buried hoards could well be the plunder of local brigands who burgled villas or robbed travellers, hiding their loot in isolated places, to be retrieved after a discreet interval. The hoards found were perhaps never collected because the thieves were either arrested, or too frightened to go back for them.

Where the old ways survived

Despite the Romanisation – either swift or gradual – of central and southern Britain, older ways persisted almost unchanged in vast areas. In the west and north – on the uplands of Devon and Cornwall, in Wales, along the Pennines and in southern Scotland – towns and villas were few, and the army provided the only permanent Roman presence. It was in these regions that the Celtic pattern of life survived.

West of Exeter, country settlements were, with one exception, unchanged. The exception was a ten-roomed villa house built in the mid-2nd century at Magor, in Cornwall – probably the home of a local Dumnonian tribesman who had made good in Exeter or in the Roman army.

The villa would have been a strange sight to the other tribesmen, who mostly still lived like their ancestors, in oval enclosures known now as 'rounds'. Each was surrounded by a bank and ditch which helped to protect it from the elements, marauders and wild animals. Huts, sheds and pens hugged the inside of the bank, to gain as much shelter as possible from the sweeping winds and rains.

One of these 'rounds', at Trethurgy near St Austell, has been investigated thoroughly enough to reveal the pattern of everyday life there. Its timber gates were set into a stone-faced earth bank 6½ ft high, with small store sheds on either side. The gateway led into an open yard where beyond the sheds to the left, and set against the bank, were three oval one-roomed houses. The houses were of timber, and two had strong stone foundations. Outside them women would squat grinding corn while their children played near by; inside each, a fire blazed on the hearth in the centre of the room, while ovens warmed for the day's baking.

To the right of the gateway stood two more houses and a large oval cattle byre. It was probably the women's task to clear out manure and straw from the byre to be carted off and spread on the

Houses that were built to last
In the south-west, in Wales and in the north, Britons had for centuries before the Roman conquest been building circular huts with solid stone walls. Stone was abundant and suitable wood scarce in these areas; in any case, stone-built houses probably lasted much longer without repairs and rebuilding than timber-framed huts. Not surprisingly the traditional type of house persisted in these parts of Britain throughout the Roman occupation.

From fort to farm
When the Roman army rolled through the south-west peninsula it encountered small fortified settlements, such as that at Tregeare, Cornwall. Celts continued to occupy some settlements, but abandoned others. After the conquest there was, particularly in Cornwall, a growth in the number of farming settlements known as 'rounds' – oval enclosures, surrounded by a single bank or wall, which contained up to a dozen huts.

fields around. In a corner of the yard, someone with patience – probably an old man – laboriously carved stone bowls and dishes from elvan, a local granite. These bowls, together with beef, hides and a little tin, brought in enough money for the people of Trethurgy to buy cooking pots from Dorset potteries, and even samian tableware from the Continent. Outside the enclosure some of the men ploughed small fields covering a total of 40 or 50 acres, while others drove cattle to new pastures or rebuilt any of the walls surrounding their fields that had been damaged.

Scenes like this were common throughout the south-west, but in the far west of Cornwall and on the Scilly Isles people built quite different homes. These were courtyard houses – living-rooms, workshops, stores and even small stables, all built into the inside face of a thick wall and facing a central yard. Some were enclosed by a bank and ditch; others were in unprotected villages such as Chysauster, near Penzance, where four courtyard houses stood each side of a street.

Between 20 and 40 people lived in each of these Cornish 'rounds' and courtyard villages.

Rome and the Welsh peasantry

The Silurian tribesmen of south-east Wales fought hard against the Romans, and later were granted local self-government. Their capital was at Caerwent, and villa estates slowly grew around it – particularly along the coast.

Many peasants became tenants or labourers on these estates. At one, in Llantwit Major, they lived in a large half-timbered building across the farmyard from the villa itself. This building was spacious and airy, with cement floors and plastered walls, and was conveniently near the sheds, stables, smithy and workshops where much of the day's work was done.

Mussels, whelks, limpets, cockles and winkles were collected from the seashore 1½ miles away to make a tasty addition to the regular fare of beef and mutton. Deer and hares were also hunted for the table.

The villa was a close-knit little community of 20 or 30 people, preoccupied with their everyday routine and little concerned with events in Caerwent, 35 miles east. Their only regular contact with the world outside came when surplus produce was sold to local garrisons, or shipped elsewhere.

The territory of the Silures was watched over by about a dozen forts for most of the time the Romans occupied Britain. But there

Island farm hut
At Din Lligwy on Anglesey there can still be seen the stone foundations of a circular hut which was once part of a thriving Welsh farm. The farmyard also contained another house and four oblong buildings which were used as

216

are few signs of forts in south-west Wales, where the Demetae tribe offered little opposition: a local tribal authority centred on Carmarthen was set up in the 2nd century, showing that by then the Romans trusted the Demetae to run their own affairs with a minimum of supervision.

The Demetae had for centuries lived in small, roughly circular enclosures protected by a bank and ditch, and continued to do so. But some of their farmsteads were altered in ways that reveal Roman influence. In several settlements, including one at Cwmbrwyn, near Laugharne, the inhabitants no longer lived in circular timber-framed huts, but in a single long building with stone walls, glazed windows, and a stone-tiled roof. Cattle raised there would have been driven 10 miles to Carmarthen for sale in the market.

Things were very different further north, in the Cambrian Mountains and Snowdonia, where the Ordovices, like the Silures, fought ferociously for their territory. It was finally surrounded and controlled by a strong network of forts that was maintained throughout the occupation. Few Ordovician settlements of the period have been discovered – possibly because these mountain shepherds led simple, rootless lives, moving between summer and winter pastures and leaving little evidence behind them. Those settlements that have been found are clusters of huts around Roman forts, where the people may have been forced to live so that the garrisons could keep an eye on them. Some forts in the territory show signs of having been damaged at the end of the 2nd century and rebuilt a little later: precautions of one kind or another may have been well justified.

Farmers in north-west Wales and Anglesey seem to have relied mainly on cattle or sheep for their living, though most farms included up to 15 acres of small terraced fields, and traces of copper and iron working have been found on some. There were half a dozen forts in the area, indicating strict government control. High taxes in kind on top of a shortage of good farming land may explain the poverty of these people. They had few trinkets and personal luxuries, and even pots seem to have been scarce and carefully looked after to last for years. On a farmstead at Caer Mynydd, in Gwynedd, the remains of only 15 pots were found, though the place had been lived in for 150 years.

But there were some who managed to get rich. The wealthiest peasant family yet identified in north Wales lived in a large farmstead at Din Lligwy, on Anglesey. The farm was surrounded by a great five-sided wall and consisted of two houses, several workshops, a smithy with six smelting hearths, and a store shed.

stores and workshops. One of these was the smithy, where blacksmiths forged iron tools for the farm; they may also have produced some for exchange. In return for these and for wool, beef and hides, the farmers obtained cash, silver and pottery.

Mines and cave-homes

In the Pennines lived the aggressive tribe of the Brigantes. Their hostility to the invaders was such that Rome was obliged to keep a large garrison in the region, in forts like those at Slack and Brough-on-Noe. For as well as fierce tribesmen, the Pennines had valuable lead and silver mines, which were under overall control of the army and had to be kept in production.

Roman patrols and wagons moving slowly along the bleak mountain and moorland roads were a common sight, as they carried the supplies that enabled forts to survive the rigours of winter.

The peasantry had long since learned how to combat rain and cold as they herded their cattle and ploughed their few poor fields. Under their tunics they wore loose-fitting trousers or sometimes knee-breeches, and around their shoulders a *cucullus*, or hooded cape, or a *byrrus*, a long heavy cloak with a hood. Some Derbyshire shepherds who moved their flocks of tough brown-woolled sheep between high and low pastures seem to have lived in caves for part of the year, as they had done before the Romans came.

Caves gave excellent protection both from bad weather and from wild animals, but these shepherds were no primitive 'cave-men'. They left behind in their caves samian pottery, coins, bone combs and many bronze brooches, showing that they were just as

Food for the forces
The abandoned homes of thousands of British farmers are scattered across the hills of Cumbria. Their inhabitants produced much of the beef and some of the grain that kept the Roman army in the north alive throughout three and a half centuries of occupation. The settlement of Ewe Close, Cumbria (left) is one of the best examples of this type of farming. Once it consisted of a tight cluster of circular living huts and sheds, small cultivated enclosures and larger stock pens, surrounded by acres of open pastureland. The haphazard arrangement of the buildings and enclosures contrasts sharply with the uncompromising straightness of the Roman road which runs only a few yards from the native huts.

The imprint of the Romans is much clearer on the other side of the Pennines at Grassington, North Yorkshire (above right). Here, acres of regular, rectangular fields form a highly organised landscape in which, despite the unsuitable climate, large quantities of grain were produced. It is likely that, in this area, the demand for corn to feed the northern garrison completely altered the traditional farming practices of the native Brigantes.

218

Protective clothing
Long before the conquest the peasant families who farmed the upland areas of Britain had worn heavy woollen cloaks to protect them from the harsh climate. The hooded cloaks, which reached below the knees, looked like the one worn by a merchant named Philus, depicted on this tombstone found in Gloucestershire. During the occupation, cloaks from the north of Britain were exported to other parts of the Roman Empire.

wealthy as farmers in some other regions of Britain. They also had permanent homes, perhaps like the substantial stone farm buildings discovered at Roystone Grange in Derbyshire. There, in a remote, wind-swept valley, traces of several homesteads, their enclosing walls and their fields have survived. At the centre of one cobbled yard stood a large, strongly built farmhouse, one end of which was paved and perhaps used for storing hay and corn; the remainder had an earth floor, and was the living area, with a hearth.

Outside were a few small fields enclosed by stone walls, showing that a little corn was grown, but mainly the land was unsuited to anything other than pasture. Apart from trading their meat and hides, the farmers could have made some extra cash by mining the lead veins in local rocks. Life there must have been rigorous, and the peasants may not have lived much beyond their mid-30s. Some were buried in a little family cemetery just beyond the farmyard, others in barrows – burial mounds – built more than 2,000 years before.

Fraternising around the forts

In the wild uplands of Cumbria and North Yorkshire, a working relationship built up between the peasant farmers and the auxiliary garrisons that were permanently settled in the region's strong network of forts. The troops kept up regular patrols in the countryside around their forts and the local people got to know them. The farmers supplied the garrisons with beef, mutton, corn and hides – either for cash or as payment-in-kind taxes.

When tax payments were due, or the farmers had cattle to sell, herds and laden wagons thronged the roads to the forts, around which, in time, grew civilian settlements. This sort of settlement was called a *vicus*, and in it the country people opened up shops, taverns and brothels, where off-duty soldiers could spend some of their pay, and travellers relax. Here, too, many Roman soldiers met and courted local girls who later became their wives.

Villa estates were unknown in these regions, and the *vicus* was the one place where peasants could make peaceful contact with the Roman way of life. Away from the forts they lived in isolated homesteads and small hamlets and villages of between 10 and 20 round, stone-walled huts. At Ewe Close and Crosby Garrett, in Cumbria, such hamlets can still be seen: close-knit, inward-looking communities, huts clustered together in groups of three or four, surrounded by animal pens and vegetable plots. Beyond them were

Garrison town
In many parts of northern and western Britain the only towns to flourish were those that grew up alongside the walls of

Roman forts. Such towns grew quite large if the nearby fort was occupied for a period of two or three centuries. At Chesterholm, Northumberland, a settlement consisting of shops, taverns, houses, a staging post and a bath-house clustered closely around the west gate of the Roman fort of Vindolanda – a support for the frontier garrisons. There was even a brewery, but it was probably retired soldiers who dedicated an altar to Vulcan that was also found. The upstanding walls and towers are, however, modern reconstructions.

221

small, squarish fields, then open pastures, bounded only by dykes to mark farms' boundaries or to keep cattle off the more exposed hill-tops.

Fort settlements often became quite sizeable – 15 to 30 acres or more, with several hundred inhabitants. Though they were peasant communities, they resembled in many ways the small towns of southern Britain. The *vicus* at Carlisle was really large, covering 70 acres, and probably became a tribal capital – the centre of a *civitas*, or self-governing tribal region with its own council and magistrates.

Murder on Hadrian's Wall

In the *vicus* outside Housesteads fort on Hadrian's Wall were a boot and shoe shop, a smithy, and several taverns, among other buildings. Dice found there suggest that the soldiers were given to gambling as they drank, and their comrades may well have been called out from time to time to deal with arguments that had ended in brawls. But there is some grim evidence proving that the presence of nearly 1,000 Roman soldiers still did not guarantee the safety of civilians at Housesteads. Beneath the floorboards of a back-room in a building less than 100 paces from the sentries at the south gate were found the bodies of a man and a woman who had been stabbed to death and quickly hidden away by the murderers. Who they were, who knifed them and why will never be known, but the fact that their bodies were hidden successfully suggests either that they were dispatched swiftly and silently, or that their screams went unheard above the din of night life in the taverns.

Another large *vicus* surrounded the fort of Chesterholm, south of the Wall alongside the busy Stanegate road. There was a sizeable inn, narrow one-roomed shops that included a leather-worker's, and the usual taverns. The taverns sold not only wine but also beer brewed in Chesterholm's own brewery, a small building containing two stone vats built over a heating flue.

New windows on the world

Chesterholm's *vicus* seems, in fact, to have been a quite sophisti-cated little settlement: gourmet delicacies such as *Gari Flos Scombri* – prime mackerel sauce – were served in the taverns, probably to tickle the discriminating palates of Gaulish soldiers; and as well as a jar that once held mackerel sauce, several pieces of expensive

On a farm in the hills
The harvest is in and summer is ending on a small hill farm at Cefn Graeanog in north Wales in the 3rd century AD, shown in the reconstruction on pages 224–5. The family that works it is busy preparing for winter. Within the walled farmyard (1), which is about 100 ft square, are three stone-walled and thatched round houses (2). Smoke rises from their chimney holes as the women inside cure meat to store against the hard days ahead. Logs for fuel have been gathered and stacked in the store-sheds (3), and the barn, which forms the gateway to the farmhouse, is already part filled with hay to keep the cattle fed. But its roof is in need of mending, so two of the men are busy repairing the thatch (4). The market-garden patch to the right (5) is empty, its vegetables gathered in, but its fence will doubtless be repaired before spring. More urgent, however, is the need to store away the last of the wheat and barley crop; a man is busy winnowing it in the middle of the yard, tossing it into the air (6) with a two-pronged fork to let the breeze blow away the chaff. The small fields outside the enclosure (7) are bare after the harvest, and cattle may soon be brought down from outlying pastures to

jewellery have been found. They include a fine gold ring set with a red stone and inscribed *anima mea* – 'my life' – a silver ornament dedicated 'to the God Maponus', and a jet finger ring with the name 'Gatinius'.

These discoveries show that many of the people there understood Latin, and the locals would have picked up at least a few words of the language on this northern frontier. But it was probably retired soldiers who played the most prominent role in the village council, and set up altars like that from Chesterholm carrying a dedication from the inhabitants: 'For the divine house and the deities of the emperors, the villagers of Vindolanda set up this sacred offering to Vulcan, willingly and deservedly fulfilling their vow.'

Taken as a whole, the evidence available makes it abundantly clear that even in the west and wild north, the tribesmen found new windows on the world in the company of soldiers and veterans from strange, far-away places. But they still clung more tenaciously than elsewhere to their ancient ways of farming, eating and dressing; and to their own Celtic gods and spirits. It was among the bleak high places of Britain that the Celtic heritage was most strongly preserved during the four centuries of Roman rule.

graze on the stubble. Four other men have tied two pigs to long poles (8) and are carrying them back to the enclosure, where they will be carefully fattened up for slaughter later in the year. Honey from the beehives sheltered by the farmyard wall (9) will supplement the family's diet, and some of the sheep grazing on the lower hills (10) will also be slaughtered for meat.

THE LAND THAT TIME FORGOT

Remote corners of rural Britain that tell the story of country life almost 2,000 years ago

The curious oval houses that flank the village street of Chysauster in Cornwall have been deserted for 1,700 years. In Roman times they were the homes of families who farmed the surrounding land. The family lived in the largest of the rooms, cooking over the open hearth, spinning wool and sleeping on beds of bracken covered with skins and blankets. Next door was the workshop, and across the central yard stood a lean-to shed. An underground chamber, close to the houses, was probably the communal cold-store.

Despite changes in agriculture over the centuries, thousands of acres of fields that were cultivated during the Roman occupation can be seen in Britain today. There are two distinct types. The Celts continued to farm square fields surrounded by stone walls or banks. However, when the more efficient but much heavier plough was introduced by the Romans, it became even more difficult to turn plough and oxen round at each furrow's end. Many farmers of imperial or villa estates, therefore, began to farm much longer and narrower fields so that fewer turns were needed. Some of these fields, which were only about 30 yds wide, survive in the Cotswolds and on Salisbury Plain.

Celtic cultivation
Native Celtic farmers generally cultivated their fields with simple wooden ploughs, tipped with iron shares and pulled by a pair of oxen. The hoe was more often used for the cultivation of garden plots.

Farming village
The Celtic community which settled at Chysauster (below left) in the Iron Age continued to farm there during the Roman occupation. Eight stone-walled houses, each consisting of three or four cell-like rooms, are ranged along either side of the street.

Hard labour
This small bronze model of a native ploughman captures a day in the life of a village farmer. The wooden plough is pulled by a team of oxen and guided from behind by the ploughman. The ploughing season lasted only three weeks, in which time a team such as this would have ploughed no more than 20 acres.

CHAPTER EIGHT

An industrial revolution

Along with the Roman invasion came an industrial revolution, as a new breed of technicians and businessmen marshalled manpower, skills and resources

Native skills and new ideas
Canterbury glassware was one of several industries that blossomed under Roman encouragement. The bronze stud inlaid with glass (left) is another fine example of the Romano-British craftsman's work.

SOME OF THE FINEST GOLD JEWELLERY OF ROMAN BRITAIN HAS BEEN FOUND NOT, AS MIGHT BE EXPECTED, IN THE grand villas of the south, but in remote corners of western Wales, where the Celtic peasant farmers barely scraped a living. From Rhayader, in Powys, came a broad gold bracelet decorated with superb filigree lattice-work, and a gold necklet inlaid with blue stones set in a filigree border. Two solid gold bracelets in the form of serpents, with two gold chains and pendants, were found less than 30 miles away at Dolaucothi, in Dyfed.

An explanation for such wealth in a poor area can be found on the mountain slopes at Dolaucothi, overlooking the modern village of Pumpsaint, where the Romans worked their only real gold-mine in Britain. Small amounts of gold may have come from the streams of Cornwall, Scotland and Ireland – and had done for 2,000 years before the Roman conquest – but at Dolaucothi the gold was not panned in ounces from alluvial gravel; it was mined in quantity by sophisticated techniques in which hundreds of thousands of tons of earth and rock were removed.

Immediately after the final conquest of Wales around AD 70, Roman hydraulic engineers moved into the Cothi valley and built aqueducts to bring water from as far as 7 miles away, up the mountain-side and into a series of reservoirs. It was then released to pour down the mountain, stripping away vegetation and topsoil to reveal gold-bearing veins in the rocks beneath.

Treasure trove
These pieces of jewellery are perfect specimens of the goldsmith's delicate craftsmanship. They were found at Rhayader in Wales, and may have been stolen from travellers by brigands. The bracelet is decorated with filigree – intertwined ribbons of gold – and scrolls at each end which suggest that it was the work of a native Celtic craftsman. The other piece, which might be a necklet or a bracelet, is set with carnelians or with 'stones' of blue paste.

Sweated labour in the mines

The skills of the engineers who laid bare the veins of gold at Dolaucothi were backed by a massive labour force of miners hacking away below ground. Gold veins were followed by open-cast quarrying and by shafts driven through the rocks. The shafts were cut with iron picks, hammers and wedges, and by a process known as fire-setting, which involved heating up the rock with wood fires, then pouring cold water over the hot rock, cracking it apart so that it could be removed. Convicts and slaves drove these shafts to depths of more than 100 ft, removing on the way gold-bearing ore and shovelling it on to sledges to be hauled to the surface.

The sweating miners laboured in darkness relieved only by tiny oil-lamps, cramped by rock debris, choking in foul air and threatened constantly by collapsing shafts and tunnels. As they dug deeper, rising water added to their dangers and discomforts. Engineers would then install large wooden water-wheels, driven by more slaves, to lift the water in buckets and tip it out higher up.

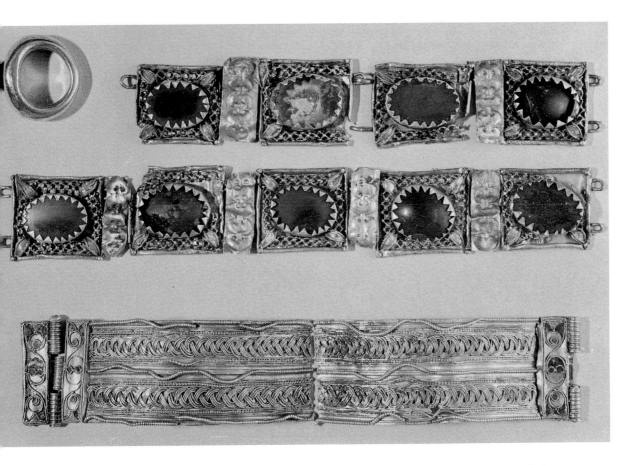

The goldsmith's craft
There were goldsmiths' workshops in London and at Malton, North Yorkshire. Day-to-day life in one of these workshops is portrayed on this Roman relief. The goldsmith is hammering an ingot on a small anvil; above him hang the scales on which the precious metal is weighed.

At the surface, gold-bearing rock was emptied on to a crushing floor and pounded into small pieces, which were put into a wooden cradle and thoroughly washed with water channelled from tanks cut in the rock. The heavy gold dust and nuggets settled on the floor of the cradle, to be collected and passed to goldsmiths, who melted it in crucibles and cast it into ingots. Much was shipped off to the imperial treasury or mint, but gold jewellery found in these Welsh hills suggest that some was worked locally.

All British mines – gold, silver, copper, lead, iron and tin – were state property, and some were permanently supervised by Roman soldiers and officials, although others were worked by private enterprise on payment of rent and a share of the proceeds.

Near the Dolaucothi mine, beneath Pumpsaint village, lie the remains of a fort. Outside the fort's southern gateway, on the banks of the River Cothi, was a timber-built civilian settlement, and further away a bath-house for the troops and engineers. The wretched miners probably washed the mud and grit from their aching bodies in the cold waters of the Cothi.

Silver for the Empire's coins

Even more important than gold, however, was lead. This was used for pipes and gutters, and alloyed with tin to make pewter. But its real value lay in the silver extracted from it to mint coins. The Mendip lead-mines were in production within six years of the invasion: a pig – or ingot – of lead found at Wookey Hole cavern was cast in AD 49. By Nero's time – AD 54–68 – such ingots were being exported to Gaul, and by around AD 70 British production was high enough to make Spanish mine-owners complain to the emperor. He set a limit on British output, but before the century ended miners were operating in Clwyd, Yorkshire and Derbyshire.

Silver was so vital to the monetary system that lead-mines were always kept under close supervision to prevent fraud or theft. In their early years the Mendip mines, centred on Charterhouse, were overseen by troops of the Second Legion Augusta, whose name was stamped on some of the lead ingots produced there. About AD 60, responsibility seems to have been transferred to imperial agents, for the names of two men – Gaius Nipius Ascanius and Tiberius Claudius Triferna – were stamped on some ingots of the AD 60s and 70s.

When the lead-mines were leased out to private individuals and companies, men like Ascanius and Triferna seem to have put their considerable experience to a profitable use and set up in business themselves. The name of Ascanius reappears on a lead ingot from the Clwyd mines later in the century, while Triferna's name is on ingots from Derbyshire. These men paid a rent for use of the mines, passed over to the imperial procurator half the ore they mined – and were kept under close supervision by government officers to make sure they did not cheat the emperor.

However, Triferna did get away with some silver; four of the lead ingots stamped with his name were found hidden under a stone cairn at Green Ore, in the Mendips. Three were stamped once, in the normal way, but the fourth was stamped four times. When analysed, the first three proved to be made of lead from which the silver had been extracted; the fourth, however, was still rich in silver. Triferna and his cronies seem to have hidden the ingots, to be recovered later when the silver could be extracted in secret. The specially marked ingot held enough silver to make about eight *denarii* – ten days' pay for a legionary.

Anyone caught defrauding the emperor of silver faced execution, or was condemned to work in the mines. Toiling alongside other criminals, slaves and prisoners-of-war, he faced a life of back-

The way to work
This low, dark cave is an entrance to the Roman gold-mine at Dolaucothi in central Wales. Through this entrance trudged the criminals, prisoners of war and slaves who worked out their weary lives in the appalling, cramped conditions of the narrow shafts below. The work was overseen by soldiers who were based in the nearby fort at Pumpsaint.

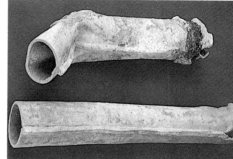

breaking labour under harsh conditions. In some lead-mines, 12 out of every 100 workers died each year, but as almost all British lead-mines were open-cast workings, chances of survival were probably better than in the shafts and tunnels of Dolaucothi.

Winning the silver

Lead ore was mined in much the same way as gold, but unlike gold, lead was extracted from its ore by smelting in a furnace, rather than crushing. A second stage, known as cupellation, was then needed to extract the silver from it. The lead was heated in a shallow hearth to a temperature of around 1,100°C, by using bellows, which also provided the blast of air needed to separate the silver from the lead. The silver was left to be picked out of the hearth. Finally, in a third stage, the lead was re-smelted to remove remaining impurities, and the pure metal could then be poured into ingot moulds. Roman technicians taught all these skills to the British workers.

Everyday life in the Charterhouse lead-mining settlement can be reconstructed from finds there, and surviving records of similar

A self-made man

Lead was usually smelted and cast into 'pigs', or ingots. This one weighs about 135 lb and bears the stamp of Gaius Nipius Ascanius. He began life as a slave, but was later freed and rose to become an imperial agent overseeing work at the lead-mines. Eventually he was rich enough to take out an independent lease on mines in the Clwyd region of Wales.

ones in Spain. Charterhouse covered about 30 acres, partly laid out in the Roman grid-system. Timber and stone buildings housed officials and civil servants who ran the mines, and workers employed by the lessees.

Other buildings would have been workshops where lead was smelted and silver extracted from it. Cobblers, launderers, bakers and other tradesmen paid fees to the government to set up shop there, and were granted monopolies of their trade in return. Baths, probably privately run, would have been for officials and other settlers, while just west of the settlement stood a small amphitheatre where the entire population could watch entertainments like animal-baiting or wrestling on public holidays. At such times even the long-suffering miners would have a break, and the ring and clatter of picks and shovels, the roar of furnaces and the harsh commands of the guards would cease for a few hours.

Iron – an expanding industry

Unlike gold and lead, iron can be found in many parts of Britain, so iron mines were less closely controlled, although as a mineral resource it belonged nominally to the emperor and those smelting it would have been expected to rent rights from the government. Iron was mined in most regions, but the main sources were the Weald of Kent, the Forest of Dean and the East Midlands. An iron industry existed in the Forest of Dean in pre-Roman times, but stimulated by the occupation, it grew rapidly – more than 200 acres of slag heaps survive there.

Iron furnaces and workshops were more scattered in the east Midlands, and some iron may have been produced there by itinerant workers moving from one source of ore to another, and building furnaces for just one or two smeltings. Some furnaces, however, seem to have been more permanent, built close to workshops and settlements. At Sacrewell, in Cambridgeshire, the furnaces stood in the open, and the labourers who worked them lived close by in long, one-roomed buildings with bare cement and stone floors.

Another settlement at Wakerley, Northamptonshire, had a long tradition of iron-working, which was carried out on a large scale and by much more elaborate methods. There were several long, narrow channel-hearths for roasting ore, eight or nine shaft-furnaces for smelting it, and circular hearths for forging the iron that collected at the bottom of the furnaces. Shaft furnaces, introduced by the Romans, were more efficient than Celtic furnaces, because they generated more draught, working up higher temperatures.

Precious metals
The Romans had been aware of Britain's abundant mineral supplies – gold, bronze, tin, iron and silver – more than a century before the conquest. The prospect of new supplies of silver may have been particularly enticing to the Roman government, which

An iron-worker's day

needed ever greater quantities of the metal in order to mint coins like this with which to pay the army. Although political reasons may have been the immediate motive for the invasion of Britain, the lure of its alleged wealth may well have been an added incentive to the conquerors.

A British iron-smelter's day began early. Wearing a thick tunic and stout hob-nailed boots for protection, he and his workmates filled the roasting hearth with iron ore and charcoal fuel, both obtained locally. The ore was dug from an outcrop with hammers and picks, and the wood for charcoal was collected from neighbouring woodland and scrub. Roasting the ore made it easier to break up,

Buying loyalty
Roman emperors were expected to buy the support of their troops; by the late 4th century a new emperor would give each of his soldiers five gold coins and 1 lb of silver. This silver ingot from the Thames at London, one of two dozen similar ingots found in Britain, is probably an example of these hand-outs. Its official stamp suggests that it was made around AD 395.

Mining in the Mendips
Lead had already been mined at Charterhouse in the Mendip Hills before the Roman invasion. Today the area is pitted with quarries and works that date mainly from the Roman and medieval periods.

and before going into the furnace it was graded into equal-size lumps so that the furnace could be packed evenly.

With the roasting hearths burning well, the shaft-furnaces near by were prepared for firing. Slag, ash and other debris from the previous day's work was dumped to one side, and the clay shaft of each furnace was packed with a charge of charcoal. Once the furnace fire was lit, bellows raised the temperature to about 1,300°C, and after about half an hour, lumps of roasted ore and more charcoal were added. Gradually a spongy mass of iron – the 'bloom' – began to form at the base of the shaft, while slag was tapped and allowed to run out into a collecting channel. More ore and charcoal were added, until after six or seven hours the bloom had grown to fill the base of the shaft.

As the furnace cooled, the bloom, now weighing between 13 lb and 26 lb, was removed with large tongs to a forging hearth. There it was heated and repeatedly hammered to remove remaining slag and waste. The iron was then either turned over to a blacksmith on the spot, or sold to one in a nearby town. The blacksmith worked it into a variety of useful implements ranging from ploughshares and spade-blades, through kitchen knives and craftsmen's tools, to the humble but vital nails that fastened building timbers.

The process of roasting and grading the ore, charging and firing the furnaces, and heating and hammering the bloom needed a team of eight to ten men, who had to work hard and fast to produce enough to make a fair living. That they succeeded is evident from the number of bronze brooches, bracelets, rings and pins found at Wakerley. Two pointed writing instruments found there were probably used to record the quantities of iron produced and the prices obtained.

Compared with the great iron-works in the Weald of Kent, however, other operations were on a very small scale. The Weald – another area where iron was worked long before the Romans came – was ideal because of its rich ore deposits, hardwood forests for charcoal, and clay suitable for building furnaces. A large part of the Weald became an imperial estate, apparently supervised by the Classis Britannica – the British fleet, which possessed major naval bases at Richborough and Dover. Roofing tiles found on smelting sites at Bardown and Cranbrook were stamped 'CL.BR', meaning they were naval property.

Shaft-furnaces were built in hundreds in the Weald. From the huge slag heaps found at Oaklands Park it can be calculated that this one centre alone turned out 200 to 500 tons of iron a year. Fleet blacksmiths were probably stationed at Bardown and Cranbrook, making tons of nails, weapons and anchors for naval bases.

Working the tin in Cornwall

The Romans must have anticipated a rich reward from Britain's tin deposits. Before they arrived, the tin of the south-west, so important to prehistoric man for alloying to make his bronze tools and weapons, had been referred to in the works of such classical authors as Diodorus Siculus, Strabo and Julius Caesar. From these reports, the invaders may well have expected it to help significantly towards meeting the cost of garrisoning their new province.

These hopes were not immediately fulfilled. When the south-west was incorporated into the province in the mid-60s, troops stationed at Nanstallon fort made some attempt to work the local tin. But the effort needed for the small amount found, together with the large quantities being produced in Spain, caused the government to lose interest. For two centuries, tin-mining was left to local communities like those at Chysauster and Castle Gotha, who continued to work it as a sideline to farming.

But in the 3rd century Spanish output declined steeply and the Romans took a fresh interest in the Cornish sources. Evidence of new and repaired roads with inscribed milestones shows considerable government activity in the south-west at this time; and there was a marked rise in the amount of money circulating or being hoarded away. This new wealth in an otherwise poor region was surely derived from tin-mining. A hoard of coins found at Caerhayes was actually hidden in a jug made of tin. Some of the metal was shipped up the Bristol Channel to Sea Mills, and found its way to Bath, Camerton and other settlements near modern Bristol, to be used in the pewter industry.

Pottery – the growth industry

Another traditional British craft, the manufacture of pottery, was given a tremendous boost as the Roman army presented it with 50,000 new customers – all handily grouped in forts housing between 500 and 6,000 men, and in constant need of new pieces. Some units brought their own potters with them, or were followed by those who had worked for them on the Continent. But immigrant potters could not meet the total demand, and British craftsmen soon mastered the improved techniques of manufacture and firing which these men brought with them. As the Britons learned how to shape and finish their vessels to the liking of the troops, they won a growing share of the military market.

237

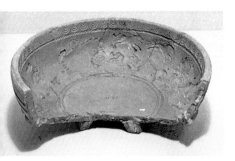

Samian ware
The success of Gallic samian pottery in British markets inspired native potters to try to imitate the imported vessels. In the late 2nd century, at least one pottery producing samian ware was established at Colchester, where clay moulds such as this one were used. The venture was not a success, however, and the kiln soon closed down.

Kitchen equipment
Forts and towns required a constant supply of kitchen ware. To a large extent local potteries satisfied their demands, producing a standard range of storage jars, bowls, dishes, jugs and cooking pots. Many small potteries also produced mortaria – *grit-surfaced grinding bowls which looked like the vessel in the centre of this group of domestic pottery articles. But they had to compete with the highly successful mass-manufacturers in Oxfordshire, who also produced imitation samian ware.*

Furthermore, soldiers were not their only customers. The growth of towns brought with it large numbers of new civilian shoppers, and market places where people from the countryside around could buy. As the British adopted Roman ways of cooking, eating and drinking, they wanted the appropriate kitchen pots and tableware – *mortaria* (grinding bowls), pie-dishes and wine beakers. A wide range of pottery was used in every house, and as it was fragile constant replacements were needed. For all of these reasons, pottery manufacture became the fastest-growing industry in Roman Britain, and the biggest industrial employer.

Most of the pottery used was made in small local workshops serving a town and the rural settlements around it. Three or four small kilns, each firing around 200 vessels at a time, were used to make a wide range of coarse kitchen ware of the kinds most constantly in demand – cooking pots, storage jars, dishes, bowls, flagons and jugs. Kilns found outside St Albans were only 10 or 15 minutes' journey from the shops and the forum where their wares were sold; thousands of fragments of these pots have been found in the town.

The fortunes of pottery centres fluctuated from century to century. At one stage, kilns at Radlett and Brockley Hill served a far wider area than the markets of nearby St Albans. Together with another large pottery at Colchester, they made most of the *mortaria* used in southern Britain – and a good number used even as far away as the northern frontier. The men who made these popular grinding bowls were household names and stamped their wares with 'signatures' so that customers knew they were buying the genuine article.

One businessman named Albinus, with potteries at Radlett and Brockley Hill, sold more *mortaria* between AD 90 and 100 than any other potter. When he retired, his son Matugenus carried on the business. A local rival was Castus, who continued in production until about AD 140. One of Castus's kilns found at Radlett was still stacked with partly fired pots, including more than 20 *mortaria* carrying his name. Later, however, the kilns in this area went into decline. By the mid-2nd century they served only a local market, their *mortaria* apparently made by potters who were barely literate, to judge by their name-stamps.

Coloured bowls and beakers

From the mid-2nd century, Oxfordshire kilns became by far the biggest producers of *mortaria* for markets in the south. These kilns were centred on Headington, Churchill and Cowley, and they also developed imitation samian ware. Imports of samian pottery dwindled rapidly in the 3rd century, probably through unrest in Gaul, where it was made. So potters copied the most popular samian shapes and vessels – mainly distinctive bowls and dishes –

A growing concern
Early in the 2nd century potteries were established around Cowley and Headington in Oxfordshire which produced the sort of kitchen ware usually made by local workshops. Initially these potteries supplied a local market. By the middle of the 3rd century, however, the Oxfordshire kilns had become a major centre of pottery production in Britain, and mortaria, *or grinding bowls, from Oxfordshire were being sold throughout the south. As the samian factories in Gaul went into decline, native imitations such as these cornered an increasing share of the British market.*

239

New Forest pottery
In the 3rd and 4th centuries a pottery-producing centre was established in the New Forest area which rivalled the potteries of Oxfordshire. The potters there attempted to produce passable imitations of samian ware, but outside their own region neither their imitations nor their grinding bowls were able to match the superior quality of Oxfordshire products. The Hampshire kilns, however, were considerably more successful with their drinking beakers and with colour-coated vessels such as this one, which were bought and used throughout much of southern Britain.

and tried also to match their bright red colour. They could not, however, reproduce the hard glossy surface of the real thing. Oxfordshire 'samian' nevertheless became a popular tableware in late 3rd century and 4th-century Britain.

Competition came from New Forest potteries around Linwood and Ashley Rails, which made not only many similar-shaped vessels, but also turned out a set of tableware – and particularly drinking beakers – distinguished by a colour-coated surface. The colours varied from matt black through brown and red to a lustrous purple, often overlaid with white-painted festoons, circles and other motifs. This colour ware may have been copied from the popular and similar products of potteries further north in the Nene Valley, which were set up about 100 years earlier.

The New Forest kilns also made the usual range of cheaper coarse kitchen ware, and from the variety of their products it appears that the industry was started by men with considerable business acumen. They deliberately set themselves to make pottery that had either proved popular elsewhere, or would be needed in quantity by every local household. Their kilns were in an area with abundant clay and ample woodland for fuel. They were also at a great distance from the potteries whose products they were copying, enabling them to undercut the prices of these competitors.

Villas for the pottery magnates

Good business sense was also evident in the Nene Valley potteries, whose similar range had in addition some superb drinking beakers. These had a lustrous black or deep brown finish, and were decorated most attractively with raised figures of hares, hounds, stags and, occasionally, chariots; some also had finely painted white scroll-work. These beakers were shaped like tableware imported from the Rhineland, though not of such high quality, and it is possible that the Nene Valley industry developed its potential only when immigrant potters arrived from the Continent in the late 2nd century. Dozens of potteries sprang up along the river, especially around Water Newton, and good-quality clay was ferried in from the Wansford area, while finished products were ferried out.

The valley also boasted some great villa estates created by wealthy pottery magnates. Of the 20 or 30 major potteries in the area, the most impressive must have been one at Castor, in Cambridgeshire, where traces of a luxurious house have been found. Built around a central courtyard, it was lavishly decorated, with painted walls and mosaic floors.

Nene Valley pottery
Drinking beakers from the New Forest area, though widely used, were rarely as attractive as the best beakers produced in the Nene Valley. Kilns near Water Newton in Cambridgeshire produced colour-coated pottery, grinding bowls and coarse grey and buff ware on a large scale. It is possible that the Nene Valley potters copied the shapes and dark brown or black colouring of pottery imported from the Rhineland, for products from both areas are often very similar. Nene Valley beakers, which were especially popular, are often decorated with sporting themes.

Designs that echo Celtic art
The elegant lines of the deer, hare and hunting dog on drinking cups used in Roman Britain, and the flowing painted scrolls on cups and jars such as this, echo the native Celtic artistry seen on the pottery and metal-work of the pre-Roman Iron Age. It says much for the high standards of craftsmanship maintained by the potters who made these vessels that they could invent such attractive, and often dynamic, designs.

The daily life of the potter

The Nene Valley potters lived and worked in half-timbered buildings about 30 yds long and half as wide, with a single wide doorway in one wall. The inside was often divided along its length, with aisles each side formed by pairs of roof supports. Close by were the kilns – circular and built of clay, with a flue and stoke-hole.

One group of men shaped the pots, taking weathered clay from a dump in their yard, working it into a suitable consistency, and then throwing the pot on a wheel. Finished vessels were dried, either in the sun or in drying sheds, after which colour coating or other forms of decoration were added. At this stage, another group of men took a batch of pots to fire them. After arranging fuel carefully in the base of the kiln, they began the long and skilled task of stacking the dried pots inside, making sure that all would be evenly fired, and none damaged. As many as 500 pots might be fired at one time.

The top of the kiln was covered with a temporary dome of clay or turf, leaving vents to encourage a draught, then the fire was lit. Some men would have to tend the fire carefully for two or three hours, while it reached maximum temperature, but most of the others would turn to other tasks – perhaps unloading another kiln, fired the day before and left to cool overnight. Finally, the finished pots would be packed in wooden crates, loaded on to wagons and taken to the river, where boats carried them quickly and cheaply to their markets.

Black pots from Poole

Vast as the Nene Valley potteries were, they were not the largest: this distinction fell to those making the black burnished, or polished, cooking pots used in almost every household and fort. Several potteries made this sort of ware, but the one in Poole, Dorset, was pre-eminent. Concentrated in the harbour area, from which its wares could be sent by sea to most parts of Britain, this hugely successful industry was, paradoxically, quite primitive in its technology and organisation. Its pots seem to have been fired not in kilns but in bonfires; its vast output, rather than being the product of a centrally organised industry, came probably from small, independent local workshops.

The Dorset black-burnished potteries concentrated on a small range of vessels, and almost nothing else.

Potter at work
A number of potters' workshops have been excavated in the Nene Valley and elsewhere. This painting from Pompeii evokes a vivid picture of what daily life in one of these establishments may have been like. A young apprentice throws a pot on the wheel, while the foreman or master potter oversees him.

The potters' kilns
Two well-preserved kilns and the remains of a workshop were uncovered in 1969 at Stibbington in Cambridgeshire. Both the stoke-holes and the raised floors of the chambers can be clearly seen today. Once the pots had been loaded into the chamber, the upper parts of the kiln would have been covered with clay or turf. This particular firm used one kiln for kitchen ware and the other for firing colour-coated pots.

Some potteries, on the other hand, also made tiles for roofing and underfloor heating flues. These tiles were probably formed in wooden moulds, turned out, and left to dry before firing. At this stage the workers often scrawled comments on the end tile of a row – the last to be counted. One Dover tile-worker boasted: 'I made 550 box tiles'; another man added: 'I smashed 51.' No doubt the cost was docked from his wages. Cats and dogs frequently strayed across the drying tiles, and several tiles that have been found carry not only their paw marks, but also the dents made by stones thrown at them by the workers.

Quarrying – a new industry

The vast building programmes put in hand needed huge quantities of tiles, though demand was greater in the south and east than in the north and west, where large quantities of stone were available for roofing and for heating systems. Spacious stone-built public buildings and private homes transformed stone-quarrying into an industry employing thousands. For the quantities of stone required were also enormous: the walls of Silchester took nearly 1½ million cu. ft of stone, and those at Cirencester more than twice as much. Cirencester had hundreds of shops and houses, as well as numerous public buildings. Building the town may have called for around 18 million cu. ft of stone – enough to have built nearly half of Hadrian's Wall.

The type of stone used varied considerably from one part of Britain to another – as it does today – according to local sources available. In the south-east, flint and chalk were used, while high-quality Greensand and Kentish Rag were ferried up the Thames for use in London. In the east Midlands, the limestones around Ketton and Barnack were used not only for building, but also for sculpture and making stone coffins. Slate from Charnwood Forest in Leicestershire was popular for roofing, and was carried as far south as St Albans. Further west, limestone was the most popular for major structural work. This included the distinctive golden stone from Ham Hill, the famous Bath freestone, and the oolitic limestone of the Cotswolds. Buildings in these areas were roofed with slates of pennant grit from Bristol, or Stonesfield sandstone from Oxfordshire.

Another important stone was Purbeck marble, from Dorset, favoured for decorative work such as inscriptions and wall surrounds. So popular was this substitute for expensive Italian marble that it was sent as far afield as Chester and Colchester. Two well-known examples of its use are the forum inscription from St Albans and the Cogidubnus inscription from Chichester. Since Purbeck marble is found only on the Isle of Purbeck, it has been possible to identify its quarries at Worbarrow and Wilkswood. Elsewhere, however, few quarries can be positively identified as Roman, as they have since been exploited by generations of stone-workers, destroying any evidence that might have remained.

Quarrymen and masons

Two quarries where Roman methods can be detected are at Handbridge, near Chester, and at Barcombe Down, near Hadrian's Wall. Slabs were split from the bedrock by driving in a line of wedges, then roughly dressed with pick, adze, mallet and chisel, before being loaded on to wagons and carted either direct to a building site or to a mason's yard. Only one stonemason of Roman Britain is known by name – Priscus, who came originally from

Roofing tiles
Clay tiles were the usual roofing material for both town houses and villas, and tile-manufacturing centres sprang up everywhere. This tile is stamped 'Arveri', showing that it was produced at the tile-works of Arverus – a manufacturer who seems to have supplied tiles to Cirencester and the surrounding countryside.

Chartres, in Gaul. He set up an inscribed stone to the goddess Sulis-Minerva at Bath, and may have settled near by in order to work the Bath freestone. His workshop has not been found, but part of one used by another mason lies beneath the remains of Fishbourne palace, where he had helped to build an earlier house. Evidence found at Fishbourne, and finished masonry elsewhere, makes it possible to describe how these masons prepared stone.

The blocks were brought in roughly dressed by the wagon-load and stacked ready for use. They were then worked into regular shapes with hammers and a variety of chisels, including the claw-chisel, which leaves distinctive multiple 'teeth' marks. Most of the pieces were then ready for use, but others would be held back for further working. Some, such as lintels and the bases of columns, might need dowel-holes drilled in them with a bow-drill, while others might be sawn into thin flooring slabs, using an iron saw with multiple blades. Fine sand was used as an abrasive to speed the work. In most cases, limestone for columns was laboriously worked with hammer and chisel, but small columns used for verandas and some column capitals appear to have been turned on a large hand-driven lathe.

Once building began, the site became crowded. As well as ready-dressed stone, large quantities of lime mortar, timber and roofing slates or tiles would pile up. Sometimes scaffolding was needed – a row of holes to take scaffold posts was found in the floor foundations of the Latimer villa. Half-timbered buildings called for even greater quantities of timber, and the gaps between posts were filled by panels of wattle – interwoven twigs, over which clay and plaster were applied.

Plaster and paint for the wall

Plastering was skilled work, and the plasterers' craft is well illustrated in a design carved on the tombstone of a house painter at Sens, near Paris. It shows four Roman plasterers at work on a wall. Two of them stand on a trestle-table set alongside the wall, one applying plaster with a 'float' identical to those still used today, and to a Roman one found in St Albans. Next to him, the second man is painting the wall, probably to a design drawn on the scroll lying at his feet. On the floor, a third is mixing plaster, while in the background a fourth man – probably the master plasterer – is sitting studying another scroll, perhaps with the design for the room on it.

Two or three layers of plaster would be applied, and afterwards the painter's brush would follow the outline of a design

Art of the mason
Huge quantities of stone were quarried for building purposes in Roman Britain. Stone was used not only in the construction of houses and public buildings, but also for town walls. Better-quality stone was used for architectural embellishments, such as this elaborately carved column capital for Cirencester in Gloucestershire.

Painted plaster
Interior decorating was not practised in Iron Age Britain, but within a few decades of the conquest, painted wall-plaster was a common feature of the British town house and country villa. Some walls were decorated with pictures; it was more usual, however, to find plain panels imitating marble and other veneers, such as this Cirencester wall-panel.

already scratched on with a pointed tool or sketched in pale paint. Colours for decoration were prepared with stone grinders on soapstone or marble palettes. The range available was remarkable; by careful mixing, all sorts of delicate shades could be achieved. Paints were made up mostly from minerals: chalk and lime for white, lead and ochre for red and yellow, malachite for green, and a fusion of copper, silica and calcium for blue. With them the wall-painters managed to create elaborate and varied designs, including imitation marble panels and stone columns, scrolls decorated with birds and animals, scenes from mythology and even portraits of the house owner and his family.

247

Mosaics for the villa floor

Another major group of interior decorators were the mosaic craftsmen, who made intricately patterned floors for the houses of the wealthy. They worked, like the plasterers, in teams. Apprentices were probably put to cutting stones and pottery into the tesserae, or tiny cubes, which made up the pattern. They were also allowed to gain experience by working on the border of the pattern, where the design was simpler and mistakes less likely to be noticed.

Not all these floors were individually designed for a particular room and laid directly on site. There were workshops in the larger towns, where borders and certain standard panels of geometric design were prepared for sale 'off the peg'. Occasionally, one of these pre-fabricated panels can be discerned by poor or incorrect fitting in a floor: for instance, a panel in the mosaic showing Orpheus and the animals at Newton St Loe villa, in Avon, is laid the wrong way round.

In the yard of the mosaic craftsman would lie stocks of materials for making tesserae: limestone and sandstone for yellows and browns, ironstone for reds and browns, slate for blues and black, and usually chalk for the white pieces. Other materials were also used, such as the remnants of red pottery and pieces of fired tiles, which were particularly useful, giving colours ranging from red and orange through pink to grey and black.

A mosaic craftsman commissioned to lay a floor would first visit the house-owner to talk over designs, probably showing him scrolls illustrating other mosaics his team had laid. Then he had to prepare a sound base for the mosaic, as subsidence could soon ruin the finest craftsman's handiwork. Over a foundation of rubble, a layer of cement was spread, and when this began to harden, the outline of the design was sketched on to it with paint or a sharp tool. A solution of lime and water was then poured over the cement, and into this the master mosaicist and his skilled workmen laid the thousands of tiny squares of stone and pottery which made up the design. A floor 15 ft by 9 ft might need 120,000 individual pieces.

Some firms made such a great reputation that they became much sought-after by the wealthy house-owners of the neighbourhood. They also developed their own peculiar styles or trademarks – distinctive arrangements of panels or favourite motifs – by which their work can still be recognised. The most successful, to judge by the number of floors commissioned, was a Cirencester firm known to have laid about 50. Most of these floors are around Cirencester, but there are others in Avon, Wiltshire and Oxfordshire.

248

Recurring pattern
This detail from the Aldborough mosaic in North Yorkshire shows the intricacy of the work involved in laying a floor even with such a commonly used motif as this three-stranded pattern, which is known as a guilloche. Sections of the border pattern used in mosaic floors may well have been ready-made in workshops, and then transported to the site where they were to be laid. Occasionally it is possible to spot poorly or wrongly fitted sections. Sometimes the work of an apprentice can be seen in borders that are less neatly laid than the central panels and scenes created by the master craftsmen.

Sculpture for house and temple

Other craftsmen who worked to beautify fashionable British homes were the sculptors. They carved statues, reliefs and architectural decorations in their workshops, where they also made altars for temples, domestic shrines and tombstones. One workshop at Lanchester, in Durham, produced at least 50 altars which have been identified in forts and civilian settlements across the Pennines in the north-west. Another workshop at Carlisle concentrated on the production of tombstones.

A specialised craft was the carving of shale – a soft, flaky stone resembling slate that was quarried and worked mainly around Kimmeridge, in Dorset. Shale was used to make arms and legs for couches and chairs, and three-legged, round-topped tables. Shale workers also made trays, bowls and plates for the dining table, and rings, pins, bangles and spindle whorls. Most of the larger shale objects were made on a lathe, using a chisel-shaped flint as a cutting edge. Many of the shale workers' techniques were similar to those used by wood-turners – as were some of the products.

Decoration for a floor
The Romano-British house-owner could choose from a wide range of floor surfaces, but the most prestigious and the most expensive was the mosaic floor – comprising small cubes of stone, brick, tile, pottery or glass and laid by teams of workmen under the direction of a master craftsman. This floor, at Aldborough, North Yorkshire, is typical of the more simple geometric patterns that were produced to relatively standardised designs.

A Roman 'industrial estate'

In some towns, so many different crafts were carried on that the workshops formed a sort of industrial estate. At Camerton, a small town alongside the Fosse Way in Avon, craftsmen plied their different trades in long, one-roomed stone workshops at the roadside.

They included several blacksmiths, and a pewter manufacturer from whose workshop have come stone moulds for making dishes and saucepans. The Romans also used pewter to make jugs, flagons and large dinner-plates. Another Camerton workshop contained an oven of a type often used for malting, so there may also have been a brewery in the town. Possibly these craftsmen were working not for themselves, but for one or two wealthy landowners who employed them – or even owned them if they were slaves.

A similar settlement at Wilderspool, in Cheshire, embraced an even wider range of crafts and industries. Timber-framed workshops, each standing in its own yard, stretched for more than 300 yds on both sides of the road. Iron-workers, bronze and lead-workers, potters and glass-workers combined to create a scene that must have been one of indescribable noise, heat and near-confusion, shrouded in pungent smoke and lit by the leaping flames.

Some products of the glass-workers and the bronzesmiths of Wilderspool were used on the spot by local craftsmen, some of whom specialised in the manufacture of enamelled brooches. Raw materials for all these workers, and finished products ready for market, came and went on wagons or in boats and barges on the Mersey, which ran beside the settlement. As at Camerton, capitalist middlemen may have been behind the success of this industrial estate: fragments of stone columns and an elaborately carved capital discovered there must have come from a large building.

The settlements at Camerton and Wilderspool are typical examples of the immense impact made by the Romans on industry and crafts. For the first time, workshops were being concentrated in one place, their production organised, and a wide range of goods and raw materals turned out on a large scale. These commodities sold in new markets where buyers were brought together in unprecedented numbers, while the markets were linked to manufacturers by an efficient system of roads and waterways.

Britain remained an agricultural society for more than 1,400 years after the Romans left. But under Roman rule, workers in the more Romanised parts of Britain moved out of the peasant's hut and into the contemporary equivalent of the factory and industrial estate: they wrought, in their way, an industrial revolution.

CRAFTS FOR EXPORT

Jet from the beaches and dales of the north found its way to new markets throughout the Roman Empire

During the Bronze Age the families of local chieftains from northern Britain had sometimes been buried with elaborately carved jet necklaces. It was not until after the Roman conquest, however, that a flourishing jet craft developed in Yorkshire.

The industry probably centred on York itself, where the remains of at least one jet-worker's premises have been discovered. Most of the raw jet came from around Robin Hood's Bay near Whitby, but quantities were also found in the dales.

Jet was used primarily in jewellery – bangles, armlets, pins and rings. During the occupation the tradition of making jet necklaces was revived; Roman necklaces, which consisted of strings of spherical and oval beads, were, however, less elaborate than the prehistoric ones. Simple patterns or small pictures of a god were carved on some signet rings while some medallions, probably betrothal gifts, showed a man and a woman on one side and a device of intertwined hands on the other.

Warding off ill-fortune
Medusa medallions such as this were probably worn in Roman Britain as a protection from evil. One explanation for the popularity of jet as a material for jewellery was that it was thought to possess magic powers. It is a form of fossilised and water-worn wood, and like amber it becomes charged with electricity when rubbed.

Yorkshire craft
Relics of Romano-British jet workshops have been found within the walls of York. Jet from Whitby was not only sold in the markets of Roman Britain but also exported to the Rhineland. British jet was sufficiently well known in the 3rd century for the Roman writer Solinus to note its good quality. These pieces of jewellery are typical of the more popular items made from jet. Bangles, finger rings and necklaces composed of jet beads were worn by many well-dressed ladies in Roman Britain. Pins such as this one, carved with a grinning face, were rather scarcer. These products of Yorkshire craftsmen probably travelled to southern Britain packed into wool and linen shipments.

CHAPTER NINE

Religion and the after-life

The British pay homage to fierce Celtic war-gods and remote Roman divinities – but from the East come new faiths and new hope for life after death

Cult of Mithras the bull-slayer
Along with a pantheon of Greek and Roman gods, the invaders imported the Persian cult of Mithras – seen here slaying a bull – to areas of Britain where horned warrior gods and stone heads were still worshipped by the Celts.

Cult of the severed head
*The Druids take a sinister
prominence in comments by
Caesar and other Roman
writers on the Celtic religion.
Some Druidic rituals seem to
have involved human sacrifice,
and other fearful practices
related to the cult of the severed
head. There are few surviving
pictures of Druids, and little
material evidence of their
existence. A glimpse of a Druid
may, however, be discerned on
this bronze coin of the
Catuvellaunian king
Cunobelinus, who ruled much
of south-east England before
the Romans arrived. The
standing figure seems to be
holding a severed head – taken
perhaps from a sacrificial
victim. The barbaric rites in
which the Druids indulged,
rather than any threat posed by
their political power, probably
gave the Romans the motive for
taking ruthless action against
them. Another of the Druids'
methods of appealing to their
gods was to burn a victim alive
in a man-shaped wicker-work
cage.*

AVING CONSIDERED THE GREAT STONE CIRCLES AT STONEHENGE AND AVEBURY, THE 17TH-CENTURY ANTI-quarian John Aubrey pronounced that there was 'clear evidence' that the monuments were pagan temples, probably the 'Temples of the Druids'. It was Aubrey's statement that gave rise to the widely held conviction that Stonehenge was the centre of the Druidic cult that held Britain in its grip at the time of Julius Caesar's invasion.

In fact, there is no evidence connecting either monument with the Druids. Built some 4,000 years ago, their purpose was accomplished long before the arrival of either Caesar or the Druids. There is little doubt, however, that the Druids played an important role in the religious life of the Celts, though what this role was can only be pieced together from a few scraps of information gleaned from Roman writers and from much later evidence in Irish literature.

From these varied sources it seems that the Druid priests practised magic and rituals that took many years to learn, and officiated at the sacrifice of both human and animal victims. Portraits of these awesome and powerful figures are of course rare, but one scene that may include a Druid appears on the reverse of a coin minted by the British king Cunobelinus. This depicts an altar, beside which stands a priest gripping a severed head, probably that of a sacrificial victim.

A gentler ritual, as described by the Roman author Pliny, tells how white-robed Druids climbed oak trees and cut ceremonial sprigs of mistletoe with a golden sickle. The oak was sacred to the Druids, and mistletoe was a magical antidote to all poisons. Many trees, it seems, were sacred to the Celts; early Irish literature refers to the sanctity of ash and yew, while Tacitus, in describing the attack on Anglesey by the Roman Governor Suetonius Paulinus, tells of sacred Druidic groves on the island. The Roman names for Buxton, Willoughby, in Nottinghamshire, and North Tawton in Devon contain elements recalling sacred groves, and dedications found at Nettleham, near Lincoln, and at Bath imply the nearby presence of further sites.

Springs and rivers also figured in the religion of the Celts. The healing springs at Bath and Buxton were both holy places, and Celtic warriors appear to have cast valuable arms and equipment into the River Thames as offerings to the gods who dwelt there. The Celtic river goddesses Deva and Sabrina are remembered in the river names of Dee and Severn, and close to the stern walls of Carrawburgh fort on Hadrian's Wall there are wells rather charmingly dedicated to water nymphs, and to Coventina, a local female deity, whose sacred spring still bubbles up into its stone tank.

Horned god of war
The Celts worshipped their horned warrior god under many different names in different parts of the island. This relief from Maryport, in Cumbria, is one of a group of finds from the north-west which show the god, known locally as Belatucadros. His shield and spear suggest the warrior, but other attributes emphasise fertility.

As a general rule, the Roman civic and military authorities were fairly tolerant of the religious practices of the peoples they conquered, but the Druids they stamped upon with unwonted ferocity. The priesthood was almost certainly behind the tough Welsh resistance movement, and was probably responsible, too, for the sacrificial deaths of Roman veterans and citizens at Colchester in AD 60, during Boudicca's revolt. But once the power of the Druids had been broken, the Romans reverted to their usual policy of religious toleration – of assimilating, if possible, the gods of conquered territories into their own religious system. This is why the gods of groves, springs, rivers and wells continued to be worshipped during the Roman occupation.

The crowded heavens

The Romans themselves worshipped many gods, but even they must have been astonished by the number of gods and goddesses in the Celtic world. Surviving inscriptions give the names of more than 50 native gods; most of them appear to have been very localised, though it is likely that there were four or five deities that were worshipped under many different names in different parts of the country. Inscriptions show, for example, that the Britons were able to identify some 20 male deities with the Roman Mars. Some, like Toutatis and Camulos, were probably worshipped over a wide area, but others, such as Belatucadros and Cocidius, were known only within a small neighbourhood – in their cases, the vicinity of Hadrian's Wall. The mention of these gods in Roman inscriptions confirms that the imperial government made no attempt to suppress these native cults.

It is not surprising, therefore, that Romano-Celtic temples were often built over the remains of Iron Age sanctuaries – there are examples at Harlow, at Frilford in Oxfordshire, and at Hayling Island. At Hayling Island the pre-Roman shrine was a round timber hut: the circular shrine was retained under the occupation, but rebuilt in stone and given double enclosing walls, an impressive entrance porch, a painted interior and a tiled floor.

Most of the British temples of Roman times consisted of circular, square or polygonal shrines surrounded by either a veranda or a covered cloister of similar shape. The walls of the shrine were generally painted, the floors sometimes laid with mosaic, and in some cases, the entrances were flanked by imposing columns. More than 50 temples of this type have been found, both in towns and at isolated places deep in the countryside.

Although the shrines of Roman Britain were inspired by pre-Roman patterns, their new façades gave them an air that was not at all out of place among the smart town buildings, or even the country villas. By the same token, the gods worshipped in them were a fusion of both Classical and Celtic deities. At the temple at Nettleton in Wiltshire, for instance, was an altar dedicated to 'Apollo-Cunomaglus'. Since Apollo was the Roman sun-god, Cunomaglus was presumably his local Celtic equivalent. The Roman war-god Mars appears in different parts of Britain as Mars-Toutatis, Mars-Alator, and Mars-Lenus, and the woodland god Silvanus as Silvanus-Callirius. One of the temples found at Brigstock in Northamptonshire was probably dedicated to the local wargod Mars-Corotiacus, for four bronze statuettes of him –

A god of the Wall
This rather dumpy little deity is Cocidius, one of the native gods worshipped in the area around Hadrian's Wall. Unusually, he is not only pictured on this silver plaque from Bewcastle, in Cumbria, but also named in the inscription punched on the bottom of the piece. He seems to be wearing an armoured corselet, holding a spear in one hand and resting the other on the rim of his shield. This and a similar plaque showing the same god probably decorated ritual furniture in a shrine dedicated to Cocidius.

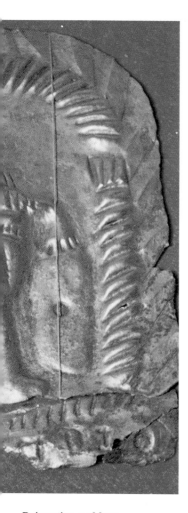

Brigantian goddess
Another sturdy figure, though much more sophisticated in its execution, is the goddess on the right. She is Brigantia, personification of the powerful tribe of the Brigantes, who occupied much of northern England. It is significant that at the time of the conquest the tribe was ruled by a queen, Cartimandua. The carving clearly demonstrates Roman influence in its style: the posture and dress of the goddess are Classical, and she was equated with the Roman deity Minerva, and Victory

represented as a Celtic warrior mounted on a horse – were discovered there.

In most places, however, the statues and religious symbols that have survived identify only the Roman god and not his Celtic counterpart. The temple site at Gosbecks near Colchester, which had been a holy place to the British before the Romans came, can only be identified with Mercury, of whom a superb 21 in. high bronze statue was found. It is not known which Celtic god was equated here with Mercury and shared his shrine.

More than one Roman god might share a shrine with a Celtic divinity: a temple dedicated to Mercury at Uley in Gloucestershire also contained a bust of Jupiter, foremost of the Roman gods. At a temple at Bruton in Somerset were found bronze statuettes of Hercules, Minerva and Mercury, and one of the Silchester temples is believed to have held statues of Peace, Victory and Mars. These cheerful combinations clearly demonstrate the Roman authorities' easy-going attitude towards the native Celtic religions. In a single small shrine, a Briton could worship not only the gods of his ancestors but also four or five different Roman divinities.

In the presence of the gods

Excavations at temple sites give some idea of Romano-British religious ritual. It was, it seems, customary at some shrines for a worshipper to drop copper coins along the path leading to the temple, as offerings to the spirits of the place. At the door he was met by a robed priest, whose brows bore a bronze or silver diadem, and beyond whom lay the dim and mysterious interior of the shrine. To the rear of the temple, almost lost in the smoky darkness, were the statues of the god, before which stood an altar on which offerings were laid. In pre-Roman days supplicants brought swords, spears and horse-trappings for the god: but after the invasion, small figurines, miniature pots, bronze jewellery, or a live sheep or goat were more usual. The offerings were later removed and either stored in a repository or buried in the temple precincts. At Uley, Gloucestershire, were found 150,000 animal bones, most of them from sacrificed sheep and goats.

Some offerings were made in a less generous spirit. These were the 'curse tablets' – rolled up sheets of lead on which were scratched invocations of divine wrath upon some enemy. Generally, the curses were aimed at a rival in love, in a lawsuit, or at the games. One dolorous lover seems to have covered most of his acquaintances in a curse found at Bath: 'May he who carried off Vilbia

A curse invoked
Curses are called down on the heads of several people suspected of trifling with a loved one's affections, in this appeal for retribution from on high found in the temple of Sulis-Minerva at Bath. The words are lightly incised on a small piece of lead – one of several such personal invocations that have been discovered. Poorly written and often difficult to translate, they were left in the shrines of the god or goddess whose help was being so ardently sought.

from me become as liquid as water. May she who obscenely devoured her become dumb. Whether Velvimna, Exsuperus, Verianus, Severinus, Augustalis, Comitianus, Catusmimanus, Gemanilla or Jovina.' On the other hand, one Sylvanus who had a ring stolen from him seems to have been quite certain of the culprit when he left a curse tablet at the temple at Lydney, Gloucestershire: 'Among those who are called Senicianus do not allow health, until he brings the ring to the temple of Nodens.'

Nodens was a Celtic god closely related to the Irish hunting god Nuada. His splendid temple overlooking the Severn was furnished with mosaics, altars and bronzes whose nautical motifs suggest he was associated with seafaring. The hundreds of offerings found at the temple, however, included a dozen model dogs, 300 pins and bracelets, an oculist's identification stamp, and a model of an arm. These gifts to the god indicate that Nodens was thought to add healing to his other powers, for in Classical religion dogs are commonly associated with healing. The model arm was meant to indicate to the god the location of the sufferer's ailment; perhaps he was seeking relief from rheumatism.

The Lydney temple obviously had a considerable reputation as a faith-healing centre. Beside the shrine was a guest house with an impressive entrance hall, central courtyard, principal dining-room and suites of bedrooms, clearly meant to accommodate large numbers of visitors. Close by stood a fully equipped bath-house, while behind the temple ran a long, narrow building with about a

A temple survives
Classical Roman temples were probably more numerous in Britain than their scanty remains would suggest. A podium – the platform upon which the building and its surrounding colonnade were built – has been found at Colchester, St Albans, Wroxeter and Bath, but only fragments of the temples have survived. Originally all would have looked something like the building on the left – the so-called 'Maison Carree' at Nîmes in France. This almost miraculously preserved temple dates from 16 BC, when it was raised as a tribute to Rome and Augustus.

259

dozen small rooms linked by a veranda. These rooms were probably let to pilgrims seeking cures so that the god might continue to exercise his healing powers upon them while they slept.

At Springhead in Kent and Nettleton in Wiltshire groups of shrines were surrounded by shops and other buildings, forming small settlements that depended for their livelihood on a steady flow of pilgrims. These settlements and other isolated temples may also have been the scene of country fairs and markets on certain days of the year. One major fairground is now occupied by Gosbeck's Farm, near Colchester, where the temple of Mercury was surrounded by an enclosure more than 100 yds square, while baths, accommodation for visitors, a market place and a theatre stood near by.

God and Mammon

Bath is the supreme British example of a town that grew up as the centre of a popular religious cult and became rich by supplying services to pilgrims. Within the town's 25 acres were the temple precinct of the presiding goddess, Sulis-Minerva, a number of other places of worship, at least two large public buildings and three bathing establishments, including the vast hot baths fed by underground springs. One of the public buildings was probably a theatre; temples and theatres were often associated in the Roman world since many dramatic performances were based on a religious theme.

To serve all these buildings there were priests, attendants, slaves and officials, all of whom must have lived within the town walls. There were hostels and inns, and for the many pilgrims there were shops where they could buy offerings for dedication in the temples. Although the surrounding villas no doubt sold much of their produce to the people of Bath and to its inn-keepers, the town can hardly have served as a market in the usual sense. There is no trace of a forum or market square, and there would have been little space for one; the central area which in most Roman towns was occupied by a forum was here completely dominated by the baths, theatre and the principal temple.

The public baths were built in the late 1st century AD and developed and expanded in later years, providing a luxurious range of turkish and sauna baths, including hot and cold mineral-water bathing. The focus was the great hot swimming bath, more than 60 ft long, 30 ft wide and 5 ft deep. It was lined entirely with Mendip lead, and fed with mineral water from a warm spring enclosed within an adjoining reservoir. This supplied water naturally heated to some 120°F, at a rate of about 250,000 gallons a day. Many of those who

Homage to Isis
This Herculaneum wall-painting depicts a scene in a temple dedicated to the Egyptian goddess Isis, whose worship was one of the many foreign cults enthusiastically adopted by the Romans. It is known that a temple to Isis was established in London,

lay in the arcade around the great bath, or swam in its waters, were there not for pleasure but in the hope of being cured of whatever ailed them. Apart from bathing in the spa waters, the pilgrims made divine help doubly sure by throwing offerings into the bath and reservoir as well. Coins, jewellery, gemstones and pewter cups, dishes and flagons have been found in both places.

Homage to Sulis-Minerva

The presiding goddess of Bath to whom all these offerings were made was Sulis-Minerva – a combination of Minerva, the Roman goddess of healing, with Sulis, her native Celtic counterpart. It was to Sulis-Minerva that the great temple next to the baths was dedicated.

This stood within a double-walled enclosure and was fronted by a large open-air altar, the corners of which bore carvings of gods and goddesses, including Apollo, Bacchus and Jupiter. The temple was not built to the usual Romano-Celtic design, but copied Classical temples, with a raised platform approached by a broad flight of steps. On this stood the *cella*, or shrine, with a columned porch or portico. Above the 26 ft high portico was a sculpture of two winged figures representing Victory, and flanked by half-human sea creatures, holding aloft the shield of Minerva, decorated with the head of the Gorgon. But this Gorgon is not the female head of Classical mythology, but that of a fearsome Celt, adorned with luxuriant moustache and flowing hair.

Within the temple was a near life-size gilded bronze statue of Sulis-Minerva, whose head is now in the Bath museum. Religious ceremonies within and without the shrine were conducted by priests, one of whom, Gaius Calpurnius Receptus, lived to the age of 75, and was buried just outside the town by his wife Calpurnia. Bath was a sufficiently important cult centre to have such resident soothsayers as Marcius Memor, whose task it was to ensure that the animals offered for sacrifice were of a suitable standard, and to interpret omens.

Emperors divine

The best known Classical temple in Britain, however, was not that of Sulis-Minerva at Bath, but the temple of Emperor Claudius at Colchester, whose massive, vaulted platform was later incorporated into the great Norman castle. It is still possible to visit the Roman

perhaps as early as the 1st century AD. Since her cult had a particular appeal to women, her worshippers would have included the wives of soldiers, officials and merchants from the East; the rites they participated in were extremely complex, and older than Egyptian civilisation itself.

261

vaults beneath the spot where the legionary veterans made their forlorn stand against Boudicca. Since Claudius's divinity was not declared until after his death in AD 54, the building could have been only just completed when Boudicca's warriors slew the last of the defenders in AD 60.

All the same, Colchester probably remained the centre of emperor-worship throughout the occupation, though the honour had its drawbacks since the town was expected to provide a regular annual programme of festivals and games. These were paid for partly by the tribe in whose territory the cult centre lay, and partly by the *Seviri augustales* – wealthy merchants or landowners elected for a year to the priesthood.

Emperor-worship was observed throughout the Empire and was one of its most powerful unifying forces. Most emperors were declared to be gods after death, but the cult also incorporated the worship of the *numen*, the spiritual power of the living emperor, to which the people of the Empire could offer prayers and material goods as expressions of their devotion to the current occupant of the imperial throne. Emperor-worship was especially encouraged among the troops. An example of a public declaration of loyalty comes from the legionary fortress at Caerleon:

> 'To the Deities of the Emperors and the Genius of the Second Legion Augusta, in honour of the Eagle, the senior centurion gave this gift: dedicated on September 23 in the consulship of Peregrinus and Aemilianus, under the charge of Ursus Actarius of the same legion.'

September 23 was the birthday of Augustus, the first and most revered of all the deified emperors, and therefore a particularly auspicious day for the centurion to make his offering.

'Jupiter, best and greatest'

The army, recruited as it was from all parts of the Empire, brought many new gods to Britain, but officially at least the legions owed their chief devotion to Jupiter. New altars were dedicated to Jupiter Optimus Maximus ('the Best and Greatest') each New Year's Day, the old altars being ritually buried at the edge of the parade ground. The inscription on one of these discarded altars, found with 16 others in pits outside the fort at Maryport in Cumbria, records that it was set up when the garrison, the First Cohort of Spaniards, was commanded by Marcus Maenius Agrippa, an officer who progressed from this small auxiliary fort to become admiral of the British fleet and procurator of the province.

Messenger of the gods
This fine bronze figure of fleet-footed Mercury was found close by the Romano-Celtic temple at Gosbecks, near Colchester.

Mighty Jupiter
Jupiter, or Jove, first god of the Roman pantheon, would certainly have been worshipped in the coloniae and larger towns of Roman Britain. This miniature of Jove with his thunderbolt was found at Colchester.

God of war
Mars was popular both with the legions and with the Britons, who equated him with their own Celtic war gods. In northern Britain, his cult may have provided a sympathetic link between the natives and the occupying power. Further south, a number of temples were dedicated jointly to Mars and one or other of his local equivalents.

263

The troops, and in particular the officers, were no doubt largely responsible for introducing Roman gods to the British, though there is little evidence of any sudden mass conversions. In their hearts the Britons still clung to the gods of their ancestors. It is true that more than 70 mosaics in Romano-British houses depict Roman deities; indeed some, like the mosaic of the gods and seasons from Pitney villa in Somerset, show as many as a dozen in a single design. However, it is likely that their purpose was not to demonstrate the piety of the villa-owner, but to provide an attractive and stimulating conversation-piece in the dining-room. Similarly, the stone sculptures of Roman gods and goddesses that graced the living-rooms of the more sumptuous villas and town houses were probably regarded more as fashionable decorations rather than objects of veneration.

The worship of Classical gods in Britain was probably a public, rather than a personal, gesture. Better-off communities expressed their acceptance of the Roman way of life by building and dedicating a temple to one of the major gods of the Roman pantheon, or to the triad whose temple stood on the Capitoline Hill in Rome – Jupiter, Juno and Minerva. Such temples, dedicated to Classical gods alone, stood in St Albans, Wroxeter and Chichester, and probably in other towns as well. In cosmopolitan towns like London, and in the *coloniae* where army veterans were settled, a high proportion of the population were of Mediterranean origin, and groups of citizens there appear to have formed guilds to foster the worship of one or other of the Classical gods. Otherwise, it was in the ranks of the legions that the gods of Rome found their most faithful adherents.

The bull of Mithras

Many of the auxiliaries worshipped very different gods and brought them to the bleak island shores from their far-off sunny homelands. At Corbridge, dedications were made to Hercules of Tyre and to Astarte, of Phoenician origin, while at Carvoran a group of Syrian archers set up an altar to 'The Syrian Goddess'. An inscribed jug found in London shows that a temple there was dedicated to the Egyptian goddess Isis; originally, she may have been introduced to Britain by soldiers stationed in the Cripplegate fort, by civilians of the imperial administration, or by merchants from the eastern Mediterranean. A second Egyptian god, Serapis, may have also had a temple in London, and an inscription shows that a temple to him stood in the *colonia* at York.

A cult from Egypt
The scratches on this 1st-century jug read Londini ad fanum Isidis – *'London, by the temple to Isis'. It is the earliest-known reference to the cult of the Egyptian goddess in Britain.*

Soldiers' guardian
The cult of Mithras, Persian god of light, had many adherents among the troops of the western empire, and about a dozen temples were raised to him in Britain. This bust of the god, wearing his traditional Phrygian cap, comes from his temple in London.

Serapis the bountiful
*Among the relics concealed
beneath the temple of Mithras
in London was this handsome
representation of Serapis,
Egyptian god of fertility, whose
role is symbolised by the corn
measure on his head. Though
the head was found in London,
the only known temple to
Serapis was in York.*

But the cult that found the greatest favour with the army, transcending sometimes even that of the gods of Rome, was the worship of Mithras. Mithras was the Persian god of light and truth, and was introduced to Britain and the other western provinces by the forces of occupation. The cult encouraged physical and moral strength in its followers, and excluded women – all features that might have appealed to soldiers who were not permitted to marry before the conclusion of their 25 years' service. Five Mithraic temples have been found in Britain – four near the forts at Caernarfon, Housesteads, Rudchester and Carrawburgh, and the fifth the famous London temple, which may have been supported by troops of the Cripplegate garrison. Evidence, principally inscriptions and sculptures, suggests there may have been at least seven or eight other temples to Mithras in the province.

Membership of a Mithraic temple was usually confined to some 20 or 30 initiates, divided into seven grades, of which the names of six are known – the Raven, the Lion, the Soldier, the Bride, the Persian and the Father. Initiation into each successive grade was determined by tests of courage and endurance, all of which took place within the shadowed secrecy of the temple. This was usually a small building with a minimum of light and ventilation, sunk a little into the ground to represent the cave where Mithras slew the sacrificial bull – the central symbolic act of the cult.

The temples were built to a common design. Beyond an antechamber was the sanctuary, divided into a central nave flanked by two low benches. At the far end, a recess contained a sculpture of Mithras slaying the bull, and altars dedicated by members of the cult stood before it. One such temple at Carrawburgh, is sufficiently well preserved to conjure up a picture of the initiation ceremonies that took place there.

The members of the temple used to arrive in twos and threes, wrapped in their cloaks to keep out the chill wind that gusted around the foot of the slope on which the fort stood. Inside the antechamber they put on the masks of their grades, and awaited the arrival of the novice and his sponsors. Once the whole company was assembled, the initiate was taken through the oath that bound him never to reveal the rites and ceremonies of the cult.

Before he could be admitted to the sanctuary, the novice had to prove that his courage was worthy of the god. He was led to a 6 ft long pit next to the fireplace, and directed to lie down in it, as though in the grave. He was then covered with stone slabs and subjected to the heat of the fire and the cold of the pit.

Emerging as if from the tomb, the initiate was then escorted into the inner sanctuary. At first he could see little, for apart from

God of light
One of the altars at the Carrawburgh temple bore an image of Mithras, whose head was surmounted by a perforated crown. At some point in the ceremonies, a torch or lamp was passed behind the altar, giving the impression that the god was surrounded by a pulsating halo.

A secret kept
Though now open to the sky, the tiny temple of Mithras at Carrawburgh fort on Hadrian's Wall still retains something of its ancient mystery. Celebrants took part in rites that centred upon the group of altars at the far end. Since initiates were sworn to secrecy, many of the details of the rites are forever lost.

Birth of Mithras
According to his followers, Mithras was born on a rock at the time of the winter solstice and was armed with a sword and a torch at birth. He fought to deliver the world from evil and achieved salvation for humanity by slaying a bull whose life-blood fertilised the Earth. In his battle against evil, he came to epitomise both moral and physical courage, qualities that had a particular appeal to the professional soldiers of Rome. As can be seen from this sculpture, his cult absorbed other eastern religions; hence the zodiacal signs surrounding him.

one or two torches carried by members of the cult, the only light came from tiny windows set high in the roof. The place was silent – footfalls were muffled by the blanket of heather spread thickly on the floor – and in his nostrils was the sharp reek of pine cones burning on an altar at the far end of the room. As his eyes became accustomed to the gloom, he picked out, to his left and right, the statues of Cautes and Cautopates, the torch-bearing attendants of Mithras. Cautes held his torch upwards, representing light and dawn, while Cautopates held his torch towards the floor, signifying darkness and twilight.

Beyond the statues, members of the cult reclined on the benches flanking the nave, while at the far end three altars stood in line before a curtained recess. As the novice was led before the altars, the worshippers recited the Mithraic prayer that began:

'Thou shalt see a young god, fair of aspect with flaming locks, clad in white robe and scarlet cloak and having a crown of fire...'

True enough, for the altar on the left bore a relief of Mithras clothed in white and red, and crowned by a halo lit from behind by a flaming torch. As the new member was welcomed by his fellows and placed offerings on the altars, the curtains before him parted to reveal the sacred relief of the bull-slaying, from which an even more imposing representation of Mithras gazed out at his convert. Prayers and hymns followed, and the ceremony concluded with a ritual feast in which all members joined.

Unlike the temples serving the legionary forts, whose membership was entirely military, the Mithraic temple in London might also have included wealthy merchants and civilian administrators among its initiates. The London temple was not only much larger and more elaborate than that at Carrawburgh, but was also lavishly furnished with statues and sculptures. Apart from the customary relief of the bull-slaying, dedicated by a veteran of the Second Legion Augusta, contributions to the temple included a bust of Serapis, a superb head of Mithras, a seated statuette of Mercury, a head of Minerva, and a lively group depicting Bacchus and Pan. The number and quality of these objects show them to have been the offerings of men of substance.

During the 3rd century, the prestige of Mithras was considerably enhanced by his identification with Sol, the Invincible Sun God, who was also of Persian origin. The worship of Sol became increasingly popular with the Romans, and the Emperor Aurelian built a great temple to him in Rome in AD 274. The god left marks on the calendar that remain to this day; Sunday is named after him, and his birthday, December 25, is now celebrated as the birthday of

The coming of Christianity
By the 4th century, Christianity was spreading through the Empire, including Britain, its outermost province. It was at this time that a room in the villa at Lullingstone, Kent, seems to have been dedicated to

Christian worship. Wall-paintings may be portraits of the family who owned the villa; the one shown here probably depicts a deceased member, since the figure stands before curtains or a screen, which in Roman art symbolised death.

Christ. At Carrawburgh, the Mithraic temple was extended and rebuilt in the late 3rd century for the worship of the unified Mithras and Sol, and was reconstructed again a few years later after its destruction by raiders.

However, the cults of both Sol and Mithras were very soon to be eclipsed by the rise and official adoption of another eastern religion: Christianity. Christians appear to have been less tolerant of Mithraism than of other pagan cults of the Roman Empire, perhaps because it closely resembled the new religion both in its teachings and even in the architecture of its temples. All the Mithraic temples found so far show signs of desecration by Christians during the 4th century. That the London sculptures survived was due entirely to the devotees of the god who hid them beneath the temple floor. The temples at Rudchester and Caernarfon were both desecrated by the middle of the 4th century, while at Carrawburgh, the bull-slaying relief and the statue of Cautopates were smashed into fragments and Cautes was beheaded. By a remarkable reversal of fortunes, Christianity rose to a position of unprecedented power, while the followers of Mithras suffered persecution.

The rise of Christianity

Unlike the followers of the many other faiths of the Empire, the Christians accepted neither the divinity of the emperors, nor even their supreme authority in worldly matters. Their god ruled on earth as in heaven, and they had therefore long been persecuted as political subversives. The persecution was fairly sporadic, beginning when Nero made the Christians scapegoats for the great fire of Rome in AD 64, and ending in a bloodbath conducted by Galerius, the heir of Emperor Diocletian, early in the 4th century.

By this time a Christian community had been established in Britain for at least 100 years, for there are references to it in the writings of Tertullian and Origen in the early part of the 3rd century. The execution of St Alban, the first martyr in Britain, probably took place during Severus's persecutions in AD 209. However, in AD 313 Emperor Constantine issued the Edict of Milan, giving the Christians freedom of worship, and in 314, British bishops attended the Council of the Church at Arles.

When Constantine was himself converted, Christianity became the official religion of the Roman Empire, and by about AD 375, despite setbacks, it had emerged as the Empire's leading faith. At the end of the 4th century, Emperor Theodosius banned pagan worship and closed all pagan temples.

Devotions public and private

The British clergy who went to Arles in AD 314 probably came from the four provincial capitals that had by then been established in Britain – York, London, Lincoln and Cirencester. Almost certainly, Christian churches had been established in all these towns by that date, though so far no trace of their buildings has been discovered. Remains of what may have been churches have been found at Silchester, St Albans and within the shore fort of Richborough. The Silchester building, incorporating vestibule, nave, aisles, transepts and apse, bears the closest resemblance to the modern notion of a church, and though no Christian symbols or objects were found there, its overall design leaves little doubt that this is the place where local Christians worshipped.

Within the remains of the villa at Lullingstone, Kent, are those of a private Christian chapel. The family and their friends came to the chapel by way of an antechamber, on whose wall was a wreath enclosing the *Chi-Rho* monogram, the first two letters of Christ's name in the Greek alphabet, and flanked by the letters *Alpha* and *Omega* ('the Beginning and the End'). On one wall of the chapel itself were six full-length portraits, of which three stood with their arms outstretched, in the early Christian attitude of prayer. One of the figures was shown standing in front of curtains, indicating that the person depicted had died.

No doubt many similar chapels were built elsewhere in the province during the 4th century, as more and more wealthy Britons

Symbol of Christ
On a chapel wall in the villa at Lullingstone, the Chi-Rho *monogram – the first two letters of Christ's name in Greek – is flanked by* Alpha *and* Omega, *the beginning and the end.*

Christian treasure
This selection from the hoard of Christian silverware found at Water Newton, Cambridgeshire, includes a chalice, a wine strainer, a flask and bowl, and plaques bearing the Chi-Rho *symbol.*

A Roman Christ

Portraits of Christ surviving from the early Christian era are rare, and this is the only one so far identified in Britain. Set in the centre of a mosaic floor in the villa at Hinton St Mary, Dorset, and backed by the Chi-Rho *symbol, this was a public declaration of faith by the villa's owner, who obviously pictured Christ as a clean-shaven Roman.*

made public commitment to the new religion. In mosaics at the Dorset villas of Frampton and Hinton St Mary, the *Chi-Rho* monogram figures prominently. At the latter, it appears behind the portrait of a man who is probably to be identified as Christ, although he is dressed in the Roman fashion and is beardless – in contrast to the later, medieval ideal.

The mosaics at all three villas, including Lullingstone, also feature a scene from pagan mythology; that of the hero Bellerophon slaying the monster Chimaera. The scene was probably intended as an allegory of the triumph of good over evil. Similarly, the mosaics depicting Orpheus surrounded by animals that were popular in villas in the neighbourhood of Cirencester may have represented the idea of Christ as the good shepherd. The same symbol had been used by Christians in other parts of the Empire as long ago as the 2nd century.

The needle's eye

Apart from these expensive mosaics, there is other evidence, too, to suggest that the Christian Church in Britain had no lack of wealthy patrons. At Water Newton in Cambridgeshire, a hoard of silverware was found consisting of three wine-mixing bowls, two flagons, a wine strainer, a chalice, a circular dish, and 17 triangular plaques of the type once fixed to the walls of pagan temples to demonstrate the fulfilment of a vow. Seven of these plaques carried the *Chi-Rho* monogram, which also appeared on the bowls and strainer. Whether the silver was communion plate or not is uncertain, but there is no doubt that it was used in some form of Christian ceremonial, perhaps in commemoration of the Last Supper. At least two of the bowls were gifts – presumably made to a church. Inscriptions on one of them record that one was given by Innocentia and Viventia, and the other by Publianus.

Fine pewter ware of Christian origin has been unearthed in other parts of the country, some bearing the *Chi-Rho* monogram, and others the early Christian motif of a fish or with peacocks, which were symbols of immortality.

Evidence of Christian baptism in Roman Britain survives in a font in the church at Richborough, and in what may be a baptistry at Silchester. In addition, some 20 circular lead tanks have been found on Roman sites, large enough for a convert to stand in while water was poured over him; half a dozen bear prominent *Chi-Rho* monograms in relief on their sides. Some silver spoons and gold rings bearing not only the monogram but also brief inscriptions such as *Vivas in Deo* ('Live in God') and *Spes in Deo* ('Hope in God') may have been baptismal gifts.

The poorer brethren

Christianity began as a religion of the poor, and it is certain that not all British Christians were rich. It was surely poorer men and women who scratched *Chi-Rho* and *Alpha-Omega* symbols on the pots, tiles, pewter plates and cups and other everyday articles that

Coffin of a child
Wealthier Romano-Britons were buried in coffins of stone or lead, like this one found in the Minories, London. Intended for a young man whose idealised portrait appears on an enclosing stone sarcophagus, the coffin actually contained the bones of a boy of 11 or 12.

have come to light. Such finds have been made throughout Britain, and all the evidence indicates that Christianity was widespread socially and geographically by the 4th century. It is more difficult to judge how many Christians there were, though evidence that may throw light on this has been unearthed in a cemetery at Poundbury, just outside Dorchester in Dorset.

As many as 5,000 people are thought to have been buried in the Poundbury cemetery during the Roman period, mostly during the late 3rd and 4th centuries. The graves in one small group were haphazardly arranged and contained weapons or utensils for use in the after-life, which suggests that the people buried here were pagans. But most of the burials were laid out in ordered rows, and the bodies were oriented east–west and only very rarely accompanied by artefacts. All these were features of Christian rather than pagan burial – evidence that there was a large Christian community in Dorchester from the late 3rd century onwards.

Some bodies at Poundbury were buried in coffins lined with lead and filled with gypsum plaster. Roman coffins were commonly lead-lined, or even made entirely of lead, but the added precaution of using gypsum may indicate that Christian resurrection of the body was expected. The attempt to preserve the bodies at Poundbury was partly successful, for the hair was intact on the heads of several skeletons when they were disinterred in modern times – one woman still possessed two fine six-strand braids of brown hair. Other gypsum burials have been found at York, where one woman's auburn hair was so well preserved that it still held her jet hairpins in place. Another burial at York contained a strip of bone inscribed, 'Sister, hail, may you live in God', proof that there was a Christian community here, too.

Simple burial
The poor of the Roman era received short shrift after death, though in pagan times they were at least provided with a coin to pay for their passage over the Styx. Many burials contained no grave goods at all, as can be seen from this interment at Fishbourne.

Pomp and piety
Few provincial funerals could equal the grandeur of this one depicted on a Roman sarcophagus. Professional mourners and musicians drown the lamentations.

Last rites

All the popular religions of the Roman Empire agreed that proper burial of the body was important. The Christians wanted their bodies preserved for the Resurrection, while worshippers of the Classical gods were convinced that the souls of those who went unburied were left to wander aimlessly on the banks of the Styx for 100 years before being ferried across to Hades, the first stage on a journey that led, for the fortunate, to the Elysian Fields. Inevitably, therefore, Roman settlements of any size and permanency soon began to acquire large cemeteries.

The law laid down that all bodies had to be buried outside the town limits, so in Roman Britain cemeteries lined the principal roads out of the towns. A traveller leaving York for Tadcaster would immediately begin passing vaults and family cemeteries belonging to the wealthier members of York society such as Julia Velva, the legionary veterans Aeresius Saenus and Cresces, or the *decurion* (councillor) Flavius Bellator. Further along the road he would come to a large cemetery where the poorer townspeople were buried, where tombstones were rare and graves shallow and haphazardly arranged. In the countryside, every farmstead and villa estate seems to have had an area set aside for the burial of its dead: a walled family cemetery, such as the one at Litlington villa in Cambridgeshire, and mausoleums, like those at Keston and Lullingstone in Kent, were built and used by villa-owning families.

Since the Britons took so readily to Roman ways of burying the dead, it is likely that some adopted Roman funeral rites as well. Immediately after death, the deceased was loudly mourned by all present, in order to convince him of everyone's grief at his passing. He would then be laid out, either in his best clothes or in a shroud. Arrangements for his funeral and for the erection of his tombstone were inscribed on tablets and properly witnessed; the responsibility of carrying out his instructions rested with his heir.

If a man was concerned that his estate was too small to provide for a proper funeral, he would probably have joined one of the many burial clubs. These were often 'trade' clubs, restricted to people in a particular craft. The clubs had a social function, for their members met regularly to offer sacrifices and hold feasts; but their main purpose was to arrange for the burial of a member when he died. The expenses were met from entrance fees and subscriptions. Each burial club wrote its own rules, which commonly included 'exclusion clauses' for members who were in arrears with subscriptions or had committed suicide.

The face on the urn
Cremation was the most popular form of burial among the Belgic peoples of south-eastern Britain at the time of the Roman conquest, and continued to be practised

Two burial clubs are known to have existed in Britain, though there were certainly others. The club at Halton Chester on Hadrian's Wall was a guild of slaves, who could not possibly have afforded as individuals to pay for their funerals. The other, at Bath, was a guild of armourers who put up a tombstone to one of their colleagues, Julius Vitalis, who died after nine years' service in the Twentieth Legion.

The corpse was carried to the cemetery in a procession led by professional mourners and followed by the family, the heir and close friends. When the service was over, the body was disposed of. Cremation was most popular in the 1st and 2nd centuries, and burial in the 3rd and 4th. For cremations, a pyre was built at the cemetery and the body placed on top of it. The ashes were collected, and after being ritually purified or washed, they were put into an urn, or a leaden casket, and buried.

When the body was buried intact, the better-off families would choose a wooden or stone coffin lined with lead, or one made entirely of lead. These were very expensive, and were often richly ornamented with Medusa heads and lions to ward off evil, or with Bacchic scenes depicting the pleasures of the hereafter.

The articles buried with the dead display great confidence in the after-life. The deceased was sent on his way not only with food and drink for his journey, but also with favourite belongings, such as the gaming board and pieces left on top of a lead coffin in the vault at Lullingstone villa. The dead were generally provided with a coin to pay the ferryman Charon for their passage across the River Styx into Hades, and also with cakes to feed Cerberus, the guard-dog of the Underworld. Since it was believed that the traveller would have his hands full feeding Cerberus, the coin for Charon was usually placed in his mouth.

Immortality in stone

Richer folk, and those who had belonged to burial clubs, were commemorated by tombstones. These were generally of local stone and bore inscriptions which began with the formula 'To the Spirits of the departed'. This was followed by the name and age of the deceased, his profession or titles, and the name of the person who had raised the monument. Many tombstones carried a portrait, though this was rarely intended to be an accurate depiction of the departed; such tombstones were produced in quantity and kept as stock-in-trade by local masons. A mason working near a cavalry fort could safely produce a dozen tombstones showing a trooper riding

until the 3rd century. Often a household pot sufficed to hold the ashes. More elaborate urns such as this one, decorated with the portrait of a young girl, were comparatively rare. It may well have held her ashes.

down an enemy – a favourite theme for the memorials of cavalry-men. For civilian customers the masons could with equal confidence turn out the standard seated or standing frontal portrait, the head and shoulders bust, or the figure reclining on a couch, often with wine cup in hand.

In poor families there might be little in the way of a monument, although sometimes, in a pathetic attempt to provide a memorial, brief details of the deceased were written on the side of the funeral urn. At Ilchester, for example, a parent scratched 'for little Vrilucolus' on a child's urn. Frequently, the poorest classes could afford neither coffin nor tombstone, and for them, too, there was always the danger of gravediggers disturbing the corpse in order to make way for another burial. Disturbed skeletons found in some British cemeteries had clearly been thrown about while there was still tissue in place to hold them together. Paupers were probably buried in no more than a shroud or perhaps, if the body was contracted, in a sack. Even the poorest folk, however, were often accompanied by a few simple articles when they were buried – a bangle or a brooch, and a pot or two that, when found, sometimes still contain traces of the food left with the corpse.

After the burial, a funeral feast was held and offerings made to the earth goddess Ceres. People who had attended the funeral were regarded as having been touched by death and had to be ritually purified. Following the funeral there would be nine days of mourning, ending with a second feast and final sacrifices.

Thereafter it was intended that the dead should be left in peace; in fact, this did not always happen, for many tombs were robbed and desecrated, as in the cemetery at York where several of the richer tombs were broken into. A number of coffins at York were apparently re-used, the remains in them presumably being thrown away. The coffin provided by Septimius Lupianus for his wife Julia Victorina and their four-year-old son Constantius was found to contain only one skeleton, and that was of an adult male.

The evidence of death and burial throws a clearer light on the hearts and minds of the people of Roman Britain than all the majesty of Hadrian's Wall or the magnificence of Fishbourne Palace. No one can fail to be moved by the words of Quintus Fortis of York, who, when his beloved daughter Corellia died at the age of 13, had inscribed on her tombstone:

> 'You mysterious spirits of the departed ... who are sought by the paltry ashes and by the shade, the phantom of the body, after the brief light of life; I, the father of an innocent daughter, a pitiable victim of unfair hope, lament this, her final end.'

RIDDLE OF THE HEADLESS BURIALS

Celts venerated the head as the seat of the soul, and carved heads were used in rituals

It seems likely that Celts used human heads – particularly those of defeated enemies – as well as carved ones in their ceremonies: the Romans would undoubtedly have forbidden this practice, but there is evidence that the cult of the head continued to flourish. A few carved heads have been found inside temples, but it is uncertain whether there is any connection between the cult and the frequency of burials in which the head is either missing or separated from the body. At Guilden Morden, in Cambridgeshire, for example, two women and a man were found beheaded: one woman's head was at her feet; the other had her head placed in her lap.

Expressions in stone
Crude carvings of heads which are clearly not intended as portraits, but rather as stylised representations, have been found on many Roman sites, particularly in northern England. A good example is one from Corbridge, just south of Hadrian's Wall, which appears to show a male head with a healthy moustache. Most of these heads do not depict the neck or shoulders, and so they cannot be regarded as busts or fragments of larger statues. However, the two heads on this page are both from the south: the smoothly carved and rather pious looking, rounded face above comes from Eype, near Bridport, in Dorset; the forcefully carved, ferocious head on the left, teeth bared in a savage grimace, was found in the Forest of Dean.

CHAPTER TEN

The end of Roman Britain

As Rome crumbles, warriors from the Empire's fringes take over the land to create a new society. But Rome's legacy lives on . . .

Out of the ashes
The eroded, tree-grown defences of St Albans recall the slow decay of Roman Britain. But as the walls crumbled, the same era saw the resurrection of the Church, epitomised here in the 7th-century chapel at Bradwell-on-Sea.

THE DEMISE OF THE 400 YEAR PAX ROMANA, THE LONGEST PERIOD OF UNIFICATION THE WESTERN WORLD HAS EVER known, began slowly. From the middle of the 3rd century onwards, the garrison of the province of Britain was gradually weakened by the demand for troops on other frontiers and by the removal of units to support pretenders to the imperial throne. At the same time, its coasts were constantly threatened by raiders from the Low Countries, the Western Isles and Ireland who constantly probed for loopholes in the island's defences.

All the same, the Channel still preserved the country from the kind of concerted barbarian attacks that ravaged the eastern borders of Gaul. The 12 great forts that were built along the coast from Brancaster to Portchester – the forts of the Saxon Shore – kept Saxon and Frankish raiders at bay, while Hadrian's Wall secured the northern frontier. Even with a depleted garrison, the province was fairly safe – provided that its enemies never acted in unison.

However, in AD 367, this was precisely what happened. Whether through conspiracy or chance, north, south, east and west all suffered simultaneous and determined attacks; Scots and Attacotti swept across the Irish Sea, the Picts overran the Wall, and Saxons and Franks overwhelmed the coastal forts of the south and east. The province lay plump for the plucking. Its army was largely powerless before the invaders, and its once-warlike inhabitants, forbidden to carry arms for 300 years, were defenceless. Bands of escaped slaves and army deserters joined with the barbarians in a year-long bout of plunder and anarchy.

For the first time, the very fabric of Romanised life in Britain was threatened. Rome appointed three generals in quick succession in an attempt to save the province. The last of these, Theodosius, drove out the invaders, and as far as can be seen from the archaeological evidence, reorganised the defences of north and south, improved the fortifications of the towns and perhaps installed small permanent garrisons in them.

In Britain, outlying villas were in an especially hazardous position. They were almost impossible to defend, and appear to have suffered the most during the great raid of 367. Two villas on the navigable stretch of the River Avon near Bristol – easy targets for raiders from across the Irish Sea – were among those that came under attack. At King's Weston the west wing of the villa was burnt down; and at Brislington villa at least two rooms were destroyed by fire, and the bodies of four of its inhabitants were thrown down a well in the back yard. Further inland, the villas at Keynsham and Box were also fired, and three more skeletons were found in a well at North Wraxall in Wiltshire.

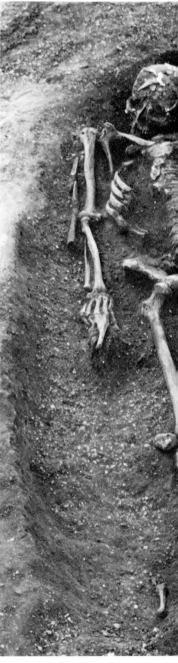

Armed for eternity
In the large and recently excavated Saxon cemetery at Berinsfield, Oxfordshire, lie the remains of a Saxon warrior. Probably in his

The villas decay

With further raids likely and security forces concentrated on the frontiers and the towns, wealthy landowners became less inclined to live in their villas or to spend money on maintaining them. Life was safer in the towns and most of the villas excavated so far show signs of gradual abandonment or decline in the last 30 years of the 4th century. At King's Weston and Keynsham, the buildings were re-occupied, presumably by squatters who built kitchen ovens in the once-elegant colonnaded verandas. At Painswick a room with a mosaic floor appears to have been used as a stable or cow-shed. The villa estates were still being farmed, and the villa houses were frequently still occupied, but living standards were fast declining.

Within the security of town walls, things were rather better and, as more and more rich villa owners crowded into them, some of the larger towns may even have enjoyed a temporary boom. At St Albans new houses were built after the terrors of 367, and where small garrisons were installed in towns, their regular pay helped to stimulate the local economy. The presence of professional soldiers is suggested by the projecting bastions built on to town defences in the late 4th century. If, as has been claimed, these were platforms for catapults, then such weapons required trained artillerymen for their operation and maintenance. The discovery of late 4th-century military-style buckles on the sites of towns, forts and villas may confirm the army's widespread role in the period. But these troops were no longer the regular forces of earlier days. These late reinforcements consisted largely of Germans recruited on – or beyond – the borders of the Empire, some of whom accepted military service in Britain in return for grants of land.

By AD 410 the last of the regular army had departed, and so too had the Roman administration. From now on, it seems, the British had to look to their own devices, both for defence and government. After about 402, no new imperial coinage entered Britain, and this drastically affected the economy. Four centuries of Roman rule had established a monetary value for every commodity, greasing the wheels of the imperial common market. But as money became more scarce, factories selling to anything more than local markets began to close down. The quality of local pottery declined, at first perhaps because of the lack of strong competition, and later because skills were gradually lost. No one made window-glass or mosaic floors any more, and even the techniques of building with stone and mortar were lost, as fewer British householders were able to pay for the maintenance of their Romanised homes.

twenties, he was covered by his shield before burial and his spears were laid beside him. Only the shield-boss and spear heads remain, the wooden parts having rotted away.

Grass in the streets

In some towns, the Roman system of local government was maintained at least until the mid-5th century. At St Albans, for instance, water mains were still being laid by the council at this time. But elsewhere it was a very different story. At Canterbury and Dorchester (Oxfordshire), small huts with timber walls, thatched roofs and sunken floors, very like those in Germanic settlements on the Continent, began to appear inside the Roman defences. There is no evidence of destruction or massacre, but rather the impression of gradual run-down.

Late 4th-century uniform buckles have also been found at Canterbury and Dorchester, reinforcing the impression that Germanic mercenaries and their families took over these communities gradually. They erected their own traditional kind of houses as the Roman buildings fell into disrepair, and grass and weeds forced their way up through the pavements. In Dorchester the huts were built along the edges of the old Roman streets.

Since public shows and public buildings such as the baths were already things of the past, the towns' roles as social centres also waned. No one knows how long Roman local government organisation lasted, but with the breakdown of central government and an increasing number of aliens settling both within and without the towns, such authority as councils still exercised must have grown ever more fragile.

Pestilence and famine brought the final curtain down upon a number of towns. Several late Roman writers refer to plagues in the western provinces in the 5th and 6th centuries, and the Venerable Bede, the English chronicler who wrote a history of the English church up to the early 8th century, says: 'Suddenly a terrible plague struck . . . and in a short while destroyed so large a number that the living could scarcely bury the dead' – a reference to an outbreak that took place shortly before AD 450. Perhaps the unburied skeletons found among the remains of Wroxeter, Cirencester and Caerwent are those of the victims of Bede's plague.

The Saxon tide

By the mid-5th century, the mercenaries and their families brought in by the Romans to bolster the defences of Britain late in the previous century had been joined by further waves of Germanic immigrants. Some were doubtless invited by the British to help

Pagan splendour
The dress of the Continental soldiers brought in to bolster Britain's defences in the late 4th century had little in common with the austere uniforms of the legions. Heavy bronze ornaments, like these found in Dorchester, seem to have been correct wear for these troops.

Churchman and chronicler
Much of what is known of Britain in the 5th and 6th centuries comes from the writings of the Venerable Bede (673–735). His history of the Church to 731 made him the first English historian.

282

them in their defence, while others came seeking new land to settle. Some of the Saxon settlements on the east coast, and especially those on the approaches to the Thames estuary, were almost certainly established in this way. In return for land the newcomers probably took on an obligation of military service, fighting for the local British rulers.

One such ruler was Vortigern, who ruled in Kent. It was he who brought in Saxons under the famous Hengist and Horsa – the first Saxons in Britain whose names are recorded. Where they settled is not known, but a Saxon settlement at Mucking overlooking the Thames estuary near Tilbury must have been very much like the one occupied by Hengist and Horsa's people. More than 100 Saxon huts and two Saxon cemeteries had been constructed at Mucking by around AD 400.

Saxon cemeteries dating from around the middle of the 5th century have been found scattered through the Thames Valley, East Anglia, Kent and the southern Midlands, all of which must have had settlements near by. Surprisingly, in the early days at least, there are few signs of hostility between the British and the newcomers. Initially Briton and Saxon seem to have peacefully co-existed;

frequently they lived in the same settlements and inter-married. Villa estates changed hands, but their fields continued to be cultivated, even while the villa buildings themselves fell into ruin.

The battle for Britain

Inevitably as more and more Saxons arrived in the late 5th century, Saxon land-hunger awoke British resentment and a dormant fighting spirit. The *Anglo-Saxon Chronicle*, compiled possibly in the 9th century from earlier sources, tells of many battles and many British defeats between 450 and 600. In 491, apparently, the Saxons Aelle and Cissa 'besieged Andredescester (Pevensey Castle in East Sussex) and slew all the inhabitants; there was not even one Briton left there'.

Further west, however, some of the British were swift to re-learn long-forgotten military skills, and in the south-west at least put up a spirited resistance until the second half of the 6th century. There, local leaders, called 'kings' in the *Anglo-Saxon Chronicle*, assumed the mantle of government. Bede names the most successful of them as Ambrosius, apparently a Roman of noble descent, who may or may not have been the Arthur of legend. Pre-Roman British hill-forts at Castle Dore in Cornwall (traditionally the capital of one of Arthur's contemporaries, King Mark), and at South Cadbury and Congresbury in Somerset were re-occupied in the late 5th century by Britons who wore Roman accoutrements, and who still managed to acquire wine and pottery from the Mediterranean.

All these places were massively re-fortified, and within the defences handsome timber buildings were erected. At South Cadbury a big rectangular hall about 65 ft long and half as broad was built at the centre of the fortified settlement, most probably as the home of the local chieftain. Later tradition unswervingly names him as King Arthur, and the site of his wooden hall as Camelot.

In this part of the country the British seem to have maintained their independence by reverting to living in hill-forts similar to those

Site of the last stand
Pevensey was one of the forts of the Saxon Shore built to defend the south and east coasts against pirates. Probably it was the last of these forts to hold out against the Saxon invaders; the Anglo-Saxon Chronicle *records that it fell in AD 491, and that not one of the defenders was left alive.*

Many-tower'd Camelot?
In the west, the hard-pressed Britons refurbished and reoccupied some of the old hill-forts. One such was South Cadbury fort in Somerset, persistently identified as Arthur's Camelot. Certainly it was occupied in the period traditionally associated with the hero.

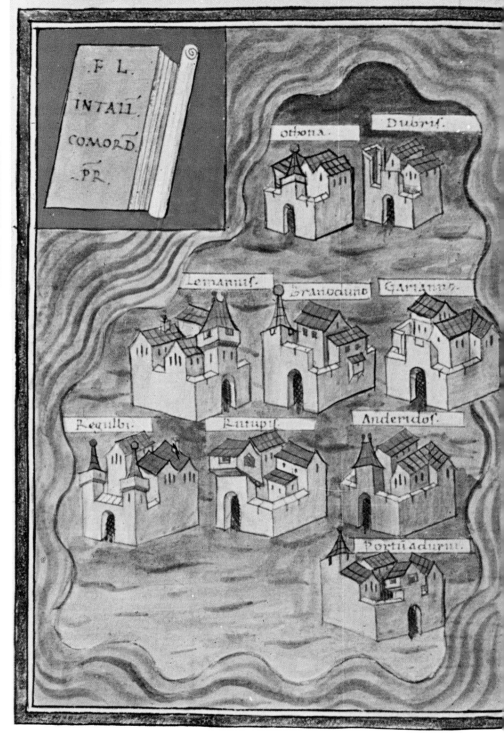

COMES LITORIS SAXON PER BRITANIAM.

Defence of the province
The Notitia Dignitatum, *a digest of civil and military returns compiled around AD 400, lists the various commands and units serving in the western Empire. It contains this delightful, if inaccurate, sketch map of the defences on Britain's south-east coast, with some Latin place-names unconventionally spelt. At the top of the map are Othona (Bradwell) and Dubris (Dover). Next come Lemanuis (Lympne), Branoduno (Brancaster) and Garriano (Burgh Castle). Beneath lie Regulbi (Reculver), Rutupis (Richborough) and Anderidos (Pevensey). By itself is Portuadurum, modern Portchester.*

285

abandoned by their ancestors' five centuries before. In the far west, the south-west peninsula and Wales, many of the ancient British villages and farmsteads remained for a time as untouched by the Saxons as they had been by the Romans. At Pant-y-Saer on Anglesey are the remains of a typical western homestead, consisting of two circular stone houses and some smaller rectangular sheds surrounded by a stone wall – no different in layout from others in the region that were occupied throughout the Roman period. But in one of the sheds, someone lost a fine silver brooch of 6th-century design in the mud of the floor, showing that the place was lived in a century or more after the Romans left.

Heirs of the Romans

By the early 6th century southern, eastern and central Britain had been widely settled by the Saxons, and their villages had multiplied. In the villages of Charlton in Hampshire, West Stow in Suffolk and Catholme in Staffordshire each family lived in a timber house or hall often more than 30 ft long. A strong timber frame supported walls of clay-daubed wattle and a thatched roof. Light and air were provided by a door in the middle of each long wall, and all the family's activities took place within the single large room. What privacy there was might be provided by a partitioned area at one end; but the women of the house did their cooking indoors on open hearths just to one side of the doorways. The jewellery they wore and the tools they used differed from those of the Romano-Britons. Equally unfamiliar were the newcomers' handmade pots and glass drinking beakers, but some of the other odds and ends they accumulated belonged to a Britain of a century or so earlier – Roman coins, keys and hair tweezers.

Around the house were grouped the farm buildings, perhaps an open-ended barn, a small granary for the barley; and two or three small workshops where wool was spun and woven, iron was forged and corn ground. The whole complex was surrounded by fences and ditches, separating it from its neighbours in a scene reminiscent of the days before the occupation.

The entire life-style of the people who lived in these villages was foreign to the British, and they were not yet Christians; but they were far from being the barbarians the Romans thought them. They had their own skills and crafts and their own political and economic systems which, as they settled down and mingled with the British, matured and developed to produce a culture and a landscape that were distinctively English.

Nearly full circle
In many respects, life in a Saxon settlement was akin to that in an Iron Age village on the eve of the Roman invasion some 400 years earlier. In both cases the settlements were small, and the buildings in them consisted of a mixture of living huts, workrooms and storerooms. However, as can be seen from these reconstructions at West Stow, the Saxons brought their own building styles and clever use of timbers. Constructed over a trough that acted as a damp course, the walls and floors of the huts were made of oak, and the rafters of ash. The thatched roofs were supported on hazel hurdling.

The legacy of Rome

In spite of the centuries of great change that followed the departure of the Romans, their occupation of Britain left a legacy that has survived to the present day. Some of this legacy Britain shares with the rest of the civilised world. Museum showcases contain not only Roman sculpture and painting, but also the excellent copies of Greek masterpieces made by Roman artists.

Latin literature kept the lamp of human knowledge alight through the dark years that followed the collapse of the Empire. The language itself was international, and formed the basis of modern French, Spanish, Italian and Portuguese; even in English, one word in three comes from Latin. It was a language that crossed all frontiers, enabling churchmen, doctors, men of law and scholars of all kinds to converse freely with one another.

That both the speech and literature of Rome survived was due in no small part to the tenacity of the Christian Church. Although Christianity was not Roman in origin, once adopted it was fiercely protected, and withstood the political upheavals of the 5th and 6th centuries. Even in remote parts of the Empire such as Britain, Christianity appears to have lived on throughout the so-called Dark Ages, and its traditions survived with it.

This legacy has a direct bearing on Britain, for among some of the earliest British writings known are those of Gildas, a Welsh priest of the 6th century, and the Venerable Bede (AD 673–735),

Saxon skills

The legend of the ale-swilling, sword-swinging Saxon plunderers, a people possessed of only the most rudimentary skills, dies hard. Yet from evidence gathered at early Saxon sites, it would seem that they were hard-working farmers and good craftsmen. A foot-operated lathe stands in a corner of a reconstructed hut at West Stow, Suffolk; metalworking, pottery making and weaving would also have been carried on in the village.

287

both of whom wrote in Latin. Without Bede's classic work – *A History of the English Church and People*, much of the islands' story would have been irretrievably lost.

Just as the Church survived, so too did some of the towns. What happened to them during the Saxon period is often uncertain, though some clearly suffered a serious decline and others were certainly abandoned. But evidence is accumulating to show that some towns, such as London, York and Canterbury, were occupied continuously from Roman times through to the present day. Other Roman towns enjoyed a prosperous rebirth in the Middle Ages.

Furthermore, the Roman impact on these towns is still visible. The present-day layout of, for example, Colchester, Cirencester and Exeter does not, it is true, duplicate the neat grid-system of the Roman town; but the High Street frequently lies over the principal Roman street, and the town's modern entrances and exits stand on the same sites as those of Roman times.

Beyond the gateways, where streets become roads, the Roman influence is even more apparent. Slowly, archaeologists and historians are piecing together the network of Roman roads which lie beneath many minor highways, and the major roads too, dozens of which have long been known to coincide with Roman trunk roads. On its journey from Seaton, near Exeter, to Lincoln, the Fosse Way often vanishes beneath farmland, and in one place an airfield, but it always triumphantly and variously reappears as the A358, the A37, the A429, the A46 and several other major roads. The A2 from Dover to London and the A5 from London to Shrewsbury are for most of their distance superimposed directly on Watling Street – laid out in the middle years of the 1st century AD to supply the Fourteenth Legion as it pushed westwards towards the Severn. Similarly, the line of advance of the Ninth Legion was also the line of Ermine Street, now partly overlaid by the A1 and A14.

The motorist constantly finds himself driving over the self-same roads along which the conquering legionaries marched 19 centuries ago. Occasionally, on the bleak moorlands of northern England, he might come across the exposed paving of a Roman road which has survived the modern roadbuilder's tarmac.

Standing today on these exposed stones the Roman legacy becomes visible, tangible, a living experience; and so it is throughout Britain. The life of Roman Britain is there to grasp and touch – the soldier's barracks, the townsman's temple and theatre, the landowner's villa, the peasant's hut. In museums are displayed the father's tool-kit, the mother's cosmetics, and the child's toys. The Romans have left as a legacy an immense wealth of material with which life in the first four centuries AD can be re-created.

Level 5

Level 6

Heavy iron set
(3¾ in.)

Level 7

Copper finger ring
(¾ in.)

Level 9

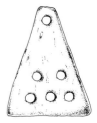

Bone pendant
(1½ in.)

Building up the picture
Tools and jewellery helped to re-create the life style and determine the occupations of the workers at Gatcombe,

Blue glass bead (¾ in.)

Bronze toilet tweezers (1½ in.)

Iron knife (5 in.)

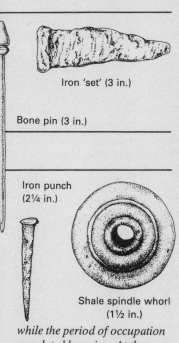
Iron 'set' (3 in.)

Bone pin (3 in.)

Iron punch (2¼ in.)

Shale spindle whorl (1½ in.)

while the period of occupation was dated by coins. At the lowest level, spindle whorls suggest wool working, while the iron tools above tell of a later metalworker.

EXPLORING A ROMAN WORKSHOP

As the Roman influence faded, so many of their buildings, great and small, fell into ruin and vanished beneath the turf, untouched for nearly 1,500 years until rediscovered by modern archaeologists. This section through a late 4th-century workshop at Gatcombe, near Bristol, shows how excavation revealed the progressive decay of the building. Beneath the modern turf level (**1**), lies soil (**2**) deposited over the centuries to cover the tumbled upper parts of the walls (**4**). At some time these had been disturbed by farmers in search of building stone (**3**). Under the rubble were successive levels of debris (**5–9**), among which were a hearth, a stone bench and a number of objects showing that the building had been a metalworker's shop for about a century. Finds beneath the flagstones (**9**) suggest that the building might earlier have seen brief service as a weaver's hut before the floor (**8**) was laid.

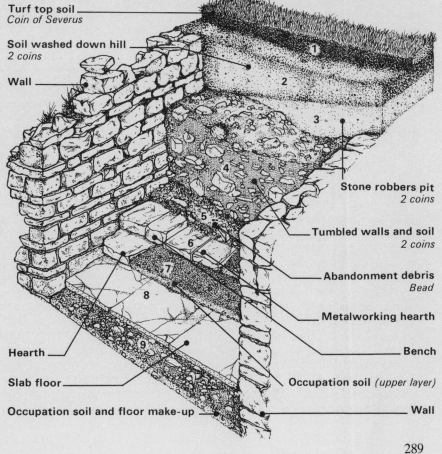

Turf top soil
Coin of Severus

Soil washed down hill
2 coins

Wall

Stone robbers pit
2 coins

Tumbled walls and soil
2 coins

Abandonment debris
Bead

Metalworking hearth

Hearth

Bench

Slab floor

Occupation soil *(upper layer)*

Occupation soil and floor make-up

Wall

Gazetteer of Roman Britain

Emperors and legionaries, merchants and craftsmen, sailors and slaves left their mark upon the province of Britain. How permanent *it was can be seen in this 2,000-year-old trail that leads down city streets, through museums and out to the wild moors and the ancient hills.*

Aldborough N. Yorks.
ISURIUM

The modern village of Aldborough was the capital of the tribe of the Brigantes. The Roman town was relatively small, covering about 55 acres, but it had a regular street system, a forum (market square), and four gates in its encircling walls. Earthen defences were superseded by masonry fortifications, of which a section can be seen near the south gate. The south-western defences are also well preserved, in the grounds of Aldborough manor house; there, the walls are still more than 8 ft high. Permission to view them should be sought at the manor house. Of the large number of square towers that formed key points in the defences only two remain.

Most of the Roman town's public buildings were uncovered during the 18th century. A number of fine mosaics were also found; two of those now on display at the site come from a private house. One depicts a lion-like animal under a tree, surrounded by patterned borders. The other is a highly ornate mosaic with two figures and the word 'Helicon' written in Greek; Mt Helicon, in Greece, was associated with the Muses of classical mythology. Another

mosaic from Aldborough is in the Kirkstall Abbey House Museum, which lies 3 miles north-west of Leeds. Aldborough lies 6 miles south-east of Ripon, 1 mile east of the A1.

Ambleside GALAVA Cumbria

Excavations at the Roman fort have revealed the remains of two gates, some angle towers and a central range of buildings which are identifiable from a plan on the site.

There are visible traces of stone structures dating from the 2nd century, but there was an earlier fort on the site, built of clay and timber. The remains of Galava lie at the northern end of Lake Windermere, 1 mile south of Ambleside.

Antonine Wall Strathclyde and Central

In AD 142 Emperor Antoninus Pius decided to shift the frontier of Roman Britain northwards from Hadrian's Wall. To mark the new frontier, he built a wall 37 miles long from Bridgeness on the Firth of Forth to Old Kilpatrick on the Firth of Clyde. The wall consisted of cut turves laid to a height of about 10 ft on a 14 ft thick stone foundation. A timber walk for patrolling

sentries ran along the top.

The Antonine Wall was garrisoned by cohorts of auxiliary troops stationed in 19 forts set at intervals of about 2 Roman miles. A few smaller fortlets and six signalling platforms have also been found along the wall. To the north of the wall was a ditch that in places was 43 ft wide and nearly 13 ft deep. Behind the wall to the south was a road linking the forts.

The Antonine Wall was occupied twice during its short strategic career. The first occupation lasted about 13 years, until troops were withdrawn to deal with a major uprising by British tribes further south. The wall was garrisoned again from about AD 160 to 163, shortly before the northernmost frontier was finally given up, possibly as a result of further unrest to the south.

As the wall was made only of turf, little of it has survived. The ditch, however, is still clearly visible, the most impressive stretch being at Watling Lodge, 1¼ miles west of Falkirk behind the trees on the south side of the road that runs south of the former Forth and Clyde canal. For the picturesque Tentfield Plantation stretch of the wall, continue west along this road and turn right at the next crossroads.

From here both ditch and wall can be followed for about 1 mile.

The most outstanding remains of the Antonine barrier lie 1 mile east of Bonnybridge, south of the Glasgow to Stirling railway line, and can be reached from Bonnybridge by crossing the canal southwards and taking the first turning on the left. The wall and ditch are visible half a mile along this road, beyond the railway line. At the car park, the wall is 5 ft high and in a better state of preservation than anywhere else; but here again it is the massive ditch that particularly catches the imagination. On the other side of a stream are the prominent earth ramparts that defended the small Roman fort of Rough Castle. Twenty yards to the north, just beyond the ditch, can be seen a series of the small rectangular pits that were once planted with pointed stakes and covered with brushwood, as traps to help break the momentum of any massed attack. Between the pits and the ditch would be the killing-ground, well within range of Roman artillery.

Other fine stretches of ditch can be followed on Croy Hill north of the village of Croy, which is 1 mile south-east of Kilsyth. Pieces of the wall's stone foundations can be seen in New Kilpatrick cemetery half a mile east of the A81 at Bearsden. In Bearsden itself can be viewed the remains of a Roman bath-house belonging to a fort. Another fort bath-house has been found at Cramond, a village 5 miles west of Edinburgh at the mouth of the River Almond. The fort here was an outlier east of the wall itself, and a plan of some of its buildings can be seen near the church.

Ardoch   *Tayside*

The first Roman fort at Ardoch was built by the Governor of Britain, Julius Agricola, during his campaign in Scotland in AD 84. It was abandoned, then reoccupied in the mid-2nd century. Most of the visible remains date from this reoccupation, when the fort was an outpost of the Antonine Wall.

The complex system of five concentric rings of defensive ditches around the fort makes it an impressive monument. The east gate and the causeway over the ditches outside it can also be seen. All around the fort are encampments for the armies led north by Agricola, and by Emperor Septimius Severus early in the 3rd century.

The Hunterian Museum at Glasgow University contains relics found at Ardoch, including the tombstone of a man belonging to a cohort of Spanish troops once stationed there.

Ardoch stands on the east side of the River Knaik at the village of Braco, 10 miles north of Stirling on the road to Crieff.

Aylesbury   *Bucks*.

The Buckinghamshire County Museum in Church Street contains a selection of finds from various villas, including those at Latimer and Hambleden, and examples of pottery from the kilns at Fulmer and Hedgerley.

The Hambleden finds include bronze brooches and iron tools, and those from Latimer a display of painted wall-plaster.

Baginton   *Warks*.

A Roman fort was constructed at Baginton after Boudicca's

rebellion of AD 60–61. It was occupied for only 15 years, during which time it was remodelled several times. For example, on the ground originally occupied by barracks a circular timber arena was later built, probably as a training ring for cavalry horses. The eastern defences were designed to curve around the arena.

The main feature of interest at Baginton today is a reconstruction of part of the defences undertaken by the Royal Engineers in 1970 using only equipment available to their Roman predecessors. This gives an accurate impression of a section of a Roman turf-and-timber rampart, with its great two-lane timber gateway. The outline of the barracks, the granaries and the headquarters building are marked out in concrete, and one granary has been reconstructed in its original form.

The village of Baginton is about 2½ miles south of Coventry, on the minor road to Coventry airport.

Bath AQUAE SULIS   *Avon*

The great complex of Roman baths at Bath has made it one of the best-known Roman towns in Europe. The presence of its natural springs, gushing water at 120°F (49°C), turned Bath into a major centre for medicinal bathing. The Romans adorned it with grandiose buildings on a scale matched only by those built during the rebirth of the spa in the 18th century.

Tombstones by the roadsides leading out of the town, as well as dedications to the gods found within its walls, indicate that the modern overseas tourist has

Roman forbears. The people who came to take the waters included a lady from Metz and a man from Trier, both in Gaul.

The Roman name means 'the waters of Sulis', the Celtic goddess of the springs. Originally, the town was less than 25 acres in area and commanded a vital bridging-point across the River Avon, in a valley where at least three pre-Roman settlements had existed. A small fragment of the Roman walls survives in the street called Upper Borough Walls. The north wall turned along the Avon near the Pulteney Bridge, and in an alleyway next to the market is a small medieval gate that lies over the Roman gate.

Many Roman town houses have been uncovered, but of their remains only the mosaics in the basement of the Royal Mineral Water Hospital can be visited. Other mosaics from the town are on show in the Roman Museum next to the baths.

Construction of the bathing complex began in the 1st century, and it continued to be used until the late 4th century. The baths were built around the Sacred Spring, which can still be seen today near the King's Bath that was once surrounded by an elegant colonnade.

The temple complex built to the glory of the goddess Sulis Minerva – a union of Sulis with the Roman goddess of health – was set on a podium, with its shrine behind an elaborate façade of four Corinthian-style columns supporting a decorative pediment. The pediment has survived, and takes pride of place in the Roman Museum; its central feature is a snake-haired figure with the Celtic features of staring eyes and a moustache.

Dominating the baths themselves was the Great Bath, which was a swimming pool. The huge lead-lined pool, fed by water from the hot springs, is remarkably well preserved. In Roman times the Great Bath, now open to the sky, had a vaulted roof of timber and tile supported by massive piers all round the edge of the pool.

Adjacent to the Great Bath are the cold room – the *frigidarium* – and a large open hall which allowed a clear view across to the temple precinct. Next to the hall were two steam baths, the *tepidarium* and *caldarium*, both of which are still visible. In the western bath-block was the *laconicum*, a circular chamber that provided dry heat. Much of the *laconicum* can still be seen.

The construction of these baths was a fine feat of engineering. The massive hypocaust system for heating water can still be seen at the western end of the baths, while in many places it is still possible to see the columns that supported the floors of the rooms, allowing hot air to circulate underneath. The drain that carried excess water off from the Great Bath was a great masonry structure with a deep plank-lined culvert. Many smaller channels can also be seen around the baths; one section still has some of the original lead piping in place. The Mendip mines were probably the main source of lead for the pipes and lining of the Great Bath.

Bath Roman Museum, Abbey Churchyard. This museum adjoins the baths. Besides the pediment depicting the snake-haired figure, the displays include a gilt bronze head of

Minerva. Sacrificial altars and tombstones discovered in other parts of the city are complemented by fine displays of jewellery, glass and pottery. There is also a lover's curse, inscribed on lead and found in the reservoir: the writer wishes a variety of fates on his many rivals for the affections of his lady.

Beckhampton   *Wilts.*

Near Beckhampton is a particularly well-preserved stretch of the Roman road that led from Bath to Silchester. The road crosses the Swindon to Devizes road about a mile south-west of its junction with the A4. It then runs eastwards across country to Silbury Hill from which, for the next mile, its course is followed by that of the A4.

The fact that it bends round Silbury Hill proved to the first scholars who studied the great artificial mound that it was of prehistoric date.

Benwell   *Tyne & Wear*
CONDERCUM

Benwell was the first major fort on Hadrian's Wall west of Newcastle upon Tyne. Still visible are the remains of a temple outside the fort walls where the garrison probably worshipped. The temple was dedicated to the god Anocticus or Antenociticus. Three altars were found on the site, and replicas have been placed where they stood.

The originals are in the Museum of Antiquities, The Quadrangle, Newcastle upon Tyne. Anocticus was a Celtic god, and a statue of him in the museum gives him a very Celtic appearance with large, staring eyes and snake-like hair.

The temple lies 2 miles west of the centre of Newcastle upon Tyne, just south of the Newcastle to Carlisle road.

Bignor *W. Sussex*

The Roman villa at Bignor is one of the largest and most thoroughly explored in Britain. Much of it is now maintained under modern huts erected on Roman foundations, and parts of one wing have been reconstructed.

The villa residence evolved from a timber cottage, constructed at the end of the 2nd century, into a stone-built house in its final 4th-century form. The superb mosaics on the floors of its rooms mainly depict mythical scenes such as the rape of Ganymede, cupids engaged in gladiatorial combat, the Four Seasons, and Venus masked. One mosaic worker immortalised himself by inscribing his initials – T.E.R. – on one of the mosaics.

Bignor lies 5 miles north of Arundel at the foot of the South Downs.

Binchester VINOVIA *Durham*

The fort was founded by the governor, Julius Agricola, in the 1st century. The north and east ramparts are still intact, but the most interesting of the Roman remains at Binchester is its hypocaust heating system which is the finest example to survive in Britain.

Eighty-eight columns of Roman tiles still hold up the original concrete floor. Many of these tiles bear the stamps of the cavalry unit that made them. The arches permitting the hot air to circulate beneath another room

still remain, as do many flue tiles. The hypocaust may also have heated the fort commander's bath-water.

Binchester fort is situated 1¼ miles north of Bishop Auckland on a hill above the River Wear. Directions to the site may be obtained at the bungalow opposite the farm at the top of the hill.

Birdoswald *Cumbria*
CAMBOGLANNA

Birdoswald fort on Hadrian's Wall is spectacularly situated above a gorge of the River Irthing. Its defences are very well preserved, especially on the north-west corner where they stand 6 ft high. Here, too, is a tower with 14 courses of masonry still intact.

The south gate still has pivot holes in its thresholds, and two guard chambers with cooking ovens. The east gate is even finer; it retains twin entrances with jambs and pivot holes, as well as part of the arch over one entrance.

Birdoswald lies on the north side of the River Irthing, 6 miles north-east of Brampton.

Bitterne CLAUSENTUM *Hants.*

On a projecting spur on the east bank of the River Itchen lie the remains of a Roman fort, built in the 1st century on the site of a port.

Visible at its western end are the foundations of a private bath-house with four rooms, built about AD 175. The building was altered several times before being demolished and replaced by another adjoining it, though this was never completed. Beyond this building lies a

fragment of the great masonry wall that cut off the spur. This is much overgrown, though Rampart Road near by marks the line of the vee-shaped ditch that lay in front of the wall.

Finds from Bitterne, including pottery, coins, tools, and pigs of Mendip lead, are on display in the God's House Tower Museum on Town Quay, Southampton.

To reach the fort, take the Portsmouth road from the centre of Southampton, and once across the Itchen turn off to Bitterne Manor House, a block of flats. The bath-house foundations are near by.

Blackstone Edge *W. Yorks.*

Scholarly battles are waged over the splendid paved road that climbs over the steep moorlands at Blackstone Edge. Some experts claim that it is medieval or even later in origin, but the more conventional view is that it is part of the Roman road that linked the fort at Manchester with the one at Ilkley on the far side of the Pennines. If so, it is the finest example of Roman road-making in Britain.

The road is 16 ft wide and paved with flagstones. A deep gully has been carved down the centre of the road at its steepest part, probably as a means of steadying the brake poles of laden wagons negotiating the descent. To judge from the ancient pathways worn into the moor near by, the gradient proved too steep for some travellers, who chose to zigzag their way uphill instead.

The road is visible as a green patch on the moors, about 2½ miles east of Littleborough, and can be reached by a path from the Rochdale to Halifax road.

Bowes LAVATRAE   *Durham*

Although a Norman castle and churchyard cover parts of the Roman fort here, it is still possible to see well-preserved sections of the rampart on the south and west sides.

Excavations have revealed that the turf rampart, built by the governor, Julius Agricola, in about AD 78, was superseded by a stone wall in the 2nd century. Wall foundations outside the ramparts are of a bath-house, datable from an inscription found on the site to the years 197–202.

The fort is 4 miles south-west of Barnard Castle and immediately west of Bowes village on the A66.

The Bowes Museum in Barnard Castle houses a shrine to a local god of hunting, as well as other finds from Lavatrae.

Brading   *Isle of Wight*

The villa at Brading is one of the finest and best preserved in Britain. Built around AD 300, the house was altered and restored several times. In its final form it consisted of a house with a corridor connecting the rooms, wings surrounding a courtyard, and an additional range of buildings at the rear. To the north were more buildings which may have been farmworkers' quarters with baths, and a shrine to the water nymphs.

Some fine mosaics are still in their original positions. Their subject matter is mainly myth: Orpheus and his lyre, Medusa with her snake-like hair, and Perseus holding the Gorgon's head; as well as a range of animals mythological and real. The villa museum houses many finds from the site, including agricultural implements.

Brading villa is situated 2 miles north-east of Sandown, west of the Sandown to Ryde road.

Bradwell-on-Sea   *Essex*
OTHONA

From the evidence of coins found inside the walls, the fort at Bradwell-on-Sea was built late in the 3rd century, as a link in the chain of shore defences against Saxon pirates. The fort stands on the edge of the marshes, overlooking the sea.

Outlines of three of the original walls survive: the remaining masonry of the fort is slipping into the sea. Fragments of the south wall reveal its inner core, with its threefold courses of roof tiles. On the west, the remains of several semi-circular towers can be seen. In this stretch of wall, the still-massive foundations of huge boulders with a core of concrete rubble are visible.

Within the fort are the ruins of St Peter's Chapel, which date from the 7th century indicating that the fort may have been inhabited into Saxon times. The chapel is constructed largely of re-used Roman materials, and is an example of the Mediterranean style of church introduced to the Saxons by St Augustine and his followers.

The fort is situated on the south side of the Blackwater estuary, 2 miles north-east of Bradwell-on-Sea.

Brecon Gaer   *Powys*

Built in AD 80 to house a cohort of cavalry, this Roman fort is strategically placed on a low spur overlooking the confluence of the Rivers Usk and Yscir. When first constructed, the fortifications consisted of an earthen bank, in front of which lay two ditches.

In the middle of the 2nd century this defence was replaced by a stone wall, sections of which are on show. At this date the bath-house was built and the headquarters building was refurbished. The remains of the south and west gates are also visible. The fort was occupied intermittently until after AD 300. Beyond the north gate was a substantial civilian settlement.

The fort lies on the north side of the River Usk, 2½ miles west of Brecon. Take the Battle road and turn left at Cradoc. The site is directly behind a farm, which has guide books for sale.

Bristol   *Avon*

The City of Bristol Museum in Queen's Road contains important relics of Roman lead-mining in the Mendips, and of the lead and pewter industry in the same area. From Charterhouse in the Mendips come several lead ingots, lead weights, a bronze head and other smaller metal objects.

Local Roman villas are also represented in the Bristol museum. There is a larchwood writing tablet from Chew Park, as well as bronze and pewter domestic utensils. From the roadside settlement at Nettleton come stone sculptures found in the shrines there, including a relief of the goddess Diana.

Burgh Castle   *Norfolk*
GARIANNORUM

Burgh Castle is a fine example of a fort built in the late 3rd century to protect the shore from Saxon raiders. The fort overlooks the River Waveney, and a rectangle of about 5 acres is enclosed within the walls.

Parts of the walls have fallen into the river, but those on the western side are very impressive, standing nearly 16½ ft high in places. Bastions are spaced along the wall; the holes in their cores may have been made for ballista pivots.

Three gateways survive; the eastern gate was 11½ ft wide, but the other two were smaller, postern gates or doors. Inside, timber barracks have been found. These may have been occupied by the auxiliary cavalry who formed the garrison in the late 3rd century. Like other Saxon Shore forts, Burgh Castle may have been lived in long after the Romans departed; in the 7th century it housed a monastic community, and a number of Saxon glass kilns were also found there.

The castle lies near the village of Burgh Castle, about 3 miles west of Great Yarmouth. The path to the site runs alongside the church.

Burnswark   *Dumfs. & Gall.*

The large pre-Roman hill-fort of Burnswark holds a commanding position over the surrounding countryside. On the north-western and south-eastern slopes below the summit are the outlines of two Roman military camps. The camp on the south-eastern flank of the hill is the best preserved, with well-defined rectangular ramparts and gateways. By the northern rampart are three mounds, which are probably the emplacements for Roman catapults.

Many lead sling projectiles were found during early excavations of the hill-fort, leading some scholars to believe that the Novantae, the local tribe, had been besieged there by the Romans. But more recent excavations revealed that the hill-fort had long been abandoned when the Roman camps were built. It is clear, therefore, that the Roman camps were used only for practice assaults on the hill-fort.

Burnswark lies 2½ miles north of Ecclefechan at the end of a minor road leading off the road to Middlebie. Look for the turning just after crossing the railway line on the east side of the A74.

Burry Holms   *W. Glam.*

On this island off the Gower Peninsula is a Welsh tribal fortification of the Roman period. One of the finest promontory forts in the area, it is protected by the sea on three sides and by ramparts on the fourth, and was intended to defend the western end of the island.

Burry Holms can be reached at low tide from Llangennith Burrows at the northern end of Rhossili Bay.

Caer Gai   *Gwynedd*

Caer Gai was a strategically placed Roman fort occupied between the years 78 and 125. The ramparts are still very clear, and the south-east entrance can also be seen. A small shrine found in the fort was dedicated to the semi-divine Hercules by an auxiliary cohort from Gaul that was once stationed there.

Caer Gai lies near the south-

western corner of Bala Lake, and is reached by taking a track from the north side of the Bala to Dolgellau road a little more than half a mile north of Llanuwchllyn.

Caer Gybi   *Anglesey*

The Roman fort of Caer Gybi, overlooking Holyhead Inner Harbour, was probably built to guard shipping on the Irish Sea. The remains of the 4th-century building are extensive. The walls are 6 ft thick, and sections on the north and west sides stand almost 15 ft high. Part of the wall-walk patrolled by sentries has been preserved, as well as the four round towers at the corners of the fort.

The fort was built surrounding a small quay, but the sea retreated. Nowadays the walls enclose the church of St Cybi, so that church and fort both stand on the west side of the old harbour.

Caerleon ISCA SILURUM   *Gwent*

Caerleon was one of the permanent legionary bases in Roman Britain, the others being Chester and York. It was occupied by the Second Legion Augusta from about AD 74 until the 4th century. The earliest defences were of earth and timber to which a stone facing was added later.

Caerleon's most notable Roman monument is its amphitheatre. The only completely excavated amphitheatre in Britain, it was erected about AD 80 and was modified several times before being abandoned when the garrison departed. The banks and wall were constructed of earth and timber faced with stone, while the seats were made of wood. The units engaged in the building operations left their marks in the walls of the arena. The originals have been removed, but casts have been put up in their places.

Only a portion of the western part of the fort now remains, out of the original 49 acres, and this section is open to visitors. Some of the ovens backing on to the rampart date from about AD 75, but those with large flues were built later. Near the cookhouses is a communal latrine, which has a stone sewer running around three sides and would, in the days of the legion, have been equipped with wooden seats. Also visible are the ground plans of several legionary barracks built inside the fort. The larger rooms at one end of each barracks were those of the centurions, while the rank and file slept in partitioned rooms occupying the rest of the block.

There is an excellent site museum at Caerleon. In it are displayed several inscriptions, among them one from the amphitheatre; a mosaic; and smaller objects including the remains of a cremated corpse in a lead canister.

The village of Caerleon, which occupies the site of the fort, is 3 miles north-east of Newport.

Caernarfon   *Gwynedd*
SEGONTIUM

Caernarfon is best known for its massive medieval castle, but it is also the site of the Roman fort built around AD 78 at a strategic position near the mouth of the River Seiont. The first fort was an earth and timber construction designed to accommodate a

'milliary cohort' of 1,000 men. Segontium was subsequently rebuilt several times, and by the end of the 2nd century all the buildings as well as the defences had been replaced in stone. The fort continued in use throughout the 3rd and 4th centuries, to be abandoned in 383 when the garrison was withdrawn.

The modern visitors' entrance is near the south-east gate, by a section of the Roman wall. At the back of the fort near the well can be seen some of the barrack blocks, each with a long partitioned section for the legionaries, and officers' quarters at one end. Near by is part of the fort's 2nd-century granary.

The remains of the north-eastern gate survive, with its twin entrances and two guard rooms. Better preserved is the north-western gate, which has a single entrance. The next building on the left is the workshop, and near by is the 4th-century fort commandant's house, which has rooms ranged around a central courtyard. In the centre of the fort is the *principia*, or headquarters building. This had a forecourt, behind which was a roofed hall and a range of rooms that included a shrine and an underground strongroom. Channels for the underfloor-heating system are still visible in this building.

Beyond the fort were discovered the remains of a civilian settlement, the forerunner of modern Caernarfon town. The Segontium Museum on the site of the fort contains most of the material from the excavations, including an altar to Minerva, a wingless bronze Cupid with a torch, daggers and other

weapons, and bronze bowls.

The fort lies on the south-eastern outskirts of Caernarfon, on the road to Beddgelert.

Caerwent   *Gwent*
VENTA SILURUM

This town, the capital of the tribe of the Silures in Roman times, was founded some time after AD 78. Although it was only a small town, 44 acres in area, there is much to see. The stone walls of the town are very impressive, standing over 16 ft high in places. This wall, more than 10 ft thick, replaced an earthen rampart and timber defence set up in the mid-2nd century. In the 4th century a series of large bastions were added to the walls: fine examples of these can be seen on the southern stretch of the wall.

The remains of the principal temple and parts of two houses or shops lie to the north of the main street. In the porch of the church in the modern village of Caerwent is an inscription in honour of Tiberius Claudius Paulinus, at one time commander of the Second Legion Augusta at Caerleon. Dating from about AD 220, it mentions the *civitas* of the Silures – their self-governing tribal area, of which Caerwent was the capital – and also the local council that ruled over it.

The National Museum of Wales in Cathays Park, Cardiff, houses many of the finds from Caerwent, including bronze brooches, coins, lead ingots, and the remains of three bronze mirrors. Some outstanding objects from Caerwent, among them the bronze head of a curly haired girl, a broken-off girl's arm holding some flowers, and a bronze ibis head are in the Museum and Art Gallery, John Frost Square, Newport.

Caerwent lies 1½ miles north of Caldicot, just south of the A48.

Caistor   *Norfolk*
VENTA ICENORUM

Caistor was the capital of the Iceni tribe. The town was apparently founded as part of the process of 'civilising' what remained of the Iceni after Boudicca's revolt of AD 60–61. Thousands of tribesmen had been slain in battle and reprisals and the survivors put under strict military surveillance. The settlement was planned with a grid pattern of streets in the 1st century, but the forum and basilica (market square and town hall) were not built until about AD 140. When the town's first defences were erected in the 3rd century, they enclosed an area of 35 acres.

The site of the Roman town has been largely ploughed over, but the circuit of the town walls, enclosing the medieval church of St Edmund, can still be followed.

Caistor St Edmund lies 3 miles south of Norwich, and the site of the Roman town is on the edge of the village on the east bank of the River Tas.

Canterbury   *Kent*
DUROVERNUM CANTIACORUM

The pre-Roman tribe of the Cantiaci had an *oppidum*, or large settlement, at this crossing-place on the River Stour. The Romans built a town on the same site and much of this has been unearthed, including its grid-pattern streets, its forum and theatre, and many of its houses.

The town's stone fortifications were erected late in the 3rd century, and enclosed an area of about 120 acres.

Although the walls have been almost completely overlaid by medieval defences, part of a Roman gateway can be seen embedded in the medieval masonry on the side of Queningate, behind the car park in Broad Street. A fine stretch of wall has also been revealed at St Mary's Church in Northgate: here, archaeologists have located the battlements of the Roman defences, now incorporated in the medieval wall of the church.

In Butchery Lane there are the remains of a Roman town house, with wings and an interconnecting corridor. In the 1st century it was a simple timber structure, but by the 3rd century it had grown into a much grander establishment with mosaic floors and a bath-house.

On a slight eminence half a mile to the east of the cathedral is the little church of St Martin, in which King Ethelbert, Saxon ruler of Kent, was baptised by St Augustine in AD 597. The fabric of the church contains much re-used Roman material, and according to the Venerable Bede it was built before the Romans quit Britain.

Royal Museum and Art Gallery, The Beaney, High Street. The major finds from the Roman town housed here include coins, pottery and fine glass. Also of interest is an exquisite flagon from Bishopsbourne and a hoard of 4th-century silver.

Cardiff   *S. Glam.*

The massive castle in the centre of modern Cardiff overlays the

remains of a Roman shore fort. The present castle was built on the original square plan; the North Gate is built on Roman foundations, and Roman masonry appears at the base of the north and east walls.

National Museum of Wales. The museum has a fine collection of Roman material from many parts of Wales. Some of the most spectacular objects come from Welshpool: these include a bronze bucket ornament in the form of an ox head, a bronze jug with an unusual handle portraying the hero Hercules as a boy killing snakes, and a bronze skillet adorned with heads of Bacchus and two Satyrs.

There are also more commonplace but interesting finds from the excavations at Caerwent and Caerleon. Caerleon provides a bust of Jupiter, a figure of Mercury and a griffin statuette, all in bronze; a glass pot in the form of a negro's head; and part of a basket chair. There is a Roman water-wheel from the gold mines of Dolaucothi, and painted wall-plaster from the fort at Gelligaer is also worthy of note.

Carisbrooke   *Isle of Wight*
Castle

The Roman fort at Carisbrooke was built as a defence against Saxon pirates. Most of it now lies beneath the medieval castle, but a few courses of Roman walling are visible where the bridge over the moat joins the gatehouse. The vicarage garden near by contains the remains of a villa in which a fragment of a mosaic depicts a vase of flowers set within a geometric design.

The Isle of Wight Museum, housed in Carisbrooke Castle,

features a number of finds from the villa and from other sites on the island.

Carlisle   *Cumbria*
LUGUVALIUM

The Carlisle Museum and Art Gallery in Castle Street contains many Roman objects discovered at Carlisle and the northern forts, including a very fine mask of a Celtic god. There is a charming bronze statuette of a dog from Kirkby Thore, and a 2nd or 3rd-century stone statue of a local divinity found at Carlisle, as well as a large number of incriptions and stone reliefs. Among the latter are portraits of a mother-goddess from Bewcastle, and of a mother and child from Murrell Hill in Cumbria.

Carrawburgh   *Northld*
BROCOLITIA

The remains of the fort lie on Hadrian's Wall, in a particularly lovely setting. The outlines of the fort can be made out, but much more remarkable, because of its excellent state of preservation, is the temple of the Persian god Mithras that lies at the rear of the fort.

The temple, with its characteristic antechamber and sanctuary, was laid out in the 3rd century. It was destroyed in 296 or 297, then rebuilt; only to be desecrated (probably by Christians) during the 4th century.

The building is roofless and the original statues and dedication slabs have been replaced with replicas, but a vivid impression of a holy place is retained. There were three altars, behind which was a relief showing Mithras

slaying a bull. The worshippers sat on the raised benches flanking the nave, while in the antechamber stood the statue of a mother-goddess.

Mithras was not the only deity worshipped at Carrawburgh, for a well just north of the temple was used as a shrine to the local goddess Coventina.

Carrawburgh lies 7 miles north-west of Hexham on the south side of the Low Brunton to Greenhead road.

Castell Collen   *Powys*

The fort at Castell Collen went through four stages of development: it was founded in the late 1st century and refurbished during the 2nd century; then again in the 3rd and the 4th centuries. The initial earthen defences were replaced by stone walls about AD 140, and the line of these is very clear today. The foundations of the buildings, including the headquarters, can also be traced.

Castell Collen lies on the west side of the River Ithon, 1 mile north of Llandrindod Wells.

Cawthorn   *N. Yorks.*

The array of earthworks at Cawthorn are the remains of four Roman marching camps, dating from between AD 90 and 100. The westernmost camp is particularly well preserved, with gateways still intact.

The Roman camps lie 4 miles north of Pickering (6 miles by road via Wrelton and Cawthorne hamlet).

Cerne Abbas   *Dorset*

The Cerne Abbas Giant is a huge hill figure that was created by

stripping turf from the chalk above the village. The Giant is nearly 200 ft tall, and his shoulders almost 46 ft broad.

On the crest of the hill above the Giant is a British temple enclosure of Roman date. The figure's sexual organs and club are given great prominence, suggesting that he is a symbol of the cult of Hercules or of a Celtic counterpart, perhaps cut into the chalk in the 2nd or 3rd centuries.

The Cerne Abbas Giant is impossible to miss; he stands just north of the village of Cerne Abbas on the Dorchester to Sherborne road.

Charterhouse   *Somerset*

Soon after the conquest of Somerset by the Romans – in other words before AD 50 – the Mendip lead-mining industry was in full swing. Ingots bearing the imperial stamp that came from there have been found as far away as central France, while it is likely that the early plumbing of the Roman baths at nearby Bath was made of Mendip lead.

The lead-working sites and industrial complex are not easy to distinguish from more recent lead-mining activities, but well repay exploration, especially when coupled with visits to the Bristol and Taunton museums where finds from the mines are on display.

From Cheddar take the road through the Gorge. After 3½ miles the road forks; take the left fork, continue for 1 mile along this road to the crossroads and turn left here on to the road to Charterhouse. Mendip Farm stands half a mile on the left, where Roman surface workings are revealed in the scars and gulleys on the landscape.

Continue along the road, past St Hugh's Church, and turn right at the crossroads; a little further on to the left, there is a clump of trees about a small earthwork that is probably the remains of the barracks that guarded the mines.

Return to the crossroads and turn right; after a quarter of a mile, turn left and the mining settlement's amphitheatre lies on the left about 500 yds up this lane. The banks which once supported seats or benches still stand 16½ ft above the arena floor. The entrances at each end are clearly defined. It is likely that the amphitheatre was originally built for the garrison, which in the late 1st century was drawn from the Second Legion Augusta.

Finds from Charterhouse are on display in the City of Bristol Museum in Queen's Road, Bristol, and in the Somerset County Museum in Taunton Castle. The exhibits include inscribed pigs or ingots of lead, lead coffins, and small articles such as horseshoes and bronze tweezers. The Somerset County Museum has fine glass objects, engraved gems and jewellery, models of tools (possibly toys) such as axes and hammers, and an oak spade.

Chedworth   *Glos.*

As well as being one of the best-preserved Roman villa residences in Britain, Chedworth lies in an exceptionally attractive situation in the wooded Coln Valley.

The first buildings to be constructed, early in the 2nd century, were a small house and its separate bath-suite (now at the west end of the north wing),

and a half-timbered building. The house was rebuilt after a fire in the early 3rd century, and a larger bath-house was added.

The most glorious period in the villa's history began in the 4th century, when it was totally transformed. The central block and two wings were joined by a covered corridor enclosing an inner garden, and an outer courtyard was created at the same time.

It was during this rebuilding that the dining-suite and a second bath-suite were added, and the remarkable mosaic floors were laid. Meanwhile, the other bath-suite had been converted into a sauna, with a water nymph's shrine outside. Almost all of the excavated rooms are open to view. The 4th-century dining-room, with its fine mosaic of the Four Seasons, is particularly worth seeing. The house was the centre of an extensive Cotswold agricultural estate, and its elegance and luxury matched its status.

The site museum contains many interesting finds, including Christian *Chi-Rho* monograms from the nymph's shrine, which was later converted to Christian usage.

The remains of the villa lie three-quarters of a mile north of Chedworth and west of the minor road connecting Yanworth and Withington.

Chee Tor   *Derbys.*

Chee Tor is a fine example of a British farming community of Roman times. It consisted of a series of sub-rectangular houses set in small enclosures, beyond which lay terraced fields. Roman pottery has been found on the site.

Chee Tor lies 4 miles east of Buxton, and half a mile south of Wormhill on the south side of the River Wye. Wormhill can be reached by leaving the A6 4 miles east of Buxton on the Tideswell road; after 1½ miles fork left under the disused railway bridge, and continue for 1¼ miles to Wormhill – from here it is possible to see the settlement as a whole. To reach the settlement, take the footpath down to Chee Dale, follow it eastwards along the river, across the river at the weirs and up the opposite slope. The settlement lies a quarter of a mile west of the path, above a loop in the river.

Chester DEVA   *Cheshire*

A legionary fortress was founded at Chester around AD 76–78 as a permanent military base to control North Wales and the Pennines. The first fort was about 60 acres in extent and was built of timber; but this structure was replaced by stone buildings, perhaps in the 2nd century. The stone walls were constructed later still.

Deva now lies beneath modern Chester. To tour the Roman walls, start at Eastgate, where the Roman east gate once stood. To the north a fine section of Roman wall is still visible. Walk on from here to Northgate, following the line of the wall which at several points is preserved to nearly its original height.

From George Street there is a particularly fine stretch to see. When parts of this wall were restored, its core was found to contain many fragments of tombstones, presumably robbed from a nearby cemetery. One such stone, a moulded cornice, is embedded in the wall near Northgate. Beyond St Martin's Gate the Roman walls have virtually disappeared.

A large headquarters building or *principia* lay between the town hall and the centre of the Rows, and fragments of this can be seen. At Hamilton Place there is part of a row of legionary offices, as well as the shrine that once housed the legionary standards. Other parts of the *principia* can also be seen at 23 Northgate Row, where the massive base of a column from the headquarters hall is kept.

At 14 Northgate Row are the remains of a hypocaust or underfloor heating system, but the most impressive hypocaust was found in St Michael's Row, which stands on the site of the legionary bath-block. Parts of its floor and columns are on show at 39 Bridge Street.

The finest relic of Roman Chester is its amphitheatre, which is the largest in Roman Britain and lies just outside Newgate. The surviving stone structure replaced an earlier timber amphitheatre in about AD 86. The arena itself is well preserved, though the external buttresses and stairs have disappeared. On the north gate of the amphitheatre can be seen the posts on which the wooden gates were hung, and behind the north gate are the steps to the seats. On the west side of this entrance is a small room that served as a shrine for Nemesis, the goddess of Fate. The altar that once stood there has been replaced by a replica.

Chester was a port as well as a fortress, and beyond it on the River Dee were the quays, of which fragments survive next to the ladies' toilets on the racecourse.

Grosvenor Museum, Grosvenor Street. The varied life of Roman Chester is reflected in the richness of the museum. There are some fine pieces of sculpture, and what is perhaps the best collection of Roman military equipment in Britain. The bronzes include mirrors, statuettes of Hercules and Juno, and figures of birds and beasts such as cockerels, eagles and bulls.

Chesterholm   *Northld*
VINDOLANDA

The fort was founded about AD 95 on the Stanegate, the east-west road that served the chain of forts then guarding Britain's northern frontier. The visible remains date from the 3rd and 4th centuries.

The fort is entered by way of the veterans' settlement that stood beside it, where numerous buildings have been uncovered. The bath-house was built by the Sixth Legion, though to judge from finds of feminine articles such as hairpins and tweezers in the drains, it was evidently used by the civilian population as well as by the troops. A 2nd-century inn laid out around a courtyard, with its own bath-block and six guest rooms, has also been found.

Two of the fort's gates have survived, together with their guard-chambers, and there is also a substantial *principia* or headquarters building.

The site museum exhibits finds from the excavations, including iron tools and weapons, jewellery, a bronze military standard, a jet betrothal medallion, and everyday objects such as textiles, leather shoes, wooden slippers and writing tablets. Replicas of sections of Hadrian's Wall to the north are also on show: a length of turf wall with a timber milecastle, and a stone wall section with a turret.

Chesterholm lies 1 mile north-west of Bardon Mill on the Carlisle to Newcastle (A69) road and half a mile south of the Low Brunton to Greenhead road.

Chesters CILURNUM   *Northld*

This cavalry fort on Hadrian's Wall was built to command a bridging point over the North Tyne. Its extensive remains include the north gateway, and the *principia*, or headquarters building, whose strong-room lies beneath the regimental shrine. East of the *principia* is the commanding officer's house, complete with bath-house and heated rooms. The northern part of the fort projects beyond Hadrian's Wall, which joins the fort at the east gate. A well-preserved bath-block stands on the river bank.

The site museum contains many sculptured and inscribed stones from the fort, together with pottery and other relics. The columns on the south side of the aisle at nearby Chollerton Church probably came from the fort.

Chesters lies on the west bank of the River North Tyne, 4 miles north of Hexham.

Chew Green   *Northld*

These impressive earthworks, perched dramatically on a rocky outcrop, are the banks and ditches of a series of marching camps built on the line of Dere

Street, the main Roman road into Scotland. The earliest camp was established around AD 80, but the most substantial ramparts belong to a fortlet built in the 2nd century.

Permission to visit the earthworks must be obtained from the Duty Officer at the entrance to Redesdale army camp on the A68, north-west of Otterburn. Chew Green lies at the head of Coquetdale, about 7 miles to the north-west of the camp along minor roads that begin with a stretch of Dere Street.

Chichester   *W. Sussex*
NOVIOMAGUS

Chichester was the capital of the Regni tribe. It seems likely that the Romans built a supply base here at an early stage of the conquest, and that this was succeeded by a town shortly afterwards. The medieval walls follow the line of the Roman walls, enclosing an area of 100 acres. The Roman street plan, too, has persisted in the location of North, South, East and West Streets.

A Roman mosaic floor can be seen in the cathedral, and a fragment of a black-and-white mosaic, part of the flooring of a bath-house, remains in a shop in West Street. Flint wall foundations have been preserved at the Dolphin and Anchor hotel.

Perhaps the greatest treasure of Roman Chichester is the dedication stone from a temple to Neptune and Minerva that now stands in the entrance to the Guildhall. The stone records that the temple was erected by the Guild of Craftsmen, and had been commissioned by King

Cogidubnus of the Atrebates, who probably ruled over the Regni as well. Cogidubnus, who had co-operated with the invading Romans, was allowed to retain his throne, and in all probability was given the means to build the palace of Fishbourne that lies to the west of Chichester as well. The dedication stone is the only certain record of this historic figure.

Chichester District Museum, 29 Little London. This museum contains most of the smaller finds from the Roman town, including jewellery, glass and bronzes.

Guildhall Museum, Priory Park. In this museum are pottery, coins, jewellery, some small stone statuettes, and fragments of three bronze mirrors.

Chysauster   *Cornwall*
(?)GULVAL

On the moorland north of Penzance is a very well-preserved British village of Roman times. It consists of ten oval, stone-built 'courtyard houses', so called because the rooms of each were clustered facing inwards around a courtyard. The houses were occupied in the 1st and 2nd centuries, but had been abandoned by about AD 300. The roofs were thatched and so have long since disappeared, but the walls still stand to a height of 4–5 ft.

The houses are arranged in pairs, eight of them forming a single 'street'. The courtyard is reached by an entrance passage on the left. At the end of the passage is a recessed room, and on the right a long, narrow chamber which may have been a workroom. The hut opposite the entrance on the far side of the

courtyard served as the main living quarters. House No. 3 in the street is unusual in having two entrances and double the number of rooms.

Another two houses stand close to the path to the site, and near by are traces of the fields cultivated by the villagers.

Chysauster lies 3 miles north of Penzance, west of the Penzance to St Ives road.

Cirencester CORINIUM   *Glos.*

The Roman town of Corinium, the capital of the Dobunni tribe, sprang up around AD 60 as a settlement serving a small fort. From this modest beginning it grew into the second largest town in Roman Britain. The town had a regular street grid, with the forum or market square at its centre.

On one side of the forum was a basilica (town hall) of considerable size; one end of its outline is marked out in a cul-de-sac opening off The Avenue, opposite Tower Street. The amphitheatre, whose banks stand 26 ft above the central arena, can still be seen off Cotswold Avenue.

Corinium's 240 acres were enclosed within 2nd-century earthen ramparts, to which a stone wall was added in the 3rd century. Within its defences were incorporated masonry towers, external ditches and a number of gates, including the massive Verulamium Gate with its twin carriageways and two round towers. The best-preserved sections of the walls are in Beeches Road; in Watermoor Gardens, south-east of London Road; and in the Abbey Grounds north-west of London Road.

Corinium Museum, Park Street. One of the richest Romano-British collections in the country. Roman Cirencester's mosaic artists supplied villas in the vicinity as well as houses in the town, and several examples of their work are on show, together with faithful reconstructions of a Roman kitchen and dining-room.

Colchester   *Essex*
CAMULODUNUM

At the time of the Roman invasion, Colchester – called Camulodunum both by its British inhabitants and their Roman successors – was the tribal capital of the Catuvellauni. In AD 43, Emperor Claudius celebrated its conquest with a triumphal entry; a *colonia*, or settlement for retired soldiers, was established there, and a great temple dedicated to the deified Claudius begun.

According to the Roman historian Tacitus, the British regarded the town as 'the stronghold of everlasting domination' – which is probably the reason for its devastation by Boudicca's rebels in AD 60. But the town was swiftly rebuilt, and had grown to more than 100 acres by the time it was fortified early in the 2nd century.

The platform of Claudius's temple lies beneath the Norman castle, but the vaults supporting it may be viewed, provided permission is obtained from the Castle Museum. So great was the weight of the temple platform that the vaults had to be filled with sand. Many houses stood around the temple; a fragment of one of them lies near the north-west corner of the castle, next to the bandstand.

A tour of the defences of Roman Colchester is best begun at the imposing entrance to the town, Balkerne Gate. A massive 115 ft wide, this well-preserved Roman gateway consisted of two central carriageways for wheeled traffic, two passages for pedestrians and was flanked by bastions incorporating guard-chambers.

There is a fine section of Roman wall along Balkerne Hill, while Castle Park contains the remains of Duncan's Gate, a postern gate set back a little from the line of the wall. Further sections of the defences are preserved beyond East Hill in Priory Street, and in Vineyard Street, where a Roman drain can be seen issuing from the wall.

Colchester and Essex Museum, The Castle. Among the major exhibits are several mosaic pavements from town houses, inscriptions, tombstones, fine bronzes and pottery and glass. A glass vessel and burial casket found in a Roman-period burial mound on Mersea Island are also in the collection, together with pre-Roman treasures from a burial mound at Lexden.

Corbridge   *Northld*
CORSTOPITUM

The great Roman fort of Corstopitum stood on the north bank of the River Tyne at the point where Dere Street, the Roman road north from York, met the Stanegate running west to Carlisle.

The first fort was built by the governor, Julius Agricola, late in the 1st century, and was superimposed by a number of others on the same site. The Stanegate bisects the excavated area. To the north of the road are the remains of two fine granaries, an elaborate fountain and a storehouse that was never completed. To the south is the headquarters building with its strong-room.

In the site museum the excavators' finds are on show. They include a range of military equipment and tools, while among the many inscribed and sculptured stones is a carved fountain head showing a lion devouring a stag.

The fort lies half a mile west of modern Corbridge, south of the Carlisle to Newcastle road.

Din Lligwy   *Anglesey*

The stone huts of Din Lligwy were built by a British farming community in the 4th century, although there may have been an earlier settlement on the site.

The remains consist of limestone blocks 4–5 ft thick, enclosing nine circular and rectangular huts. The entrance to the settlement is in the north-east wall of the enclosure, and is backed by a guardroom.

Several huts are very well preserved, with walls standing up to 6 ft high. Hearths survive in some, and iron-working was carried out in at least two of the buildings.

The settlement is situated 2½ miles north-west of Benllech, east of the Menai Bridge to Amlwch road.

Dolaucothi   *Dyfed*

The only known gold mine in Roman Britain is at Dolaucothi. The remains of the mine are situated to the south of the River Cothi, half a mile south-east of Pumpsaint, which is midway between Lampeter and Llandovery. What was the main area of industrial activity lies on National Trust property.

Several depressions mark the sites of the water tanks that fed the channels in which gold was separated from crushed ore by washing. The hillside has a terraced appearance, from the stepped washing channels cut all the way down it.

Water was brought to the reservoir by three aqueducts, one of which was several miles long. The mine shafts were drained by wooden water-wheels, and a fragment of one from the site is in the National Museum of Wales, Cathays Park, Cardiff.

Dorchester   *Dorset*
DURNOVARIA

The town grew out of an earlier fort on the site, and was the tribal capital of the Durotriges. The concrete core of the early 4th-century town wall can be seen in Albert Road. This wall replaced a late 2nd-century bank-and-timber palisade with one or two ditches in front of it.

Remains of a Roman town house are visible behind the county offices in the north-west corner of the town. This house was built late in the 2nd century to an L-shaped plan, and other rooms were added later. There are seven main rooms to be seen, and also three rooms of a bath-suite, a kitchen, domestic quarters and a veranda.

To the north-west of the town lay the late Roman cemetery of Poundbury, where about 5,000 graves were dug, and several elaborately decorated tombs erected. Beyond lies the pre-Roman fort of Poundbury, and

snaking around its walls is the best-preserved Roman aqueduct in Britain. Poundbury is situated half a mile north-west of the town centre on the south side of the River Frome. The shelf carrying the aqueduct is visible in the northern corner of the camp, its line quite distinct as it follows the hill-top.

A fine view of the aqueduct as it passes over Fordington Down may be seen half a mile further along the road from Dorchester to Poundbury. The aqueduct was constructed in the 1st century and the channel varied in width from 3–5 ft and was about 3 ft deep.

Dorset County Museum, High West Street. Roman exhibits include several mosaic pavements, lead coffins from Poundbury cemetery, and a coin hoard from Dorchester that was buried in a bronze jug. Material from the hill-fort at Maiden Castle is on display, including skeletons of battle casualties from the siege, among them a Briton with a Roman ballista bolt in his spine. Also on show is a range of objects from the local shale-working industry, such as cups, bracelets, and elaborately carved table legs.

Dover DUBRIS   *Kent*

Dover was the base of the *Classis Britannica* – the British fleet. Its headquarters were in a fort located near the modern town centre. The earthen rampart of a later fort, built to protect the coast against Saxon pirates, is preserved in Cannon Street.

Beneath the rampart was found one of Britain's finest relics of Roman times: the Painted House. This is a small town house with flint and brick

walls and a hypocaust heating system. It gets its name from some of the walls, which stand nearly 6 ft high and give a vivid impression of the interior design of a Roman house. The wall surrounds are painted to imitate marble veneers; above are fragments of paintings of human figures, leaves and brooms.

Dover's other unique Roman monument is its *pharos*, or lighthouse. This stands near the castle, on the eastern heights overlooking the harbour. It would originally have stood nearly 80 ft high, but now only the first 46 ft are of the Roman period: the rest of the masonry is later in date. The lighthouse has survived because it served as a tower for the adjacent medieval Church of St Mary-in-Castra. A second *pharos* stood on the opposite heights, and a third overlooking the harbour at Boulogne across the Channel. All were probably built soon after AD 43 to guide convoys across the Narrow Seas.

Dover Museum, Ladywell. The museum houses a good collection of locally made Roman pottery from the Dover forts.

Edinburgh   *Lothian*

Some of the most important relics of Roman times in Scotland are displayed in the National Museum of Antiquities of Scotland, in Queen Street.

Several cases have been filled with objects from the fort at Newstead, on the Tweed – notably a 1st-century cavalry parade helmet, and a large number of tools and weapons. There is also a Roman silver hoard from the hill-fort at Traprain Law, the stone from Bridgeness which marked the eastern end of the Antonine Wall, and a marble head from Hawkshaw.

Exeter
Devon

ISCA DUMNONIORUM

Exeter was the capital of the Dumnonii tribe. An early Roman fort there grew eventually into a walled town covering about 100 acres. Several sections of the town's stone walls can still be seen, though they were often refurbished in the Middle Ages. The Roman work – regularly laid blocks of purple and grey stone, often with a projecting course at the base of the wall – is unmistakable.

To tour the walls, begin in Northernhay Gardens, where some of the base is still intact, and follow it through the archway and past the War Memorial. Here a good section of wall is visible.

Another well-preserved section begins at Eastgate House, and the finest section of all, 16 ft high, is found by following Southernhay west towards the river.

Rougemont House Museum, Castle Street. Finds from Roman buildings and the fort bath-block – later the basilica, or town hall – are on display. They include small bronze figurines of animals and humans, pottery lamps, and several attractive glass vessels, among them some fluted bowls.

Fishbourne
W. Sussex

Excavations in the 1960s uncovered a building unique in Roman Britain – a magnificent palace complex, built on the site of a Roman military base in use between AD 43 and 44. In its final form, the palace consisted of four ranges of rooms enclosing a formal garden. Only part of the palace has been excavated, but the visible remains, which are covered by a modern building incorporating a museum, are outstanding.

The site of Fishbourne is some 1¼ miles west of Chichester, north of the Chichester to Southampton road.

Gatcombe
Avon

The site of this Roman villa incorporates a section of the stoutest Roman wall yet found in Britain. Nearly 15 ft thick – half as thick again as Hadrian's Wall – it was built around a complex consisting of a villa residence, farm buildings and gardens covering 18 acres in all. All other traces of the villa were destroyed during the excavation of a cutting for the Bristol to Exeter railway in 1843.

The villa site lies 4 miles south-west of Bristol, 1 mile west of Long Ashton on the road connecting Long Ashton with the Nailsea to Chew Magna road. The site can be visited by arrangement with the owners, who live at nearby Gatcombe Court.

Gelligaer
Mid Glam.

The first Roman fort at Gelligaer was built of timber late in the 1st century, but little of this survives. The most substantial remains are of the 2nd-century fort, which was occupied by a cohort of infantry. The walls enclosed an area of 3½ acres. There were four gates, four corner towers and eight turrets. To the east was a fortified extension that contained the bath-block.

The fort lies north-east of the modern town of Gelligaer, on the north side of the Treharris to Pengam road. Permission to visit the site must be obtained from Gelligaer House.

Gloucester
Glos.

NERVIA GLEVENSIUM

Modern Gloucester grew out of the Roman town, which was in turn built over a legionary fortress. Around the end of the 1st century Gloucester was constituted a *colonia*. At this time the town's original timber buildings were partly replaced by stone, and a forum was constructed.

A fragment of Roman mosaic has been relaid in the hall of the National Westminster Bank in Eastgate Street, and another fragment that was found under the New Market is on display in the market entrance. Sections of the city wall can be seen under the City Museum in Brunswick Road, and under the Midlands Electricity Board building in King's Square.

Gloucester City Museum and Art Gallery, Brunswick Road. On show here is an impressive collection from the Roman town, including fragments of a bronze equestrian statue, and the tombstone of a Thracian cavalryman of the garrison.

Goldsborough
N. Yorks.

Still visible are the prominent earthworks of this signal station, one of a chain built to guard the Yorkshire coastline late in the 4th century. It was a formidably defended structure: within a ditch 10 ft wide, thick walls with projecting bastions enclosed an area over 100 ft square. Artillery was probably mounted on the bastions.

Inside the walls was a courtyard, at the centre of which stood a watch-tower about 100 ft high. The skeletons of two men and a dog were found in a corner of the tower, grim relics of the fortress's last days, when like nearby Huntcliff, it was overwhelmed by raiders, leaving the coast undefended.

Goldsborough is 1 mile north-west of Lythe on the Whitby to Saltburn road; the remains of the signal station stand on the east side of the Goldsborough to Kettleness footpath.

Great Witcombe   *Glos.*

This beautifully situated Cotswold villa was probably built in the middle of the 3rd century, but was altered several times before being abandoned about 150 years later. Three rooms of the bath-suite are on display under cover. This suite has a sweating room and a warm room linked to a hot room. An adjoining room with niches and a basin may well have had a religious purpose. There is also a fine mosaic pavement on show, portraying a water scene with fishes, sea horses and sea serpents.

The villa remains are 1 mile south of Brockworth, and are signposted from the Gloucester to Cirencester road, a quarter of a mile south-east of the junction with the main Cheltenham to Stroud road.

Hadrian's Wall   *Cumbria*
                              Northld

Hadrian's Wall, running 73 miles from Newcastle upon Tyne to Bowness-on-Solway, is the most

impressive legacy that the Romans left in Britain. As long ago as the 8th century the Venerable Bede expressed great admiration for the wall's builders, and even today the scale of the undertaking and the administrative skills involved in its construction and maintenance are little short of awe-inspiring.

This was no ordinary wall, but a complex of fortifications that underwent many modifications over the centuries of Roman rule. Around AD 122 Emperor Hadrian visited Britain, and the wall was very much his own conception. Detachments of legionaries began building it in 122; even sailors from the British fleet were involved. By AD 136 the great work was complete.

The original scheme was for a continuous wall, fronted by a ditch, to divide the province of Britain from the independent tribes to the north. The wall was 15 ft high, and 7½–10 ft wide, with a 6 ft parapet on top. At intervals of a Roman mile – 1,620 yds – were milecastles. These were small fortlets with gates to the north and south as well as barracks for up to 30 men. Between each milecastle were spaced two turrets, used principally as watch-towers.

The history of the wall's construction shows that in practice this plan could not be carried out in full. About AD 124 major changes were made. A chain of large forts on the Stanegate, the Roman road to the south of and parallel to, the wall, seems to have been abandoned, and replacements integrated into the wall scheme.

Sixteen large front-line forts were added to the plan, causing some of the earlier milecastles and turrets to be demolished

almost as soon as they had been built. This strengthening of the wall indicates that the tribes to the north were hostile to it.

At the same time a continuous earthwork, the Vallum, was constructed south of the wall. Since part, at least, of its purpose was obviously to protect the garrison from an attack in the rear, the Pennine tribes to the south must also have resented the wall's limitation of their movements. Digging the Vallum must have been a back-breaking task, since much of it had to be quarried out of rock. It consisted of a flat-bottomed ditch about 21 ft wide and 8 ft deep. Set back from each edge was a turf bank. Causeways opposite the forts provided the Vallum's only crossing points.

It survives in many places, but Limestone Corner is particularly rewarding. In this spot the rock proved too difficult for the excavators and the work was abandoned half-completed. Limestone Corner is on the Low Brunton to Greenhead road, 3 miles west of Low Brunton. The interesting section of Vallum begins at a gate near a layby on the north side of the road. The Vallum seems ever-present, but when climbing this road from Chesters, the great grassy swathe cutting across the landscape is particularly prominent.

There is no better place to see the wall itself than when standing behind the fort at Housesteads. As it sweeps along the crags of the great rocky scarp that drops away to the north, it is a truly magnificent sight. Peel Crag and Walltown Crags also provide impressive stretches. Peel Crag can be reached from the Low Brunton to Greenhead road by taking the minor road north from

305

Twice Brewed. From a car park that lies half a mile along this road, a footpath runs to Peel Crags, about a quarter of a mile away. At Walltown Crags, 1 mile north-east of Greenhead, is a fine turret; another is at Willowford, half a mile west of Gilsland, where the wall can be followed down to the remains of a bridge over the River Irthing. Brunton Turret, which lies just south of Low Brunton, is an especially well-preserved example, where the wall itself is at its broadest. The milecastle just west of Housesteads, commanding the bleak moors to the north, is easily accessible. At Cawfields, 1½ miles north of Haltwhistle, and Poltross Burn, at Gilsland, the remains of barracks, probably belonging to milecastles, can be clearly seen.

●Information on the well-preserved wall forts at Carrawburgh, Chesters and Housesteads, and the Stanegate fort at Chesterholm, can be found in separate entries under their names.

High Rochester   Northld
BREMENIUM

The fort at High Rochester is one of the best-preserved Roman sites north of Hadrian's Wall. A fort was probably first built there in the mid-2nd century, but some masonry dates from the 3rd century. Visible remains include a rampart, part of a tower and the fine west gate. The gateway's massive flanking towers, a gate jamb and part of an arch all survive.

High Rochester stands half a mile north of Rochester village, which lies on the Corbridge to Jedburgh road. The turning is beside the war memorial.

Hardknott Castle   Cumbria

Standing on a ledge beneath Hardknott Mountain, at 800 ft above sea level, Hardknott Castle is a 3 acre Roman auxiliary fort that must be the most dramatically sited of all forts in the province.

It was built by Hadrian, only to be abandoned before the end of the 2nd century. Yet the foundations of its headquarters building and two granaries are still clearly outlined within the surviving walls and angled towers. Beyond the defences, the parade ground and bath house can be identified.

Hardknott lies off the minor road between Ambleside and Ravenglass.

Housesteads   Northld
VERCOVICIUM

This is perhaps the best-known Roman fort in Britain, and the one at which the atmosphere of Hadrian's Wall is most strongly preserved. The name Vercovicium means 'the hilly place', and excavations there have revealed the headquarters building, blocks of granaries and barracks, a latrine block and a hospital. Several of the gates remain in a fair state of preservation; indeed, in the east gateway are ruts cut into the paving by Roman cartwheels. Hadrian's Wall commands spectacular views at this point, and the milecastle near by should also be visited.

Outside the walls of the fort are the remains of a large civilian settlement; in the floor of one of its houses, known as 'Murder House', were found the remains of a man and a woman stabbed to death. The site museum houses a wide range of finds, including military equipment. The most remarkable exhibit is a sculptured relief of three cloaked figures called the 'Three Hooded Deities'. There are also reconstructions showing how the fort looked when it was occupied.

Housesteads fort lies 8 miles east of Greenhead, north of the Greenhead to Low Brunton road.

Inchtuthil   Tayside

This great legionary fortress was the base created by Julius Agricola for his campaign against the tribes of Caledonia. Sections of the rampart and ditch can still be seen.

The Romans left around AD 87, after being there only two years. But before leaving they systematically demolished the fortress, carefully retaining any timber that could be re-used. Excavations have revealed thousands of nails bent by being pulled out of the timber buildings, as well as a store of more than a million nails in a pit beneath a workshop.

Inchtuthil is on the north bank of the River Tay, 2 miles west of Meikleour village on the Coupar Angus to Dunkeld road.

King's Weston   Avon

This villa was built around an oblong yard or hall that was fronted by a colonnade, and flanked by two small wings. There were further rooms at the rear. The house was built about AD 280 and abandoned at the end of the 4th century, after being damaged in the great barbarian raid of AD 367.

The foundations of the central yard or hall, the front corridor and the north wing, include threshold stones with clear marks where wooden doors closed on them. In the corridor is a cooking hearth, a relic of the villa's decline, when the corridor was used as a kitchen. Under the floor, in the heating system, was discovered the skeleton of a man who had been cut down by a sword. He was, perhaps, killed while hiding there during the great raid.

The south wing is preserved under cover; here are displayed a mosaic from the villa, and another from the Brislington villa, on the other side of Bristol. A small part of the bath-suite, including the changing room with its bench, is also visible.

The villa remains are situated 4½ miles north-west of Bristol on the unclassified road from Lawrence Weston to Avonmouth. The key can be obtained from the warden of the site, at 17 Hopewell Gardens, King's Weston.

Kingscote   *Glos.*

Recent excavations have revealed one corner of an extensive Romano-British settlement in which the earliest buildings, probably 3rd century, are narrow-fronted houses or shops. These were replaced in the 4th century by a larger house and associated workshops, one of which may have been used for making furniture. In the main building there are three rooms with underfloor heating and mosaic floors, and from one of these rooms a restored wall-painting shows a mythological scene, perhaps including the figure of Achilles.

The site of the settlement lies 3½ miles south-west of Nailsworth, south of the Tetbury to Dursley road, and three-quarters of a mile south-west of the village of Kingscote.

Knap Hill   *Wilts.*

Commanding a fine view of the Vale of Pewsey is a Stone Age camp known as Knap Hill, and in a sheltered position behind it is a Romano-British farmstead. Its kite-shaped enclosure and the outlines of the platforms on which the houses stood are still clearly to be seen.

The site lies 3½ miles north-west of Pewsey and can be reached by taking the minor road from Pewsey to Alton Priors and then going north-east to the top of the scarp; Knap Hill is half a mile to the east along a footpath.

Leeds   *W. Yorks.*

Leeds City Museum, in the Municipal Buildings, houses a good collection of Roman finds from local sites. The most spectacular is the 4th-century mosaic from Aldborough, portraying the twins Romulus and Remus and the she-wolf that reared them.

Leicester   *Leics.*
RATAE CORITANORUM

Leicester was the capital of the Coritani tribe, and remained the administrative centre of the area under the Romans. On Aylestone Road, by the railway bridge, is a Roman earthwork known as the Raw Dykes, which may have been part of an aqueduct system.

The foundations of the public baths are visible in St Nicholas'

Circle, beside the Jewry Wall Museum. The Jewry Wall itself, a fine stretch of Roman masonry 33 ft high, formed part of a covered exercise hall for the public baths. It probably survived because the hall was incorporated in a Saxon church.

Jewry Wall Museum, St Nicholas' Circle, has two segments of painted wall-plaster from a Roman town house in Leicester. They show human figures, birds, flowers and other motifs, against a background of pillars and arches. There are also several fine mosaics.

Lincoln LINDUM   *Lincs.*

Lindum was built about AD 60 as a fortress for the Ninth Legion. About 18 years later a Roman town was founded on the hill-top site. At first the town clung to the crest of the hill, but as it flourished it spread down the hillside to the River Witham.

Many impressive stretches of the Roman town wall survive, notably in Orchard Street, and in the grounds of the Eastgate Hotel opposite the cathedral. Also in the hotel grounds are the foundations of a water-tower, into which water was pumped from a spring. The lower courses of the early 3rd-century Roman east gate, including part of the staircase, stand in the hotel forecourt.

Remains of all four gates to the town have been found: of the north gate, one arch still stands, spanning Bailgate. Called the Newport Arch, this is the only Roman town gateway in Britain to survive more or less intact – it has been partly rebuilt after being struck by a lorry. The base of the 4th-century west gate is in the forecourt of the municipal offices, in Orchard Street. Remains of the south gate can be seen on Steep Hill, below the cathedral.

The 'Mint Wall', so called because it was traditionally supposed to be part of the Roman mint at Lincoln, stands in the yard of a garage just off West Bight. Nearly 20 ft high and 25 yds long, it was probably part of a colonnaded building. A fine mosaic floor found underneath the cathedral can be seen under the stairway at the north-east corner of the cloisters.

City and County Museum, Broadgate. Remains of a major sewage system that ran beneath the streets of Roman Lincoln are on show, with fragments of the town aqueduct, a tombstone showing a boy with a hare, and a sculptured charioteer.

Littlecote   *Wilts.*

Next to, and in the grounds of, the famous Elizabethan manor, are the remains of a large Roman villa, still in the process of excavation, though the importance of the find is already obvious. The most exciting discovery so far is an elaborate mosaic depicting Orpheus and the animals; this was first unearthed in 1730, but was presumed destroyed and lost thereafter. Recent excavations, however, have uncovered the mosaic again, together with sections of the villa buildings. These are now being consolidated and restored, and are open to the public in the summer months.

The house and the villa are in Littlecote Park, signposted about 3 miles north-west of Hungerford on the Hungerford to Swindon road.

London LONDINIUM

The city of London was a creation of the Romans. Apart from a small Bronze Age settlement near St Paul's Cathedral, there is no evidence to suggest any long-term occupation of the site before the Romans recognised its strategic importance as the first possible firm bridging-point upstream on the Thames.

The new city grew quickly. Tacitus says it was already a hive of commerce packed with traders by the year 60, when it was razed by Queen Boudicca's army. London soon rose again, becoming the seat of the procurator – chief financial official of the provincial government.

It succeeded Colchester as the capital of the province, and by the end of the 1st century it had become its commercial and political centre. The Roman genius in selecting the site is borne out by the city's continuing importance today.

Of the many fine buildings which must have graced Roman Londinium little can now be seen, and not much more has been revealed by excavation. Continuous building and rebuilding over the centuries have obliterated all but a few remains of the city's early history. Yet traces have been found on Cornhill of a market square with government offices far bigger than any others in Britain. The basilica office building was as long as St Paul's Cathedral. Another remarkable building beside the Thames, with huge halls and an ornamental garden pool at least 115 ft long, may have been the official residence of the governor.

There is, however, much more to be seen of the temple of the Persian god Mithras. Its discovery in 1954 caused a sensation: 80,000 people flocked to see it, questions were asked in Parliament about preserving it, and the construction of Bucklersbury House on the site fell considerably behind schedule. The temple can now be seen in Temple Court, 11 Queen Victoria Street, having been rebuilt about 50 yds west of its original site.

Remains of a Roman house of some elegance, with a private bath-suite, can be seen beneath another modern building erected over the site in Lower Thames Street. In homes such as these a minority of Londoners enjoyed a standard of living not attained by their descendants for nearly 2,000 years.

In the crypt of All-Hallows-by-the-Tower Church is part of another Roman house, with mosaic floors and red-painted plaster. A mosaic floor can also be seen in the basement of the Bank of England, in Threadneedle Street.

The defences of Roman London have left more conspicuous traces. Early in the 2nd century a large fort, covering 11 acres, was built at the north-west corner of the city. It housed detachments of the occupying legions, including the governor's bodyguard, and its west gate can still be seen on the north side of London Wall. A long stretch of the western defences is visible from Noble Street, near by.

When a wall was built around London later in the century, it incorporated the wall of the earlier fort. The city wall can be seen, in St Alphage's churchyard, off Wood Street, by looking down from the stairway on the east side of the little garden. Other very fine stretches up to 16 ft high and crowned with medieval work can be seen in Wakefield Gardens, north of Tower Hill, and behind Midland House in Cooper's Row.

British Museum, Great Russell Street, WC1, houses Britain's principal collection of Roman antiquities. At the top of the main staircase is a large 4th-century mosaic from a villa at Hinton St Mary, in Dorset. The main Romano-British room contains the finest of the painted wall panels found in a St Albans town house, two marble portrait busts and Christian wall-painting fragments from Lullingstone villa in Kent, and the Water Newton and Mildenhall Treasures, which are hoards of high-quality silver-ware. Near by is a fine bronze head of the Emperor Claudius found in the River Alde in Suffolk – possibly loot discarded by Boudicca's rebels.

In an ante-room is the best-surviving mosaic from Roman London, depicting Bacchus riding on a tiger. At the foot of the stairs to the upper level is a milestone of Emperor Hadrian's time, from North Wales, and above it is a mosaic from a villa at Horkstow, Humberside, showing a chariot race in a circus.

On the upper level are military buckles and arrowheads from Hod Hill in Dorset, the handsome Ribchester parade helmet, a superb gilt-bronze statuette of Hercules from Hadrian's Wall, a bronze head of the Emperor Hadrian, found in the Thames, and iron nails from the legionary fortress at Inchtuthil on Tayside – all in all, a perfect summary of the Roman years.

Museum of London, Aldersgate Street, EC2. The finest collection of Roman remains from London itself is displayed in this museum. Outstanding are the Temple of Mithras sculptures – including a fine marble head of Serapis, Græco-Egyptian god of the underworld. Among other exhibits are a mosaic from Bucklersbury, and a replica of a gold medallion from Arras, in France, showing the earliest-known pictorial representation of London. A workman's graffito, scratched on a tile, records maliciously that 'Austalis has been going off on his own for 13 days'.

Simple, everyday articles include a pair of leather bikini-style briefs, an amber necklace on its original flax string, fir-wood writing tablets and an iron-tipped bronze stylus, and dice with a dice-box.

Lullingstone   *Kent*

The compact but luxurious Roman villa at Lullingstone has a complicated and eventful history, which lasted from the close of the 1st century to the end of the 4th. The first building was a simple stone house, but by the 2nd century a man of some taste had moved in, adding baths and a shrine in honour of the water nymphs, with a fresco, part of which survives. He must have had to leave in a hurry – he abandoned even the fine marble busts of his ancestors, which are now in the British Museum.

The villa was refurbished by new owners in the 3rd century, and decorated in the 4th with mosaics that are still bright today. These show Bellerophon on the winged horse Pegasus

slaying the monster Chimaera; and a lively depiction of the Rape of Europa.

Wall-paintings of praying figures and the *Chi-Rho* monogram show that later in the century a Christian chapel was built – one of the earliest known in Britain. The best fragments of these frescoes are now in the British Museum.

The villa is signposted from Eynsford on the Dartford to Sevenoaks road.

Lydney   *Glos.*

There was a fort on the hill-top at Lydney before the Romans came. Later, iron was mined there, and towards the end of the 4th century the site became a temple to Nodens, Celtic god of healing. Three inscriptions in his honour were found in this elaborate building, which was entered by steps up to a porch containing five chapels. Behind the porch was a shrine with a sanctuary.

To the rear of the temple was another building believed to have been a centre for medical treatment. It had a row of small rooms lining a corridor, a bath-block, and a building thought to have been a guest-house. The lower courses of the walls of some buildings are still visible.

A rich array of offerings was found, some of which are in the Lydney Park museum. They include not only coins, but also bronze and stone statuettes and figurines of humans and dogs.

The temple site lies 1 mile west of Lydney in Lydney Park. Permission to visit the site must be obtained from the Estate Office which is reached from the Chepstow to Gloucester road north-east of Aylburton.

309

Maiden Castle
Dorset

Between AD 43 and 47, this gigantic pre-Roman hill-fort fell to the Roman general Vespasian in a great battle at the east gate. More than 300 years later a Roman temple was built inside the fort. This shrine had plastered and painted walls, and was surrounded by a veranda. Both shrine and veranda had mosaic floors. North of the temple are the foundations of what may have been a priest's house. Visible today are low stone walls outlining the ground plan of the temple.

Dorset County Museum, in High West Street, Dorchester, contains relics from Maiden Castle, including skeletons from the battle, and pottery, coins, brooches and a small bronze bull.

Maiden Castle lies 2 miles south-west of Dorchester, and can be reached from the southern edge of the town by a minor road leading south-west off the Dorchester to Weymouth road.

Malton DERVENTIO
N. Yorks.

This Roman fort went through many transformations, starting probably as a marching camp around AD 71. But the stone defences of the fort, built in the reign of Emperor Trajan (AD 90–117), have survived best. They follow the earthen banks of an earlier fort and are fairly prominent except on the south-west. The stone wall, 10 ft thick, is now overgrown and resembles a bank. It was defended by one or two massive ditches – the outer one on the north-west side being the best preserved, and still 40 ft wide in places. A dip in the middle of the

north-eastern defences marks a gate.

Malton Museum, Milton Rooms, Market Place. Most of the finds from Roman Malton are displayed, including small antler amulets – one of them a phallic charm – stone statuettes, an inscribed altar, a tiny bear carved from Whitby jet, and a fine terracotta roof gable-end. A mould used for casting pewter ware is from a villa at Langton, near by.

Derventio lies about one-third of a mile east of the town centre on the north-west side of the River Derwent.

Maumbury Rings
Dorset

The best-known feature of Roman Dorchester – they called it Durnovaria – is its amphitheatre, built on one of the nearby Stone Age burial mounds known as the Maumbury Rings.

Its banks still stand more than 30 ft high, and are about 110 yds across. They probably supported tiers of timber seats, and a gangway with timber walls ran around the outside of the arena. This arena was entered by a large gate, beyond which was a recessed room – possibly a cage for wild animals.

Maumbury Rings is about half a mile south of the centre of modern Dorchester, beside the road to Weymouth on the east side.

Neath NIDUM
W. Glam.

The Roman fort of Nidum was the starting point for a road that led north-east to Brecon fort, and was built by a river crossing on the road that ran west to the coast. But despite its strategic location, it was occupied for only

two brief periods, in the 1st and 2nd centuries.

The remains of a stone fort dating from the later period can be seen, including the south and east gateways with their double carriageways and guardrooms.

The remains of the fort lie 1 mile west of the town centre beside the River Clydach.

Newcastle upon Tyne
PONS AELIUS
Tyne & Wear

The Museum of Antiquities, in The Quadrangle, includes some of the finest discoveries from Hadrian's Wall, and their appeal is enhanced by scale models of the wall and its forts. From South Shields has come a bronze cheek-piece from a helmet of the late 2nd or 3rd centuries, a little ivory statuette of a gladiator, and a lovely striped-onyx cameo of a bear devouring a goat.

The stone head of the local god Antenocitus, from Benwell fort, is very impressive. There are altars to Mithras from the temple at Carrawburgh, a charming relief of two nymphs from High Rochester, and two inscriptions set up by the builders of the fort at Risingham.

North Leigh
Oxon.

The Roman villa gives the visitor a clear picture of how the hub of a large farming estate was laid out at the peak of the prosperous 4th century.

The rooms are arranged round three sides of a large courtyard, bounded on the fourth side by a wall and entrance gate. They include the servants' rooms on the south-west, and the owner's main living quarters on the north-west.

There is a fine dining-room

with a mosaic floor laid by Cirencester craftsmen, and underfloor hypocaust heating.

Extensive farm buildings have been detected further west from the air, but the size of the estate is unknown. The villa lies on the south bank of the River Evenlode, 1½ miles north of North Leigh and 4 miles north-east of Witney. It is signposted from the Witney to Bicester road.

Oxford   *Oxon.*

One of Britain's finest collections of Roman art objects, from all over the Roman Empire, is displayed in the Ashmolean Museum. The many superb pieces from Britain include a glass bowl engraved with a scene of hare-hunting, discovered at Wint Hill in Somerset.

The 2nd-century bronze statuette of Cupid from Cirencester, with its inlaid silver eyes, is the finest and largest representation of this god found in Britain. From Strood, near Rochester, there is a lovely 4th-century jet medallion portraying a Medusa head.

Pevensey   *E. Sussex*
ANDERIDA

Today Pevensey lies about 1 mile inland from the Channel, but in Roman times it was on the sea.

From the 4th century its harbour mouth was defended by a massive fort, one of a chain designed to protect south-eastern Britain from Saxon pirates. The Roman walls, strengthened at intervals by great bastions, are still 28 ft high and 12 ft thick in places. They enclose an area of about 7½ acres – a superb monument to the durability of

Roman construction techniques.

However, the walls did not save Anderida in AD 491, when it was attacked by sea-raiders and its inhabitants massacred. The site lay derelict until William the Conqueror landed there in 1066, and later built a castle within the Roman walls.

The sea's retreat in the Middle Ages left Pevensey high and dry – it stands now 4 miles north-east of Eastbourne on the road between Lewes and Hastings.

Piercebridge (?)MAGIS *Durham*

Piercebridge village covers the site of an exceptionally large Roman fort built early in the 4th century. The north-east corner of the fort wall, together with a sewer and a lavatory, can be seen in a field accessible by a path just north of the church.

The most exciting recent discovery is that of the bridge which carried the Roman road across the River Tees. The south abutment, some of the piers carrying the timber super-structure, and the paved surface of the ford beside the bridge were all preserved by being buried in silt when the river changed its course.

The village of Piercebridge is situated on the north bank of the River Tees, 5 miles west of Darlington on the Darlington to Barnard Castle road. The bridge and ford remains are on the south bank of the river, near the bend in the road to Scotch Corner.

Portchester Castle   *Hants.*
(?)PORTUS ADURNI

Portchester Castle was placed strategically on a promontory jutting out into Portsmouth

harbour, guarding the head of the small estuary against incursions by Saxon pirates. So well positioned was this fort that the site was reoccupied by the Saxons, and used constantly from the Norman period until the 19th century.

Almost the entire ring of walls, including the bastions, dates from the late 3rd century, providing a true impression of a shore fort of the period.

The outer walls enclose an area of about 9 acres. Originally about 13 ft broad, these were reduced in thickness in the Middle Ages, revealing their core of Roman flint and mortar. They are still 20 ft high in places, and the original walkways on top can still be seen. Beyond the walls lies the defensive ditch – fairly substantial despite some silting-up.

The village lies 3 miles east of Fareham, south of the Fareham to Chichester road.

Rainster Rocks   *Derbys.*

On the slopes below the prominent outcrop known as Rainster Rocks are the remains of the biggest known British lead-mining village of Roman date. It may be the Lutodarum shown on the *Antonine Itinerary*, a 3rd-century Roman road book, as the centre of the Derbyshire lead-mining industry.

Rainster Rocks lie 4 miles west of Wirksworth and three-quarters of a mile north-west of Brassington. From the centre of Brassington, take the minor road west and fork right after half a mile. A quarter of a mile further along, the road turns sharp left, and a footpath leads to the settlement from this point.

The slopes beneath Rainster

Rocks are dotted with platforms on which houses stood, and with the foundations of house and boundary walls. There are also lead veins and mine shafts visible.

On a ledge on top of the Rocks was discovered a rock shelter containing bronze coins, samian pottery, mirrors, statuettes and surveying equipment. Most of the finds are on show in Derby Museum, The Strand, Derby.

Ravenglass   *Cumbria*
GLANNAVENTA

On the site of the 2nd-century Roman fort, the exterior bath-house – known locally as 'Walls Castle' – is excellently preserved. The walls stand to a height of 13 ft and contain some window openings. One specially interesting room, which has doorways and a niche in one corner, was probably a dressing room.

Ravenglass lies on the estuary of the River Esk, 15 miles south-east of Whitehaven and half a mile west of the Whitehaven to Dalton-in-Furness road. The remains of the fort are south-east of the village, on the east side of the railway.

Reculver REGULBIUM   *Kent*

The site of the Roman fort is very prominent, because inside its perimeter stand the impressive twin-towered ruins of a 7th-century Saxon church. The fort was built early in the 3rd century as a defence against Saxon pirates – and much of it has slipped into the sea as the cliffs have been eroded. But it is still possible to see from what remains of the walls that it was square in shape and probably

had four gates. The walls are almost 10 ft high in places. One gate has been excavated, and the foundations of its single arch are on display. Inside the gate was a guardroom.

Reculver is on the coast, 3½ miles east of Herne Bay, and can be approached from the Herne Bay to Margate road along a minor road via Hillborough.

Rey Cross   *Durham*

The Roman marching camp of Rey Cross is the best-preserved one of its kind in Britain. The earthworks are truly magnificent, with a bold rampart still standing nearly 6 ft high and 20 ft wide in places. Each of the nine main gates is defended by an outlying bank. This is undoubtedly one of the earliest Roman military constructions in the area, and may well have been used by the Ninth Legion under the governor, Petilius Cerialis, in his campaigns of AD 72 and 73.

The camp is clearly signposted 6 miles west of Bowes, on the north side of the A66 as it crosses Bowes Moor.

Ribchester   *Lancs.*
BREMETENNACUM

At this fort, fragments of the granaries are still visible. They had raised floors, to keep the grain aired. The museum at Ribchester is of great interest. One of its finest exhibits is a pedestal decorated with a relief of the god Apollo, and an inscription which mentions Emperor Gordian (AD 238–44) and a regiment of cavalry from the Danube who were garrisoned in the fort.

The beautifully decorated cavalry parade helmet on display

is a replica of one found at Ribchester – the original is in the British Museum.

The village lies on the north bank of the River Ribble, 5 miles north-west of Blackburn on the Longridge to Wilpshire road.

Richborough RUTUPIAE   *Kent*

Richborough has a remarkable history, spanning the entire four centuries of Roman rule in Britain. It played a major role in the initial conquest, as the base camp for Claudius's invasion in AD 43, and a short section of the double ditches which defended the base at that time can still be seen. To commemorate the conquest, a splendid 50 ft high arch was built, encased in marble and adorned with bronze statues. But only its cross-shaped foundation remains.

In the 3rd century, this arch was converted into a signal tower and surrounded by a rampart and three ditches, which are still visible.

At the end of the 1st century, Richborough became one of the chain of forts defending the south and east from Saxon raiders. Massive walls with great towers, gateways and bastions enclosed an area of 6 acres, and it is this phase of Richborough's development which survives best. The walls still stand up to 25 ft high, and it is possible to see just how they were built – of rubble and tile, faced with stone. The west gateway, and its flanking towers, has remained intact, with some parts of the bastions. The site museum displays pottery and other small finds.

Richborough stands on the west side of a loop in the River Stour, 1½ miles north of

Sandwich. It can be reached by leaving the Sandwich to Canterbury road on a minor road half a mile north-west of Sandwich.

Rockbourne   *Hants.*

In its final form, this Roman villa had three wings ranged about a courtyard. Several rooms had mosaic floors, and a bath-house has been found, as well as corn-drying kilns and farm buildings that adjoined the living quarters.

Finds from this villa – and other places – are in the site museum. They include inscribed milestones that were incorporated into the villa walls and a fine, carved stone table-top, as well as many small items such as coins and jewellery.

Rockbourne village is 3 miles north-west of Fordingbridge, on the minor road between Sandleheath and the Salisbury to Blandford Forum road. The remains of the villa lie 1 mile south-east of the village on the minor road.

St Albans VERULAMIUM *Herts.*

Before the foundation of Roman Verulamium, the Catuvellauni tribe had a great *oppidum*, or settlement, at Prae Wood, extending down the hill to the banks of the River Ver. Here the Romans built a timber fort, around which the first town grew up. This was destroyed in Boudicca's revolt in AD 60–61, but afterwards the town was rebuilt in a grand style.

One corner of the large forum and basilica, built in AD 79, is outlined on the ground next to the Verulamium Museum. Some of the rooms ranged around the forum had mosaic floors and frescoed walls.

The theatre was also built early in the town's history and is well preserved; it stands about 200 yds along the road from the museum. Immediately west of the theatre are the remains of a Roman town house. Part of its cellar and an underground shrine can be seen. The dining-room of another house, in Verulamium Park, has been preserved with its mosaic floor.

Verulamium Museum, St Michael's Street. Many discoveries from houses excavated in the town can be seen in this museum, which contains one of the best collections of Roman finds in Britain. The mosaics and painted wall-plaster are superb, while there are clear models and reconstructions of the town and one of its gateways.

Silchester   *Hants.*
CALLEVA ATREBATUM

Silchester, capital of the Atrebates, was left to decay after the Romans left: no town or village has survived on the site.

But the stone defences, built in the 3rd century, are well preserved in most places and the gates have all been excavated; it is possible to see part of the northern gate from Wall Lane.

Some of Silchester's temples lie beneath the churchyard of St Mary's in Church Lane, where there is a sundial made from a Roman column. The amphitheatre lies outside the walls, near Manor Farm, and is quite conspicuous, though it has never been excavated. The oval amphitheatre, with an entrance to the south, would have been equipped with wooden seats.

In the Calleva Museum, Rectory Grounds, Silchester Common, are casts of objects found on the site, as well as reconstructions of buildings in the Roman town. The Museum and Art Gallery in Blagrave Street, Reading, houses the main collection of Roman discoveries from Silchester. There are some fine inscriptions, and a notable display of Roman agricultural implements and craftsmen's tools.

The remains of the Roman town lie 6 miles north of Basingstoke and 1 mile east of the modern village of Silchester. It can be reached from the A340 north of Basingstoke. Turn east at Tadley and pass through Pamber Heath; the site lies 1½ miles east of here.

Somerdale   *Avon*

In Fry's chocolate factory at Somerdale, near Keynsham, are the remains of two Roman buildings, both probably villas. The foundations of a small house have been reconstructed facing the lodge at the entrance to the factory. They were discovered in 1922 and have been moved from their original location 300 yds north. A mosaic in the hall of the factory was found in another villa in Keynsham. This mosaic shows Europa being abducted by Jupiter, disguised as a bull. The museum in the factory lodge contains a selection of relics from the excavations, including further mosaic panels and two stone coffins, one with a lead lining.

These Roman remains may be seen by asking permission at the lodge, which is about half a mile north of the centre of Keynsham, beside the River Avon.

South Shields   *Tyne & Wear*
ARBEIA

A fort was built at Arbeia to supply Hadrian's Wall from the North Sea, and to guard its vulnerable eastern flank. A substantial part of this fort can be visited, including several of its numerous granaries.

In the site museum are two carved tombstones of particular interest. One commemorated a freed slave, Victor from Morocco, shown reclining at his own funeral banquet. The other is in memory of a woman named Regina, who came from the St Albans area but moved north with her husband, Barates, a standard-bearer from Palmyra, in Syria. Regina is shown sitting in a wicker chair with a wool basket beside her.

The fort is in Roman Remains Park, Baring Street.

Thornborough   *Bucks.*

One of the two massive Roman-period burial mounds at Thornborough incorporated a wooden vault covering human ashes. With the remains were pots, glasses, bronze vessels, wine jars, iron weapons and a lamp dating the burial from the 2nd century AD. These artefacts are now housed in the University Museum of Archaeology and Anthropology in Downing Street, Cambridge.

The mounds are about 200 yds east of Thornborough Bridge, 2 miles east of Buckingham on the Bletchley road.

Traprain Law   *Lothian*

The great hill-fort of Traprain Law enclosed an area of 32 acres, and was occupied from the Bronze Age into the 5th century AD. The rampart has a stone facing that runs along the whole length of the hill; at the north-eastern end is a hollow approach road bounded by large stones set on end. The gateways to the fort are flanked by strong stone banks.

Objects of the Roman period found include several glass vessels, a very elaborate bronze folding spoon, a bronze stylus or writing instrument, and samian pottery. Important as these discoveries were, they were utterly eclipsed by the hoard of late Roman silverware buried on the same site. This splendid array includes five flagons adorned with friezes, and a scalloped bowl depicting a Nereid, or sea-nymph, riding over the waves on the back of a panther. These treasures – possibly Scottish loot from a raid into the south – are now in the National Museum of Antiquities of Scotland.

Traprain Law stands in a commanding position 1½ miles south-west of East Linton.

Trecastle   *Powys*

Two very impressive Roman marching camps, one inside the other, survive on the crest of the moors overlooking the Vale of Tywi near Trecastle. Both camps probably date from about AD 47, the period of the campaign against Caratacus.

The camps lie 3½ miles west of Trecastle and can be reached by taking the Cwmwysg road from Trecastle church; after about half a mile branch right on to a track that becomes a footpath. This is a Roman road; the camps lie about 3 miles along the road on the right.

Wall LETOCETUM   *Staffs.*

The town was situated on the line of Watling Street, and the 4th-century *mansio* or inn, which can be visited, was an important relay station for the officers of the imperial courier service. The adjacent bath-house had several hot and cold rooms as well as an exercise court. The flues and part of the hypocaust system for heating the baths still exist. The site museum contains finds that include coins, pottery, tiles, brooches and a 3rd-century milestone.

Wall is 2 miles south of Lichfield.

Welwyn   *Herts.*

There is a Roman bath-house dating from the 3rd century AD that was part of a villa in Welwyn. It is possible to see the underfloor hypocaust heating system, as well as the various hot and cold rooms, whose walls still stand up to 5 ft.

The bath-house has been preserved in a concrete vault beneath the A1(M) motorway at Dicket Mead, Welwyn, near where it crosses the River Mimram.

Whitley Castle   *Northld*

The great rampart and multiple ditches of this large and impressive fort fit snugly into the curves and contours of a high hill. It was probably built during the 2nd century and, according to dedication slabs found on the site, was refurbished about 100 years later.

Whitley Castle lies 2 miles north-west of Alston, just west of the Alston to Brampton road. Take the track to Whitlow Farm, just north of the Cumbria-Northumberland border, and ask permission at the farm before following the track north to the site.

Winchester *Hants.*
VENTA BELGARUM

Winchester was the old capital of the Belgae tribe, and the Roman town was laid out about AD 90. Defences of earth and timber were superseded by masonry walls, still detectable in the line of the later medieval walls. A fragment of Roman wall can be seen beside the Wiers Footpath, 130 yds from Bridge Street. Part of a mosaic floor showing ribbon-like and leaf-in-circle patterns, found in Dome Alley, have been relaid in the entrance to the Deanery, just south of the cathedral. Permission to see this should be sought at the Deanery. Excavations in the Cathedral Green to find the Saxon minster revealed part of the forum, while many other Roman buildings have also been identified.

City Museum, The Square. The finds on display include mosaics – notably one from Sparsholt Roman villa – as well as pottery, coin hoards and an inscription.

Wroxeter *Shropshire*
VIROCONIUM CORNOVIORUM

The fort established at Wroxeter evolved into the fourth largest town in Roman Britain, and was the tribal capital of the Cornovii. The town walls enclosed an area of about 200 acres.

The most spectacular piece of Roman masonry still standing at Wroxeter is one wall of the public exercise hall, the roof of which was originally some 50 ft

above ground level. Also visible is the market hall and, behind it, the public lavatory with its sewer. The baths, built around AD 160, are perhaps the most significant Roman remains visible. They have spacious heated rooms and a swimming pool, one of the few examples found in Roman Britain.

The Viroconium Museum, adjoining the excavations, houses a collection of coins, pottery, painted plaster, and inscriptions from the Roman town. Rowley's House Museum, in Barker Street, Shrewsbury, also has some finds from Wroxeter. The most interesting of these is the dedication tablet from the market square, which records its construction in AD 130.

The village of Wroxeter is 5 miles south-east of Shrewsbury. Turn off the A5 and follow the road towards Ironbridge, then turn right at the first crossroads.

York EBORACUM *N. Yorks.*

The legionary fortress of York, founded by the Ninth Legion shortly after AD 70, was the military headquarters of northern Britain. The town grew up around the fortress, on both banks of the River Ouse, and its defences were rebuilt several times.

Those erected by Emperor Constantius, late in the 3rd century, remain the most impressive today. Constantius added a series of polygonal towers to the walls along the river front. Best preserved are the stretches in the Museum Gardens. The main entrance is near Lendal Bridge, and under the stone archway are Roman coffins and the conduit-head of

the Roman water supply.

There is also an interval tower, and a corner tower which has in its base masonry originally used in the 1st-century fortress. The Multangular Tower is one of the finest surviving reminders of Rome in York. It extends into the Museum Gardens, but may be entered from the Public Library. The tower is ten-sided; its walls are 5 ft thick and stand up to 18 ft high.

Near by is the Anglian Tower, which has roughly dressed stones. There is some dispute as to whether it is of late Roman, Anglo-Saxon or very early Viking construction. The public lavatory at the top of Bootham Bar conceals the remains of a Roman gate into the city.

Down Ogleforth, at the Treasurer's House, is the base of a column and part of a Roman street. In St Sampson's Square, in the cellar of the Roman Bath inn, are preserved the remains of the fortress bath-house. With the landlord's permission it is possible to see some rooms.

York Minster lies over the *principia*, headquarters building of the Roman fort. The site of the excavations beneath the Minster has now been turned into the Undercroft Museum. One of its columns has been re-erected opposite the south door of the Minster.

Undercroft Museum, York Minster. Among the finds to be seen are elegant wall-paintings of theatrical masks, birds, figures and architectural details, all from a room discovered at the back of the *principia*.

Yorkshire Museum, Museum Gardens. In this museum is the lion's share of finds from Roman York, including a stone head of the Emperor Constantine.

319

ACKNOWLEDGMENTS

Artwork
The reconstructions on pages *72–73, 114–15, 170–1, 224–5,* are by Ivan Lapper. Illustrations on pages *288–9* are by Steve Sturgess.

Photographs
Credits are listed from left to right across the page, regardless of vertical order. Locations of objects are given first, followed by the name of the photographer, agency or organisation supplying the photograph. Work commissioned by Reader's Digest is in *italics*. Where one name is listed for a page bearing more than one picture, all pictures are from the same source.

Page 8/9 By permission of the Trustees of the British Museum 9 Erich Lessing/Magnum 10 Ronald Sheridan 11 Ronald Sheridan; C. M. Dixon 12/13 Scala 13 By permission of the Trustees of the British Museum 14 Colchester and Essex Museum/*Patrick Thurston* 15 By permission of the Trustees of the British Museum 16, 17 Butser Ancient Farm/*Patrick Thurston* 18/19 By permission of the Trustees of the British Museum; Colchester and Essex Museum/*Patrick Thurston* 19 East Riding Archaeological Research Committee 20/21 By permission of the Trustees of the British Museum 20, 21, 22, 23 Butser Ancient Farm/*Patrick Thurston* 24, 25, 26 By permission of the Trustees of the British Museum 26/27 Scala 28 Archaeological Advisers 28/29 By permission of the Trustees of the British Museum 29, 30 Mansell Collection 31 Penny Tweedie 32/33 The Society of Antiquaries 32 The Society of Antiquaries 33 Woodspring Museum, Weston-super-Mare 34/35 Colchester and Essex Museum/*Mike Freeman* 35 By permission of the Trustees of the British Museum 36/37 West Air Photography 36 Janet and Colin Bord 37 By permission of the Trustees of the British Museum 38 East Riding Archaeological Research Committee 38/39 Peter Clayton 38 Peter Clayton 40/41 National Museum of Wales; Jim Hancock 42/43 *Anthony Howarth* 42 *Anthony Howarth* 43 Irish Tourist Board 44/45 Cambridge University Collection, copyright reserved 45 Peter Clayton 46 Peter Clayton 46/47 By permission of the Trustees of the British Museum 47 Archaeological Advisers/East Hertfordshire Archaeological Group 48/49 Ronald Sheridan 49 National Museum of Antiquities of Scotland 50/51 Mansell Collection 52 Verulamium Museum, St Albans; Yorkshire Museum/Clive Friend/Woodmansterne Ltd 53 Mansell Collection; Michael Holford 54 Grosvenor Museum, Chester 55 Colchester and Essex Museum/*Patrick Thurston*; Ronald Sheridan 56/57 C. M. Dixon 56 Mansell Collection 57 Museum of London 59 National Museum of Antiquities of Scotland/Cooper-Bridgeman Library 60 Museum of Antiquities, Newcastle upon Tyne; Roger-Viollet 61 Scala 62/63 C. M. Dixon 64/65 Airviews, Manchester 65 Cambridge University Collection, copyright reserved; Coventry Museum 66 Peter Clayton 66/67 Peter Clayton 67 Crown copyright, by permission of H.M.S.O. 68 By permission of the Trustees of the British Museum; Hunterian Museum, Glasgow/Scottish Tourist Board 69 C. M. Dixon 74/75 A. F. Kersting 76/77 National Museum, Belgrade 78/79 By permission of the Trustees of the British Museum 80 Crown copyright, by permission of H.M.S.O. 80/81 Brian Brake/John Hilleson 82/83 C. M. Dixon 83 Ronald Sheridan 84/85 C. M. Dixon 86 Peter Clayton 86/87 Michael Holford 88/89 *Philip Llewellin* 89 Cambridge University Collection, copyright reserved 90/91 Scala 92/93 Giraudon 93 Reading Museum and Art Gallery/*Patrick Thurston* 94 Ronald Sheridan 95 Giraudon 96 Museum of London/Jeremy Marks/Woodmansterne Ltd; Giraudon 97 Museum of St Germain-en-Laye/Musées Nationaux, Paris 98 Ronald Sheridan; Yorkshire Museum/*Michael Holford* 99 By permission of the Trustees of the British Museum; Yorkshire Museum/Clive Friend/Woodmansterne Ltd 100 Museum of London; Museum of London; Reading

Museum and Art Gallery/*Patrick Thurston*; Sunday Times 101 Mansell Collection 102/103 By permission of the Trustees of the British Museum 103 Museum of London/*Mike Freeman* 104/105 C. M. Dixon 106 Reading Museum and Art Gallery/*Patrick Thurston* 106/107 Museum of London/*Mike Freeman* 108/109 Archaeological Advisers 108 York Archaeological Trust 109 Ronald Sheridan 110/111 By permission of the Trustees of the British Museum 111 Yorkshire Museum/Clive Friend/Woodmansterne Ltd; British Museum/Picturepoint 116/117 Mauro Pucciarelli; Leonard von Matt 117 Mansell Collection 118/119 Austrian National Library, Vienna 119 Colchester and Essex Museum/*Mike Freeman* 120/121 *Christopher Morris* 122 Jim Hancock 122/123 Mansell Collection 124 Peterborough Museum and Art Gallery 125 *Anthony Howarth* 126/127 C. M. Dixon; By permission of the Trustees of the British Museum 128/129 Ronald Sheridan 129 Leonard von Matt 130/131 Jim Hancock; Mauro Pucciarelli 132 C. M. Dixon 132/133 C. M. Dixon 133 Aerofilms 134 Museum of London 134/135 Vatican Museum/Leonard von Matt 135 Museum of London 136 Howard C. Moore/Woodmansterne Ltd 137 Ronald Sheridan 138 Colchester and Essex Museum/Peter Clayton 139 Reading Museum and Art Gallery/*Patrick Thurston*; By permission of the Trustees of the British Museum; Reading Museum and Art Gallery/*Patrick Thurston* 140/141 Peter Clayton 141 By permission of the Trustees of the British Museum; Peter Clayton 144, 145 By permission of the Trustees of the British Museum 146/147 Sunday Times 147 Verulamium Museum, St Albans/Michael Holford 148 Mauro Pucciarelli 148/149 Giraudon 150 England Scene 150/151 Sunday Times 151 C. M. Dixon 152 Tony Rook 153 J. Arthur Dixon 154 Verulamium Museum, St Albans 154/155 J. Arthur Dixon 155 Verulamium Museum, St Albans/*Ian Yeomans* 156 Museum of London/Jeremy Marks/Woodmansterne Ltd 157, 158, 159 By permission of the Trustees of the British Museum 160 Manchester Museum 161 By permission of the Trustees of the British Museum; Peter Clayton 162/163 Mauro Pucciarelli; Jim Hancock 162 Museum of London 164/165 Museum of London 164 National Museum of Antiquities of Scotland 166/167 Bulloz 168 A. F. Kersting; David S. Neal 172/173 Yorkshire Museum/*Michael Holford* 173 Michael Holford 174, 175 Giraudon 176 Reading Museum and Art Gallery/*Patrick Thurston* 176/177 Snark International 178/179 Mauro Pucciarelli 179 Josephine Powell 180/181 Giraudon; C. M. Dixon 181 Colchester and Essex Museum/*Mike Freeman* 182 By permission of the Trustees of the British Museum; Giraudon 183 Leonard von Matt; Reading Museum and Art Gallery/*Patrick Thurston* 184/185 Jim Hancock 185 Scala; National Museum of Wales 186 Museum of Antiquities, Newcastle upon Tyne/*Michael Holford* 187 Leonard von Matt; Claus Hansmann; By permission of the Trustees of the British Museum 188/189 City Museum, Lincoln 189 Kingston-upon-Hull Museums 190/191 Reading Museum and Art Gallery/*Patrick Thurston* 191 Scala 192 Leonard von Matt 193 Corinium Museum, Cirencester/*Patrick Thurston*; Somerset County Museum 194 Reading Museum and Art Gallery/*Patrick Thurston* 195 Warburg Institute; Crown copyright, by permission of H.M.S.O. 196/197 C. M. Dixon 198/199 Yorkshire Museum/*Michael Holford* 200, 201 Giraudon 202/203 Scala 203 Giraudon; British Museum/Michael Holford 204/205 Museum of Antiquities, Newcastle upon Tyne/*Michael Holford* 204 Reading Museum and Art Gallery/*Patrick Thurston* 205 Museum of London/*Mike Freeman* 206/207 C. M. Dixon 207 David Miles 208/209 Jim Hancock 209 By permission of the Trustees of the British Museum 210/211 Colorphoto Hinz 211 Mansell Collection 212/213 C. M. Dixon 214/215 West Air Photography 215 British Tourist Authority 216/217 Janet and Colin Bord 218 Cambridge University Collection, copyright reserved 219 Cambridge University Collection, copyright reserved; Gloucester Museum/*Clive Friend* 220/221 Department of Aerial Photography, University of

Newcastle 226 Crown copyright, by permission of H.M.S.O. 226/227 By permission of the Trustees of the British Museum 227 Museum of London/*Mike Freeman* 228/229 National Museum of Wales 229 Royal Museum, Canterbury/*Penny Tweedie* 230 Mansell Collection 231 By permission of the Trustees of the British Museum 232/233 The National Trust; National Museum of Wales 233 Reading Museum and Art Gallery/*Patrick Thurston* 234/235 Michael Holford 235 Archaeological Advisers; By permission of the Trustees of the British Museum 236 By permission of the Trustees of the British Museum; By permission of the Trustees of the British Museum 236/237 Museum of London 238 Colchester and Essex Museum/*Patrick Thurston*; Reading Museum and Art Gallery/*Patrick Thurston* 239, 240, 241 By permission of the Trustees of the British Museum 243 Ronald Sheridan 244 Nene Valley Research Committee 244/245 Nene Valley Research Committee 244 Corinium Museum, Cirencester/*Clive Friend* 246, 247 Corinium Museum, Cirencester/Judges Ltd 248/249 Crown copyright, by permission of H.M.S.O. 249 David S. Neal 250, 251 Yorkshire Museum/*Mike Freeman* 252/253 Museum of London/Jeremy Marks/Woodmansterne Ltd 253 Gloucester Museum/Peter Clayton 254 By permission of the Trustees of the British Museum 255 C. M. Dixon 256/257 Peter Clayton 257 National Museum of Antiquities of Scotland 258/259 Bath Roman Museum/Michael Holford 259 Angelo Hornak 260/261 Leonard von Matt 262 Colchester and Essex Museum/*Mike Freeman* 263 Colchester and Essex Museum/*Mike Freeman*; Yorkshire Museum/Clive Friend/Woodmansterne Ltd 264 Museum of London/*Mike Freeman* 265 Museum of London; Museum of London/*Mike Freeman* 266/267 Crown copyright, by permission of H.M.S.O. 266 Peter Clayton 267 Yorkshire Museum/*Michael Holford* 268, 269, 270, 271 By permission of the Trustees of the British Museum 272 Michael Holford 273 England Scene; Mansell Collection 274/275 Yorkshire Museum/*Michael Holford* 277 Gloucester Museum/*Clive Friend*; C. M. Dixon 278/279 John Bethell 279 Richard Hodges 280/281 David Miles 282/283 Ashmolean Museum, Oxford 284 *Gordon More* 284/285 Crown copyright, by permission of H.M.S.O. 285 Bodleian Library, Oxford 286, 287 West Stow, Anglo-Saxon village/*Patrick Thurston*

The publishers also acknowledge their indebtedness to the following books, journals and organisations, which were consulted for reference or as the source of quotations:

Antiquaries Journal; *Bede: History of the English Church and People* transl. L. Sherley-Price (Penguin); *Britain in the Roman Empire* by J. Liversidge (Routledge & Kegan Paul); *Britannia* by S. S. Frere (Routledge & Kegan Paul); *Caesar: The Conquest of Gaul* transl. S. Handford (Penguin); *Country Life in Classical Times* by K. D. White (Elek); *Hadrian's Wall* by D. Breeze and B. Dobson (Allen Lane); *Iron Age Communities in Britain* by B. Cunliffe (Routledge & Kegan Paul); *The Roman Army* by John Wilkes (Cambridge University Press); *Roman Britain* by John Wacher (J. M. Dent); *The Roman Imperial Army* by G. Webster (Routledge & Kegan Paul); *Roman Inscriptions in Britain* by R. Collingwood and R. Wright (Oxford University Press); *Roman Remains in Britain* by Roger J. A. Wilson (Constable); *Roman Roads in Britain* by Ivan D. Margary (John Baker); *The Roman Villa* by J. Percival (Batsford); *The Roman Villa in South-west England* by Keith Branigan (Moonraker); *The Romans in Britain* ed. R. Moore (Methuen); *Seneca: Epistulae Morales* transl. R. Gummere (Loeb Classical Library); Society of Antiquaries of London; *Tacitus: Annals* transl. M. Grant (Penguin); *Tacitus: Britain and Germany* transl. H. Mattingly (Penguin); *Town and Country in Roman Britain* by A. L. F. Rivet (Hutchinson); *The Towns of Roman Britain* by J. S. Wacher (Batsford); Vindolanda Trust

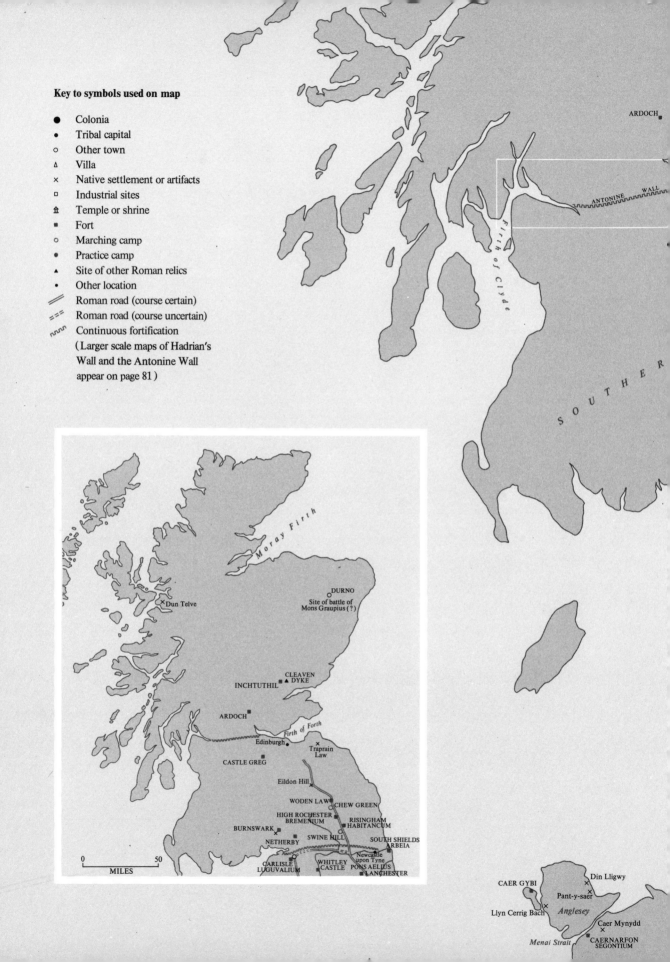

Key to symbols used on map

●   Colonia

•   Tribal capital

○   Other town

△   Villa

×   Native settlement or artifacts

▫   Industrial sites

♙   Temple or shrine

■   Fort

○   Marching camp

●   Practice camp

▲   Site of other Roman relics

•   Other location

〰   Roman road (course certain)

===   Roman road (course uncertain)

〰   Continuous fortification

    (Larger scale maps of Hadrian's
    Wall and the Antonine Wall
    appear on page 81)

ARDOCH

ANTONINE WALL

Firth of Clyde

S O U T H E R

Moray Firth

× Dun Telve

DURNO ○
Site of battle of
Mons Graupius (?)

CLEAVEN
INCHTUTHIL ▲ DYKE

ARDOCH ■

Firth of Forth

Edinburgh ○   × Traprain
         Law

CASTLE GREG ■

Eildon Hill •

WODEN LAW   CHEW GREEN

HIGH ROCHESTER   RISINGHAM
BREMENIUM   HABITANCUM

BURNSWARK   SWINE HILL

NETHERBY   SOUTH SHIELDS
                 ARBEIA
            Newcastle
            upon Tyne
CARLISLE   WHITLEY   PONS AELIUS
LUGUVALIUM   CASTLE   LANCHESTER

0   50
     MILES

CAER GYBI   Din Lligwy

          Pant-y-saer ×

Llyn Cerrig Bach ×   *Anglesey*

               Caer Mynydd ×

Menai Strait   CAERNARFON
               SEGONTIUM